Temptations in the Office

Ethical Choices and Legal Obligations

STEPHEN M. GOLDMAN

PRAEGER

Westport, Connecticut
London

Library of Congress Cataloging-in-Publication Data

Goldman, Stephen M. 1946-
  Temptations in the office : ethical choices and legal obligations / Stephen M. Goldman.
    p. cm.
  Includes bibliographical references and index.
  ISBN 978-0-275-99675-8 (alk. paper)
  1. Business ethics. 2. Corporate culture—Moral and ethical aspects. I. Title.
  HF5387.G645 2008
  174'.4—dc22   2007052854

British Library Cataloguing in Publication Data is available.

Library of Congress Catalog Card Number: 2007052854
ISBN: 978-0-275-99675-8

First published in 2008

Praeger Publishers, 88 Post Road West, Westport, CT 06881
An imprint of Greenwood Publishing Group, Inc.
www.praeger.com

Printed in the United States of America

The paper used in this book complies with the
Permanent Paper Standard issued by the National
Information Standards Organization (Z39.48–1984).

10 9 8 7 6 5 4 3 2 1

To the memory of my two grandfathers
whose lives I cherish and whose examples guide
and inspire me

Sam Beck (1888–1982)
of Denver, Colorado
Businessman
and
Frank Goldman (1890–1965)
of Lowell, Massachusetts
Lawyer

Contents

Preface

At the outset of his short study of the nineteenth-century German military thinker Karl von Clausewitz, the British military historian Sir Michael Howard wanted to make sure that his readers understood how rooted his subject was in the practical realm in which he lived and worked. Clausewitz, wrote Howard, "had the practical man's horror of abstractions that could not be directly related to the facts of the situation, of propositions that could not be illustrated by examples, or material that was not relevant to the problem at hand.... [H]e was always concerned to link theory to action, and he deliberately ignored all aspects of his subject that were not of immediate relevance to the kind of war with which he himself was familiar."[1]

Although the problems of warfare may seem to some far removed from the issues of business ethics, I share Clausewitz's horror at disembodied abstractions "not ... directly related to the facts of the situation." Many works on business ethics, especially those commonly prepared for business ethics courses in MBA programs, are heavily laced with readings from some of the world's great moral philosophers. I studied many of these writings when I was a graduate student. I found them dense and maddeningly divorced from reality. I still do. When I read these books, I wonder how much more they must seem irrelevant to business leaders and aspiring business leaders. This book will not follow that tack. Still, the concepts of such thinkers are essential to accomplish our task. But we'll address them in a manner that will help businesspeople understand how to think about such problems or, sometimes, to help them understand the rational foundation for what they already believe.

There's a second prominent genre of books on business ethics. Such works are anecdote books. Drawing heavily on descriptions of dilemmas that businessmen and businesswomen have faced, such books are largely devoid of any theoretical underpinning. Starting with real-life situations, they specialize in showing that, in the real world of business, values we care about may pull in opposite directions in tough cases. I call this the "Mary realized she had a problem" approach. To resolve such dilemmas, this approach trades on intuition. The reader is asked, essentially, to decide whether the choice made by the person in the scenario was or was not correct. The problem with this approach is that it provides little guidance for solving the different problems you inevitably encounter yourself.

This book adopts a third approach. Its aim is to improve the ability of the reader to think clearly, coherently, and effectively about concrete ethical problems faced by businesspeople. It uses the insights of the two principal disciplines that address questions of right and wrong: ethics (sometimes called moral philosophy) and law.

Ethics and law are similar in that both address what we *ought* to do. They differ in that ethics helps us to decide what we ought to do because we conclude that a given choice is morally sound. Law tells us what we *must* do to avoid a sanction, such as being held liable for damages or convicted of a crime. Still, ethics and law are linked in two ways. First, the decisions businesspeople make are interlaced with considerations from both spheres. Second, while the law's "must" nearly always derives from society's decision to put the clout of the law behind a certain ethical view, the ethical domain maintains its significance regardless of the laws content. Gender discrimination and sexual harassment did not cease to raise ethical issues just because Congress and the courts decided to write into law an ethical view prohibiting them. The relationship of both law and ethics to these questions is discussed more fully in Chapter 4.

Wags and cynics like to proclaim that the term "business ethics" is an oxymoron. But concern about individual values in business, which we sometimes refer to as business ethics, is vital for companies and for individual careers. What we do and how we do it affects our coworkers, our customers, our suppliers, our competitors, and, as recent studies prove, ourselves.

There are three principal ways that companies get into big, headline-making trouble. The first and most obvious is where a market for goods or services collapses, often because technological break-throughs render older products obsolete—remember the electric typewriter?—or, amounting to the same thing, when a competitor fills the same niche at a much more competitive price. The second is where financing, the ability to attract capital necessary for operations, fails. Look at the pinch the airlines are in now. You can't run a business without capital to sustain activities. The third way that companies court disaster, and the one in which we are interested here, is when companies or individual executives get caught up in serious ethical failures. These usually start in a mundane way, by ignoring the basic values underlying situations. As we'll see, sometimes ethical crises become legal crises, but sometimes they don't.

Unlike the first two causes, getting into trouble by ignoring basic values is *always* a self-inflicted wound. A company walks into ethical crises either by tolerating behavior that simply shouldn't be accepted, or by failing to recognize and take action when specific warning signs develop. Nothing is more crucial to the businessperson than an early warning system, a way of detecting when what seems like a perfectly straightforward business issue actually hinges on values. Sometimes mistakes in solving ethical problems damage morale, destroy an individual's career, or cripple a company's reputation in the marketplace. Sometimes the results are legal fees, legal liability, and, in extreme cases, criminal prosecution.

The old expression "Good ethics is good business" is a saw that's easily misused. A formerly prominent financial advisor in Denver, my hometown, used to make this statement all the time. He said it, but it was just a ploy. He is currently serving a hundred-year prison term after being convicted on forty-four counts for embezzling millions of dollars from his clients. Caring about values still matters, even if guys like him give the homily a bad name. Being values-savvy directly enhances the bottom line, because a company that respects people and acts with integrity is more likely to recruit and maintain a dedicated staff. It is also likely to attract and keep good clients or customers and enjoy a strong reputation. Intelligently emphasizing values while implementing business insights not only avoids trouble. It produces positive results.

This book is not about Enron or WorldCom. It's not a "scandal book." It's not about securities fraud or white-collar crime. It's about the enormous range of circumstances in which values influence what men and women do in their ordinary, as well as their extraordinary, business activities. This book's scope encompasses the kind of serious wrongdoing that whets the appetite of the news media, prosecutors, or plaintiffs' lawyers, but it's not limited to that. Instead, it focuses on people and how you treat them in everyday situations in the office.

There's another distinction upon which everything we're doing here depends. It's the distinction between intuition and rational thinking. As we'll explore in detail in Chapter 1, the three most important ways of thinking about ethical issues arise from three potent intuitions. You can't engender a corporate culture with the highest ethical standards if you treat questions of values the way you treat the acquisition of a new computer system or analyze whether expanding into a new market makes sense. Ethics don't work that way. The methodology in what I've called the "Mary realized she had a problem" approach to business ethics begins with wringing your hands and ends with pure, rarely supported, intuition. If this isn't the first book on business ethics you've picked up, you know what I mean. An executive faces a dilemma in which competing considerations pull in different directions. The executive who struggles with what to do may have trouble sleeping, or may gain or lose weight (as the case may be). And then, "Holy Toledo!" A bell rings, the light goes on and a decision is made. The rhetorical device seems to be that you or I reading the story should find ourselves agreeing that the protracted physical disruption of the executive's body produced in a flash of light, the "right" decision, one in accord with "high ethical standards." We're invited to share the executive's intuition. But why? If you're the CEO of a company, you'd be pretty unhappy if you found out that this was the process your VP of finance used to arrange a new line of credit at a bank or the manner in which your VP of marketing concluded the company should double its presence in the Pacific Northwest. Making decisions that raise ethical issues demands the same kind of hard and clear thinking required to reach any other business decision. Moral intuition is important. This book assumes yours is intact. But it's only a starting point. The book's design is to help you develop the skills to make rational, logical, and *ethical* choices—both to enable you to solve satisfactorily the problems you face and to create practical rules for your company.

THE PLAN OF THIS BOOK

The organization of this book is simple. We start with some of the key approaches that we use, whether consciously or not, to think about ethical issues. Then we discuss the most important arenas of temptation which cause ethical problems that business leaders must confront: sex, money, and power. As we will see, the presence of temptations heightens the need for approaches that are both rational and reasonable. Moreover, because succombing to temptation frequently harms other people, the law often intervenes. No business leader can function without knowing at least generally where the law will constrain his or her decisions. This book identifies some of the most critical of those laws.

Part One, Ethical Choices and Legal Obligations, sets up the conceptual background. Chapter 1 discusses the three principal ways in which we can effectively reason about ethical issues. Chapter 2 disposes of the cynical view some take that it's unnecessary to reason about stand-alone ethical issues. First, it explains why it isn't enough to say that making money justifies any actions. Second, it criticizes the derivative, and initially more plausible formulation of this position, namely, why it isn't enough to say that you can do whatever will make money provided you don't violate the law. Chapter 3 is a transitional chapter. It focuses not on direct problem areas but on the general dilemma of how a company should go about resolving the ethical issues that arise. Effective corporate ethics have a lot of "procedural fairness" about them, and the ethically savvy company will want to know how to go about resolving the problems that inevitably arise. You could easily choose to read this chapter *after* you have read the five that address the particular problems that the pursuit of sex, money, and power create. I put it up front for the benefit of those readers who, in cases where the answer isn't "Call our lawyer," will ask themselves, "How are we supposed to go about resolving a problem like this when it arises?" The critical point is this. Considering what to do in tough cases isn't simply a question of trusting your intuitions, formed in childhood and at college, however sound you feel they are. Tough questions are tough because there are *competing considerations*. Here's hoping that this book will help equip you, whether as an individual or as a manager, to resolve the difficult ethical questions you face intelligently and rationally.

Part Two, Temptations in the Office, addresses particular problem areas. In this part, we'll weave in and out of areas where the law provides guidance or makes demands that you ignore at your peril, and areas where the law is silent. I wish it were as easy as a writer in the *Harvard Business Review* put it a few years ago, saying that the need to make ethical decisions stops when conduct is "illegal."[2] It's not. But we'll identify where the law is crucial and where a manager must rely on his or her own problem-solving abilities. Part Two is organized around the three great sources of temptation in the business world: sex, money, and power. Chapter 4 discusses the problems of sex and gender in the workplace, focusing heavily on sexual harassment, though also discussing gender discrimination and the favoritism we call "paramour preference." Chapters 5 through 7 discuss the temptations of money—conflicts of interest, incentive compensation plans, and harming others in the market by inappropriate business practices, including endangering the public by selling defective products. Chapter 8 concerns one of the hidden subjects in discussions of business conduct—the abuse of power by supervisors, managers, and executives that humiliates subordinates. In this chapter, we'll also consider how racial and ethnic stereotyping can be an abuse of power.

Georges Clemenceau, the French premier at the end of the First World War, nicknamed "the Tiger," said that "war is too serious a business to be left to the generals." In the end, every choice a manager makes that affects the well-being of someone else is a lonely one. Business ethics are too serious a business to be left to the philosophers.

The purpose of this book is to help managers understand the battleground, enhancing their ability to make good choices. The conclusion is "Face the Facts, Tell the Truth, and Run on Time." Those three commands don't say it all, but they are the mantra for success in facing ethical challenges.

I hope you will find the reading ahead both enjoyable and challenging.

NOTES

1. Michael Howard, *Clausewitz: A Very Short Introduction* (Oxford: Oxford University Press, 2002), p. 2.

2. Constance E. Bagley, "Forethought: The Ethical Leader's Decision Tree," *Harvard Business Review* 81, no. 2 (February 2003):18–19.

Acknowledgments

I learned to think about ethics while I was a student at Brasenose College, Oxford. I remember with fondness and profit the discussions with teachers and fellow students, but particularly instruction in how to create an argument from the late Principal of the College, Professor H. L. A. Hart. I thank my parents, Elaine and Ed Goldman, and the Ford Foundation for the support that allowed me the chance to continue my education beyond law school. Two people who encouraged me to pursue this project at early stages, and to whom I am much indebted, are Bill Fox, former Dean of the Columbus School of Law at the Catholic University of America, and Carole Sargent, now Director of the Office of Scholarly and Literary Publications at Georgetown University. Without them, this project would never have gotten off the ground. I thank John Willig, my agent, for placing the book with Greenwood Praeger, and my editor, Jeff Olson, not only for his many helpful suggestions, but for sticking with me when the requirements of my law practice delayed my completion of the manuscript. I thank, too, my sister, Carol Maxym, who was always ready with words of encouragement.

The staff of the library of the Columbus School of Law, but particularly Steve Young, routinely fielded my research questions promptly and accurately. I very much appreciate their willingness to help. Jenny He of Sands Anderson Marks & Miller, my law firm, and Margaret Pooley at the Columbus School of Law typed and retyped my drafts, and I am grateful for their help, as well for their quizzical looks at some of the text which prompted rewriting. Lani

Pukranu, of Sands Anderson, generously took time from her busy schedule to help correct the page proofs. Pat Knox pulled the string on a title that captured what I was saying.

While preparing this book, I had the privilege of handling a major piece of litigation for Global Aerospace, Inc. Lee Demas, its general counsel, not only spent hours improving my writing skills in the briefs I wrote on the company's behalf, but also took time to read and comment on much of the manuscript. A lawyer couldn't ask for a more probing and supportive client. I cannot thank him enough. A lawyer also couldn't ask for better cocounsel than Tom Gonzalez and Nix Daniel, of Beggs & Lane, with whom I had the privilege of working on the same case, while the manuscript was finalized.

My principal intellectual debt is to Justice John Paul Stevens. In the year I spent as his law clerk in the early 1970s, I learned the true meaning of both intellectual and personal integrity. Of particular relevance here, however, is the manner in which this great and learned judge treated a wet-behind-the-ears recent law school graduate; he taught me how bosses ought to treat their employees.

I record the emotional debt that led me to a career that has involved both business and law in the Dedication.

PART ONE

ETHICAL CHOICES AND LEGAL OBLIGATIONS

CHAPTER 1

How to Think About Ethical Choices

Linda was the sales manager for the Midwest division of a company that manufactures office products. One day she had a job to do, an unpleasant one. After asking for the go-ahead to fire an underperforming salesman named Tom, she learned something terrible about his personal life, something that made his failure clear. She collected herself, changed her plan, and created an e-mail addressed to her boss Andrew, a no-nonsense national sales manager in Los Angeles. Immediately she wrote:

> Just spoke to HR about terminating Tom. Apparently his wife is gravely ill and doesn't have much time. We need to put any decisions on hold. Trust you agree. L.

She clicked the "send" button and got up from her desk to keep a luncheon appointment. When she returned to her office afterward, Linda found the following message:

> In case you haven't noticed, this is a business not the Sisters of Mercy. Fire him. Now.

As Linda sat back in her chair after reading Andrew's e-mail, she knew she had two problems. First she had a problem with her employee's performance. That's what started everything. She was used to dilemmas like this. Dealing with them was part of her job. Her second problem was thornier. Andrew had given her a flat-out order to do something she didn't feel good about doing. Anyone who has ever had a boss knows exactly how this feels. We may not like these people, or their choices in particular cases, but being the boss gives them the right to decide.

Still, immediate questions about Andrew's authority raced through Linda's mind, as they would if it were you or I who had been given such a distasteful order.

"Must I?"

"What kind of trouble will I be in if I don't?"

"Could *I* get fired myself?"

We call this type of bind a "hierarchy dilemma." After all, Linda didn't create this mess, she simply found herself sandwiched in the organizational middle, above the underperforming salesman and below the boss who was determined to force her to let him go.

Whenever you're confronted with hierarchy dilemmas, whether being asked to do something you don't want to do, or wanting to do something you cannot, your challenge is figuring out how to persuade the person whose assent you need to change his or her mind. It means finding a way to pitch it to the boss so that you get a desired outcome while keeping your metaphorical head firmly attached to your shoulders.

Sometimes, however, there's no boss telling you what to do. The decision is yours to make. This book is about how you make those decisions or, when your boss is pushing you in a direction you don't think you ought to go, the arguments you can marshal to try to persuade him or her to see it your way. What that means, in turn, is that this book is about *argument*. Now by "argument" I don't mean quarrelling with someone with whom you disagree about something. I mean making a reasoned case for a position.

Instinctively, we make cases for what we want to do or what we want others to do. In the e-mail exchange above, both Linda and Andrew have reasons, though they haven't spelled them out. In this chapter we're going to see how their reasons could be expressed. Spelling out those positions in a reasoned way is what I mean by argument.

People are schizophrenic about the need for argument where choices about values are concerned. At one level, most of us say, whether to our coworkers, our friends, or families, "You should do this *because*...." At another level, many say that a person's ethics (value system) is like his or her religion. People get to make their own choices. We praise this hands-off attitude by calling it "tolerance."

The premise of this book is twofold. The first premise is that while, at some level, people "get to make their own choices," there *are* choices that are better than others, and any company that doesn't realize, accept, and act on this fact is asking for trouble. The second premise is that the choices companies make, and the options they reject, should be a product of *thinking*. Ethical choices aren't matters of individual taste, like whether you prefer chocolate or strawberry ice cream. They are, or should be, reasoned choices. In other words, this book is about the "because" in "you should do this because...." It's about how to help you formulate your "becauses" in sound and coherent ways that will satisfy you and persuade others.

Most of us when we were young derived our initial ideas about the right thing to do from our parents, our teachers, and perhaps respected clergy. That's generally (though, I hasten to add, not always) a good thing. But it's critical to take our ethical thinking beyond what we understood when we were children. We need to challenge our rational faculties to devise solutions to the ethical problems we face in business (and elsewhere, though "elsewhere" is not the subject here) as much as we use them to solve all the other complex issues we face in business and organizational life.

In this chapter, we're going to consider three fundamental ways that people think about ethical questions. I think you'll find that your own thoughts about why you should or shouldn't do something typically fall into one of the categories, though most people find that different choices often fall into different categories. We can use the simple story about Linda, Andrew, and Tom to demonstrate all three. This story illustrates another characteristic of what we're going to be talking about in this book. When we first encounter a problem that ultimately turns out to raise significant ethical problems, the ethical issues often aren't yet crystallized. Initially, you might not even recognize that what you're confronting contains an ethical dimension. Linda's apparent duty to fire Tom looks at first like a simple management issue—firing an employee whose performance isn't up to par and who (as we'll see) hasn't improved despite having been given a number of chances. The ethical problems emerge as you start to figure out what you're going to do.

Before we explore the principal ways of ethical thinking, however, we need to define our terms. We need to understand the difference between what we mean when we say, "We should (or ought to) do X" and when we say, "We must do X."

THE DIFFERENCE BETWEEN ETHICAL CHOICES AND LEGAL OBLIGATIONS

There are two fundamental ways to think about the choices we make in business or, for that matter, in our personal lives. The first is the question of what we *must* do. The second is what we *should* do. When you ask what you must do, you are asking if you are compelled or required to do something. When you ask what you should do, you are asking about a choice that you are free to make but are not *compelled* to make.

Questions of "what you must do" come in different varieties. When you talk about what you must do, you nearly always mean that, if you don't, you'll suffer some sort of adverse consequence. Suppose a company wants to open locations in a half-dozen new states. To do so successfully, the company requires, among the mountain of needs, adequate financing, suitable knowledge of the potential markets, and sufficient management expertise to facilitate the expansion. The company *must* take care of these and other requirements, or the venture will fail. Failure is the consequence of not doing what the company must do.

The law also tells you what you *must* do, but here "must" means something different. Failure to do what the law requires means you'll suffer a sanction. The sanction, in the extreme case, can be criminal punishment. Otherwise it can mean liability for sum of money, an order forbidding you from doing something you want to do, or simply that a deal you thought you had secured is unenforceable because there's a defect in the contract.

For example, suppose a company's board asks, "Can we refuse to promote Marilyn to vice president because she's an African American female and we don't want any African American females at that level?" On one level, of course, a company has the capability in the sense of the managerial authority to promote or to refuse to promote anyone to a senior position. Legally speaking, however, as everybody today knows, the answer to the board's question is an emphatic *no*. The company *can* refuse to promote Marilyn for lots of reasons, some sound from a business point of view and some unsound, without running afoul of what the law says you can't do. But the company must not refuse to promote her *because* she's a female or because she's African American, let alone both. That's because federal and (in most places) state laws forbid discrimination on account of either gender or race. So a company can't refuse to promote Marilyn because of her gender or her race not because it lacks the managerial capability, but because, if it does so, it risks adverse legal sanctions. The law tells the company what it must, or in this case, must not do. We have a name for what the law requires you to do to avoid adverse consequences. We call it "legal obligation."

Suppose someone says, "We shouldn't take Marilyn's gender or race into account when we consider whether she's qualified for the VP post." Someone might use "shouldn't" here as a shorthand way of saying that the company has a legal obligation not to make a promotion decision based on a candidate's race or gender. But our speaker might mean something else, something very important indeed. He or she might mean, "We shouldn't take Marilyn's race or gender into account because it's *wrong* to do so. It would be wrong to do so even if there were no law against it." In this instance, our speaker is talking about what's the right thing to do regardless of whether there is or isn't a legal sanction involved. That's an ethical choice. Often what the law requires and what you'd choose ethically are the same. That's true here: Marilyn deserves a fair shot at the promotion without reference to her race or gender. But sometimes the law doesn't go as far as you think, ethically, it should. Or, perhaps, there's no legal obligation involved because Congress or the state legislature didn't create one. As we'll see in more detail below, it would have been as wrong ethically speaking not to promote Marilyn because she was an African American female in 1940 as it is today. But in 1940 there would not have been any basis for saying, "legally you mustn't do this."

The basic distinction between ethical choices and legal obligations is thus easy to see. When someone makes an ethical choice we think is wrong, we criticize the decision. Unless that ethical choice also constitutes a breach of a legal obligation, however, there's no sanction beyond our criticism. Now don't misunderstand me. Ethical criticism is a powerful tool, and no company wants to be accused of acting unethically. But it's not the same thing as a court saying, "you're going to jail," or "you're liable for $5 million."

We'll talk about sexual harassment in Chapter 4 in detail, but consider this example: No court is going to hold a male employer liable if, one time, he puts his arm around the shoulder of a female employee. But does that mean it's OK if he does so? Of course not—for two reasons. First, good and persuasive arguments can be advanced that male employees shouldn't intrude on a female employee's personal space in this way. There's an ethical objection when a male employee does so. But there's also a second reason. Certain conduct is of the kind that prompts courts to award sanctions. In some cases, however, there isn't enough bad conduct, or it's objectionable but not sufficiently bad, to warrant legal sanctions. Your company's lawyer probably will say that male employees *shouldn't* put their arms around the shoulders of female employees because if male employees do it frequently, or if a man puts his arm around a woman's waist, the likelihood of a slap from a court increases. Thus, while a male employee shouldn't behave in this way for a purely ethical reason, he also shouldn't because he might be heading down the slippery slope where an adverse liability judgment awaits. If you're a male boss, you probably can put your arm around the shoulders or even the waist of a female employee just once without risking that you, or the company, will be held liable. But you shouldn't do it, both for purely ethical reasons and because you don't want to start inching toward that line where the law says, NO FURTHER.

ETHICS, MORALS, AND VALUES

When lawyers say you "shouldn't" do something, they mean that you mustn't do it or you run the risk of a sanction. When we discuss *should* questions that don't carry legal obligations, we're using concepts that come from another discipline: ethics. When ethicists say you should or shouldn't do something, they're generally claiming that there are good reasons for doing (or not doing) it beyond that which the law prescribes. Ethicists aren't preachers. They don't tell you what to do. They're really conceptual engineers. They help to design and specify ways to think clearly, and productively, about some of the problems we face every day.

To understand how they do this, we need first to define some terms. What do we mean by ethics? And how do "ethics" differ from "morals" or "values"?

If you type "ethics" into a computer search engine, you'll see a variety of definitions, nearly all related to "right" and "wrong" conduct. That's fine, but it doesn't really help. If product development rolls out a new product and it doesn't sell, have the executives who made the choice done something wrong? They were clearly mistaken ("wrong") about what consumers in the market were prepared to buy, but nobody would say they did something wrong in an ethical sense. As we'll use the word here, "ethics" refers to choices that we make that affect others' well-being or a person's sense of his or her own self-worth. Especially in business, this generally means their financial well-being, and their individual self-respect.

This use of the word "ethics" is closely related to the terms "morals" and "morality." If you studied the subject in college, it was probably called "moral philosophy." I've generally avoided the words "morals" and "morality" because to some they have overtones related to what's called "sexual morality." It's important not to bring that baggage into what we're going to discuss.

"Values" presents an opposite problem. This word's connotations can be too broad. Although the word "values" includes ethics—"It's a core 'value' of this company not to discriminate against any employee on grounds of race, creed, or color"—the word also relates to purely business objectives. We won't be considering such important concepts as putting the customer first, prizing innovative activity, pushing stifling bureaucracy aside, and the like. Those are the "values" about which much ink has been spilled, especially since Tom Peters and Robert H. Waterman Jr. published *In Search of Excellence* more than a quarter century ago. Nobody doubts that values like these are critical for business success. But this book's focus is different; it's on right and wrong, and how we make choices where problems of right and wrong are implicated.

WHAT LINDA CAN SAY TO ANDREW

Linda's hierarchy issue is a dilemma because of its ethical dimension. Before she knew about Tom's wife's fatal illness, her decision didn't create ethical problems. To be sure, firing any employee does affect his or her financial well-being and self-esteem, but that doesn't mean there's a tough ethical problem. If you aren't doing the job, you are liable to get fired. If you're the boss, and you have an employee whose performance doesn't measure up, unpleasant though it is, you have to fire him or her. Management responsibility guides your conduct. Employers and employees alike understand that.

Linda's case, however, is no longer that simple. If she obeyed orders and fired Tom, the law would be completely on her side. Employment law doesn't protect the underperforming employee. But the question of what she truly should do is far more interesting and complex, and to her at least, equally important. Her immediate problem is what she can say to Andrew to try to get him to reverse his decision to fire Tom at once.

Can she put her concern in terms that mean anything to a boss like Andrew?

Linda must find a way to convince Andrew to delay firing Tom without openly criticizing his decision or disobeying his order. She doesn't need corporate cheerleader lines about how "people matter." And she certainly doesn't need anyone reminding her that fumbling this situation could put her own job—or at least her year-end bonus—on the line.

Let's go back to the time before Linda learned about Tom's wife. At that point she was simply a manager with an underperforming employee. Linda tried her best to get out of this problem the old-fashioned way: she tried to motivate Tom. He was once a powerhouse salesman earning a fine salary. When his performance began to slip, Linda was initially unconcerned. Even the best salesmen, she knew, could have bad quarters, from which they readily rebound. The decline in the quarterly commission bonus, which formed two-thirds of a top performer's income, usually served, along with a loss of pride, to get things turned around. For the last two and a half years, however, Tom's sales were on a consistent decline, measured both absolutely and relative to others in the region and companywide. Nothing had arrested Tom's decline. Linda tried all the usual tricks: words of encouragement, motivational seminars, and new "sales tool kits" to help increase his market penetration. She and Tom had conversations in which she sternly told him that things had to change. Nothing worked.

Three weeks after the end of a particular quarter, when Tom's sales had taken another dive, Linda reached the conclusion that things couldn't continue. She knew her own numbers, on which her incentive compensation was based, and on which the possibility of her promotion depended, would fall again—largely because of Tom. She finally had enough. When she banged out a first e-mail to Andrew, she had no qualms about what she wanted. She outlined the data and sought Andrew's permission to terminate Tom, again without knowing the circumstances behind Tom's troubles, which he'd never revealed. Andrew's reply e-mail was four letters everybody in sales management understood: "GROH"—Get Rid of Him.

Would that life were always so simple, but it seldom is. Linda immediately phoned Amanda, the human resources manager, and asked her to prepare for a termination. Like most careful companies, theirs had a set of termination procedures that needed to be followed. The procedures were there to ease what is always a painful situation and to minimize the possibility of legal difficulties.

But things didn't seem so straightforward when Amanda showed up at Linda's office. As soon as Linda told Amanda that they were meeting to discuss Tom, Amanda began to shift uncomfortably in her chair.

"What's the problem?" asked Linda. "He's under forty, he's white, and his performance has stunk for more than a year. He can't sue us."

"I—I know that," stammered Amanda. "It's just...."

Linda knew Amanda was holding something back. "Will you get to the point? How can I run this region in this economy if people don't give me full information?"

"But what I know was told to me in confidence."

"You're not his therapist. For crying out loud, out with it."

"It's Tom's wife," Amanda said softly. "She's got cancer. It's bad. She's been fighting it for a few years but, now, well...."

Linda leaned back in her chair and reflexively held her forehead.

Amanda continued: "She went back into the hospital about a week ago. They say there isn't much time." Her voice trailed off.

Linda took a deep breath. "Oh, I see," she said softly. "And Tom?"

"He didn't want anybody to know. You know how it is with him. 'Business is business' he says. He's such a private person." Then Amanda collected herself. She had dealt with such matters before and doubtless would again. She had to be tough but fair. "Whatever you and Andrew have to do, I guess you've got to do. But not now, please. If not for him, consider the effect on the sales staff."

"Of course," said Linda softly. "We can figure out what to do later, after his wife...." She did not finish the sentence.

"Thanks," said Amanda. She rose and left the office.

Linda collected herself, thought for awhile, and then created a second e-mail addressed to Andrew. On the subject line, she typed,

"Tom," and she wrote the message that opened this chapter. She thought that surely Andrew would understand the need for a compassionate delay of the inevitable. Wouldn't anyone?

Apparently not a young hotshot half a country away with quarterly regional sales figures to boost. In this instance—for reasons we will explore shortly—it would be wishful thinking to imagine that, overcome by compassion, Andrew would cancel or even delay his order to Linda to fire Tom. Andrew is what we call an EIP, an ethically indifferent person. An EIP lacks sensors and concern about others. But Linda is *not* ethically indifferent, and she found herself facing a clear-cut dilemma that impinged on her deeply held values.

THE ETHICAL LANDSCAPE

The minute anything you do affects someone else separate and apart from its effect on business, you have an issue of ethics. If you refrain from doing something because of the impact on someone else, that's an equally ethical choice. Influenced by the media, we often think that questions of business ethics concern high-profile wrongdoing—such as what went on at Enron or WorldCom, or big-ticket insider trading, or the allegations that Hewlett-Packard CEO Patricia Dunn spied on the members of the board of directors, technically her bosses. When people say, "business ethics is an oxymoron," they are referring to this. They mean that there are bad people in business, many (alas!) in highly visible positions, running major companies. But the concept of business ethics is real because the clear thinking it requires helps good people like Linda do their jobs.

Linda *can* fire Tom, we've seen, because she has the managerial capability—he's the employee and she's the boss—and because there's no legal impediment. But she believes she shouldn't. To understand it, and to figure out her best strategy to approach Andrew, we need to explore the likely bases for Linda's discomfort.

There are three basic dominant modes of thinking about ethics. Even if you've never heard the terms, my guess is that most of your training about what's right or wrong falls into one of the three categories. Borrowing from technical literature, I will call them the ethics of rights, virtue ethics, and consequentialism. We'll see that while Linda's initial reaction to Tom's situation is driven by the first two, the third provides the basis for argument which has a shot of persuading Andrew and, thus, getting the job done. Because it's the most likely way Linda might try to persuade Andrew to change his mind, it will be easiest to follow the train of thought if we start with consequentialism.

THE INSIGHT OF CONSEQUENTIALISM

If Linda can't change Andrew's mind, she's going to have a deep regret on her conscience. Firing a guy whose wife is on her deathbed is harsh, uncaring, even cruel. On the other hand, from everything she knows about Andrew, getting him to exhibit, much less act on, regret for the personal misfortunes of another person isn't a likely prospect. Andrew is an ethically indifferent person—one of the coldest of the breed—and EIPs are impervious to any kind of argument that overtly addresses concern for others. We're not going to spend much time dissecting Andrew's character. We can proceed, however, just accepting that our world contains a certain number of ethical troglodytes. But Linda has a potent argument. It's an argument that most of us respond to, and not just EIPs—though this may be the only kind of argument that reaches them. It's an argument that doesn't appeal to sentiment, compassion, human dignity, or to anything else that a tough-minded, bottom-line-oriented person might view as squishy or sentimental. But despite the fact that it makes no appeal to such an array of human values, it is—and this may surprise you—one of the most common and respected kinds of ethical arguments that exists.

Andrew's GROH e-mail and its follow-up about the Sisters of Mercy both make it clear that he has no patience with appeals to compassion, common humanity, or dignity. Indeed, if I were in Linda's situation, I'd worry that even raising such concerns to Andrew might prompt him to conclude that I wasn't tough enough for the job. So what's the most likely approach that Linda can take that has some chance of success? Part of the answer lies hidden in the plea that Amanda made to Linda before she was sure that Linda's compassion was engaged. Remember when Amanda expressed her concern about the effect on the rest of the sales staff if the company fired Tom while his wife lay dying? Suppose Linda sent a reply to the Sisters of Mercy e-mail to Andrew saying:

I hear you. But HR warns me of a negative effect on morale when the rest of the sales force learns that we terminated Tom now. Seems to make sense to wait. Less impact on staff and potential sales. Do you agree?

In making such an argument to Andrew, Linda isn't saying that firing Tom is intrinsically "wrong." Indeed, she doesn't say or imply that it's *wrong* at all. Instead, she appeals to the consequences flowing from a particular choice, and only to such consequences. Because the touchstone of this approach is to focus on the results of a possible action, we call this kind of argument *consequentialist*. Now, be aware of something very important. We're not saying that Linda's *motivation* for not wanting to fire Tom immediately is her concern about the effect on the morale of the rest of the sales force. Quite the opposite. These consequences are likely not what principally motivates Linda (and why we probably admire her more because of it). But an appeal to the consequences is an effective argument we see all the time in business. It doesn't challenge the level of the listener's compassion, nor does it overtly engage his or her emotions, and that's why it's so desirable with a boss like Andrew. It's a tough-minded response from Linda to a tough-minded directive from above. In many situations, it will work. And the approach has a long and distinguished pedigree.

A SHORT HISTORY OF CONSEQUENTIALISM

Why is consequentialism so useful? Where did it come from? Does it have limits? To answer these questions, we'll go back to the last half of the eighteenth century, at the very time when the American colonies were beginning their uprising from British rule. The American Revolution was possible in part because some of the most creative thinkers in British—or indeed world—history led a radical change about how we think about what makes one act right and another wrong. Reducing the idea of these thinkers to its essentials, the core notion is this: When faced with a choice between competing possible actions, all you have to do is determine what creates the greatest aggregate net benefit. You don't have to decide any other questions about values or morality. All you do is total your sums. Indeed, these thinkers, including such giants as Adam Smith, Jeremy Bentham, and James Mill, called this idea utilitarianism because they thought the rightness of an action was established when the total aggregate benefit—called total utility—of an act exceeded the total utility of the available alternatives. But while professional students of ethics continue to use the term "utilitarianism," I think that for our purposes "consequentialism" is better, because it clearly points to the *outcome* of an act without worrying about whether that act is innately good or bad.

Consequentialism prompts you to ask one and only one question: Does your projected course of conduct produce a greater net benefit than any alternatives? If the answer is yes, do it. You've made the right choice. Indeed, to a consequentialist, there is no other way to define the "rightness" of a choice. All people in this equation are equal in the sense that what is valuable to me is no more important than what is valuable to you. If a projected course of conduct produces consequences that are twice as valuable to you as the consequences of a different choice are to me, consequentialists know exactly what they should do. The tag line that's usually used with consequentialism is well known: "The greatest good for the greatest number." This idea seems so obvious in the twenty-first century that it is difficult to grasp how it could have sounded revolutionary two and a half centuries ago. Haven't people always thought this way? No. Smith, Bentham, Mill, and their supporters weren't called the Philosophical Radicals for nothing.

The power of this approach to ethical questions becomes vivid in the response the consequentialist gives to anyone who challenges this view. "Do you mean to say," the consequentialist might inquire, "that between two or more possible courses of action, it can sometimes be right to select a choice *other than* the one that produces the greatest benefit?" Asking this question seems to answer it. How can the right choice produce fewer good consequences than the wrong choice? How can it ever be right, when choosing between two courses of conduct, to pick the one with the fewer good consequences? Impossible. Absurd. Consequences, and only consequences, matter. Though we'll shortly take apart this simple logic, in certain limited contexts it works very well.

CONSEQUENTIALISM AS CALCULATION

This way of thinking may sound familiar to you if you took any economics courses in college or have an MBA. In fact, what I call consequentialism might sound a lot like economics, though with a broader focus. If so, you are on the money. This is no coincidence. The Adam Smith we just mentioned is the same Adam Smith (1723–1790) whose *Wealth of Nations*—coincidentally published in 1776—was the declaration of independence for a new way of thinking about economics, and (as Smith would have put it) morals.

The key to bringing this utilitarian-consequentialist approach both to ethics and economics is the importance of calculation. Whether you must choose between alternative courses of action with no apparent economic aspects, or between alternative financial choices, calculation is essential. Although there are important differences between making value choices on a consequentialist model, and making explicitly economic or financial choices, the methodology is the same. It's no wonder that consequentialism is the approach to values with which business people are most likely to feel quickly at ease.

We can see this at work if we return to Linda's last e-mail to Andrew. She didn't ask him to change his mind by making a direct appeal to his sense of values. He's an EIP, and such an appeal would be fruitless. His reply to Linda in his e-mail at the beginning of this chapter leaves no doubt that an appeal to compassion is going nowhere. It might, however, be a different story to appeal to his desire to keep intact the high morale of his sales force. That's exactly what Linda could try to accomplish when she asks Andrew to consider the effect that firing Tom is likely to have on sales force morale. And that is a consequentialist argument. Linda might well succeed in persuading Andrew that firing Tom immediately might upset his friends and colleagues in such a way as to encourage poor performance or even defection. This risk is greater than any short-term benefit the company might achieve by immediately getting rid of a subpar performer. Indeed, Andrew might not need persuading. After all, he's not being asked to do something that could get him labeled as a bleeding heart. He's just looking at the numbers.

As a practical matter, Linda's argument has a strong appeal. It has the ring of paying attention to the business's bottom line—not surprising, since consequentialism makes what are essentially economic arguments. She runs no risk that Andrew could accuse her of soft-headed thinking, or of asking him to approve something that might compromise the bottom-line good of the company. Even if he disagrees with her, he is likely to respect her argument, and he just might compromise to end the discussion.

So Linda might try to get Andrew to reverse his decision to fire Tom immediately based on a consequentialist argument. It's not a bad move. It's not in any way illegitimate. But I doubt that many people in Linda's position would be *motivated* to try to put a hold on the decision to fire Tom because of a cost-benefit calculation comparing the cost of his performance with the cost of decreased employee morale in the sales force. I wouldn't. Consequentialism is a potent idea, prompting us to assess the results of our projected acts. But the power of consequentialism, at least as a supposed complete guide to making all ethical choices, is undermined by its inability to take our ethical *motivations* into account. Consequentialism also has another serious difficulty. While the notion of calculating two kinds of benefits from an alternative course of action sounds great in principle, the story is different in practice. Before we turn to what motivated Linda to want to get Andrew to back off his order to fire Tom immediately, and why that's important for making ethical choices, let's take a look more closely at how we calculate consequences such as the supposed negative effect firing him would have on morale in the sales force.

"HARD THINKING" AND MYTHOLOGICAL NUMBERS

It seems likely to Linda and, she hopes, to Andrew that firing Tom while his wife is dying will harm the morale of the sales force. But how can we *know* that? More specifically, since consequentialism demands that we make a comparative calculation, how can we prove that the effect on sales morale will cause greater harm than will be caused by keeping an unproductive, and now distraught, Tom in place? To understand the problem of calculation in the real world—the first of the key limitations on the consequentialist approach—let's imagine that Tom's wife isn't dying. In this case, the decision-making process on whether to fire him is a straightforward attempt to find the outcome that has the best aggregate consequences. Executives and economists usually call this technique "cost-benefit analysis."

To do this, you simply plug in the competing costs and compare. Generally, people do this by looking at net benefits solely to the company. So, if we're talking about firing Tom, we'd balance the net revenue that his territory should generate for a given period against the net he has been generating. Against that we'd compare the costs associated with hiring and training his replacement, together with the anticipated difference, if any, between his current performance and what the new person would generate as a rookie until he or she comes up to the expected performance level in what was Tom's territory.

Cost-benefit analysis appears to be a clearheaded numerical calculation. But that appearance is deceptive. The costs of hiring and training a new salesperson, and introducing him or her in the territory are pretty well known. The increased revenue from a better-performing salesperson could be derived from knowledge of the territory and what other members of the sales force, on average, achieve. You'd have a good chance of coming up with a number that is genuinely grounded in reality. But as soon as the factors you have to take into account are not obviously quantifiable, you start assigning numbers that really are only an executive's estimates or guesses of costs and benefits, not a derivation from quantifiable reality. What's more, a thoroughgoing consequentialist will have to take into account the effects, financial and psychological, getting fired will have on Tom. For the consequentialist, the fact that the company has a clear legal right to fire him won't make a difference. A consequentialist manager might *say* that the good of the company will outweigh the financial and psychological difficulties Tom would suffer, but how is he or she really going to know? You can assume that the greater good to the company outweighs the harm to Tom, but you can't really know, first because it hasn't happened yet, and second because precise quantification of psychological harm is impossible.

But calculation difficulties also can involve just the company's own costs and benefits. Suppose that Tom is not a healthy white male under the age of forty. Suppose that the underperforming employee is Bob, who is either African American, or over forty, or disabled. Under federal antidiscrimination legislation, it's illegal to discriminate against persons on account of their race, their age if they are over forty, their disability status, or their gender. In any of those cases, we'd have to assign a number to the risk that firing a person who is a member of a protected class under federal antidiscrimination laws may cause the company to incur legal costs. A person in Linda's or Andrew's position might protest that the company wants

to fire Tom or Bob on the basis of poor performance, and not on anything having to do with race, creed, color, national origin, gender,
age, or disability. And, given the facts of our story so far, they'd be
right. Still, any experienced executive—especially an experienced
human resources executive—will know that firing a person who
belongs to what the law calls "a protected class" can lead to trouble.
If the documentation of Bob's subpar performance is inadequate, or if
the company has "a pattern and practice" of discriminating against
the protected class to which Bob belongs, these costs can be significant—even if the company is not ultimately found liable for discriminatory conduct.

The point here, however, is not the magnitude of the costs. It's
that they are speculative. A sales manager may be able to come up
with plausible estimates of the costs of bringing a new salesperson on
board. But legal costs? Likely damages? Lawyers know that even
with the best intent in the world and a sound foundation of experience, there's a lot of guesswork involved. Cost-benefit analysis makes
sense where the costs and benefits are capable of being pretty precisely identified. When they can't be, what we have is little more than
a bundle of hunches and intuitions masquerading under the guise of
mathematical precision.

If we return to our original story—in which Tom's wife is mortally
ill—the issue of the speculative quantification of the negative effect
on employee morale is even clearer. No one with any real-world
business experience can doubt the importance of good morale.
Human resources professionals, for example, deal with it day in and
day out, and they see the cost to companies that underrate it. Yet assigning morale a monetary value can hardly escape being arbitrary. It's like
those reputed Revolutionary War expense reports that George Washington turned over to the Continental Congress: 2 shillings, 8 pence, for
horse fodder; 1 shilling, 10 pence, for lodging; and 200 pounds for
"entertaining officers." (The father of our country was a notorious
spendthrift.) Was it really 200 pounds? What about 175? Or 225? The
"fudge factor" for such numbers is inevitably part of the equation.

The point is this: If any one of the "values" you need for a complete cost-benefit or consequentialist calculation is essentially a
guess, the "precision" of the entire calculation is bogus. You get the
result you get because of what you assumed. So, in the case of the
employee morale in Linda and Andrew's company if Tom is fired,
your result will entirely be determined by the cost you assign to bad

morale. Assign it a high cost and you are effectively saying, "Don't fire him." Give it a low cost, and you are deciding to fire him because "the benefit of getting rid of a salesman who isn't doing the job outweighs the negative effect on morale." Now, it's true that experienced managers have a platform for assigning the probabilities of the effect on morale that are more than wild guesses. The problem is that such estimates can't help but be approximations. There aren't any real, hard numbers. Your conclusion will be the result of the numbers you input. Do you think Linda and Andrew would assign the same numerical value for cost-benefit analysis purposes to firing Tom? It sounds unlikely to me. As computer people say, garbage in, garbage out.

Thus we have what appears to be an anomaly: consequentialism, the cost-benefit method of trying to solve ethical problems in a hard-bitten, tough-minded, rigorous "no room for sentiment" way turns out itself to have a speculative component in all but the easiest cases. The alleged tough-mindedness is at best an illusion, and at worst a pseudo-scientific way of disguising the intuitions, or even the biases, of the person making the calculation.

CONSEQUENCES AREN'T ALL THAT MATTER

The first objection to a rigidly consequentialist view of solving ethical problems, thus, is that it frequently fails to achieve its goal of answering questions about values based on actual, hard data rather than on speculation. Lots of damage, like the pyschological harm of losing your job, can't be quantified. Consequentialism, in short, starts to break down because so often genuine hard numbers can't be assigned to relevant factors, thus undermining the conclusions we get from our calculations. But this isn't all. Much of what concerns us when we talk about ethics, morals, and values in fact can't realistically be assigned a numerical value. There's more to the way most of us think about ethics than calculating aggregate net benefit.

Another way of putting this idea is that consequentialism simply doesn't reflect the way most people think about many issues related to values. Take Linda. Why is she unhappy about the prospect of firing Tom when his wife is on her deathbed? Because she has done a quick mental calculation and concluded that this would harm the sales force's morale? Sounds pretty implausible and, indeed, pretty distasteful. It may be the reason she gives to Andrew, but we all know what we think about Andrew. Most of us would think less of Linda if all that moved her in the face of the personal catastrophe overtaking Tom was simply that firing him would have a quantifiable negative impact on the sales force's morale.

If we are going to consider any approach to ethics other than consequentialism, we have to face what initially appears to be a worrisome fact. Any alternative approach to values other than consequentialism must hold that, *at least sometimes,* the right choice will not produce the highest aggregate new benefit. The consequentialist will say, "No way, can't happen." But can it? You be the judge.

Let's try a different example in which consequentialism faces a stiff challenge. Jack is a rising superstar executive (at another corporation) who regularly accomplishes feats above and beyond what his colleagues achieve. He sets ambitious goals for his unit and attains them. Profit margins are high. Expenses are carefully controlled. No one else matches Jack in the creation of innovative management approaches to the problems of the unit. He is a man marked for advancement in his company. Down the road, even the CEO's position looks within his reach. Jack means a lot to the success of the company, and to all who depend upon its well-being.

Jack has only one problem. While he seems to know how to behave himself around the female executives who report to him, he can't keep his words—or his hands—under control with young women who work in clerical positions. More than one administrative assistant has walked into the human resources office in tears because of Jack's sexual innuendo or outright propositions. Finally, after a number of such incidents, the HR manager decides that she must raise the issue with her boss, Elizabeth, the chief operating officer. How should Elizabeth deal with this problem?

Now, as we'll see in more detail in Chapter 4, in the real world of twenty-first-century America, this scenario would present a legal issue, because sexual harassment is illegal under Title VII of the Civil Rights Act of 1964. But it also presents an ethical issue. Elizabeth would have a choice to make even if there were no Title VII. We already know how she would approach the problem if she were a thoroughgoing consequentialist. The benefits that Jack brings to the company are huge. Firing him, or chastising him enough that he would put himself on the job market, would cost the company dearly. If the women he harassed were other executives making substantial contributions to the company, we might have a stronger consequentialist case. But no, Jack's victims are simply clerical personnel, and easily replaced. There's no room for sentiment. The facts are the facts. Superstar executives, especially potential CEOs, are worth their weight in gold. Elizabeth's consequentialist conclusion would almost certainly be to risk unhappy secretaries, but not to risk an unhappy Jack. He's too important.

This approach will make many of us squirm, or at least I hope so. To say it is heartless and unfeeling, not to mention demeaning to Jack's victims because they are relatively powerless, is an understatement. It's this exact point that makes so many people unable to accept the pure consequentialist approach. The thoroughgoing consequentialist must be willing to accept the cost of the harm to the women. To make matters more problematic, the consequentialist has to add up everything that *all* the persons involved like or want, and subtract what they dislike or what hurts them. Elizabeth, if she were a true consequentialist, would have to credit Jack's column for the powerful positive rush he evidently gets from sexual innuendo and other methods of strutting in front of powerless women. If Jack's thrills outweigh the women's collective trauma, then our pure consequentialist must give Jack even more favorable marks! But you're probably thinking, this can't be right, and I agree with you. Now let's examine why.

"LEGAL" RIGHTS AND "MORAL" RIGHTS

Let's consider the women in Jack's office. They wouldn't like Jack's repeated sexual innuendo or what the law calls "unconsented to touching." But the fact that they can't stand it wouldn't be enough to challenge Elizabeth's conclusion if she were a thoroughgoing consequentialist. As we have seen, the women's likes and dislikes (assuming they could be quantified) could simply be folded into the cost-benefit calculation. To the consequentialist, that's the only way those feelings could be relevant to Elizabeth's ethical choice about Jack's conduct. Now, it's pretty unlikely that these women would be satisfied with this, any more than Linda would be satisfied if Andrew said to her, "I don't think there's much cost associated with a temporary dip in the sales force's morale." What the women would be likely to say is that they have a *right* not to be sexually harassed in the workplace. It's critical to understand that such a claim of right could mean two different things. On one level, the women could claim that they have a *legal right* not to be sexually harassed. Whether such a claim is correct depends upon what the law is at a particular time. In early twenty-first century America, a woman does have a legal right to be free of such harassment and has since the day President Lyndon Johnson signed the Civil Rights Act of 1964. But before that date, such a claim would have been false.

Does that mean that sexual harassment was somehow OK before the Civil Rights Act became law? Of course not. It just means that there was no *legal* right. So what kind of right is it that isn't legally enforceable? The answer is what we call a *moral* right. It's a claim to be treated in a certain way because it's the right thing to do. It's an appeal to make an appropriate ethical choice, not a description of a legal obligation. As a matter of practice, most of us make such claims of rights, for ourselves and for others, all the time. If the right is also legal, the law may add substantial clout—a fact that I, as a lawyer, work with day in and day out in my practice. But the absence of a legal right doesn't diminish the claim of a moral right.

Let's go back to Tom. Linda may well think, and many of us would be likely to agree with her, that Tom has some kind of ethical claim of right not to be fired while his wife is terminally ill. Conversely, we'd probably agree with Linda that she *shouldn't* fire Tom now, that doing so wouldn't be the right thing to, even though we understand that, unlike the women Jack has sexually harassed, there's no legal right involved.

We've thus seen that consequentialists assert that acts should be chosen because of their consequences, and nothing else. We also realize that, for many of us in a variety of situations, acts should (or should not) be done because of claims that rights are involved. The next step is to understand how claims about rights interact with the claims of consequentialism.

THE CONFLICT BETWEEN CONSEQUENTIALISM AND "RIGHTS"

Everybody remembers Thomas Jefferson's words from the Declaration of Independence:

We hold these truths to be self-evident, that all men are created equal; that they are endowed by their Creator with certain

unalienable Rights, that Among these are Life, Liberty and the
pursuit of Happiness.

Unalienable rights. Rights no one can take away from you. Probably because of the Declaration, this concept forms a central part of
the creed of nearly all Americans. But here's an ironic twist. This
theory that espouses human rights is *squarely inconsistent* with the
belief that questions of values should be decided by trying to achieve
the greatest good for the greatest number! That's right. Pure consequentialism, while enormously useful in many business settings, is at
odds with our fundamental American concept of unalienable rights.
The heritage of 1776, in which both the Declaration of Independence and *The Wealth of Nations* appeared, points in two contradic-
tory directions.

When a woman claims that she has a right not to be sexually harassed by Jack, she is implicitly making a clear statement about what
effect her right—whether legal or moral—should have if the result
differs from the (calculated) conclusion of the pure consequentialist.
The logic is simple. She's saying that her claim of right prevails.
Generalizing, this means that a claim of right is a claim that a person
is entitled to be treated in a certain way even though the aggregate
computation of consequences would reject that treatment. To put it
in another way, the "right" claimed is a right to receive a decision
even though "maximizing aggregate beneficial consequences" would
dictate a different result. So if you have a recognized right, you have
a trump card. A woman whom Jack harasses thus says that she has a
right not to be propositioned or touched in the workplace, regardless of whether she can easily be replaced and whether Jack, the rising superstar, can't be.

A right, then, is a claim to ignore the choice dictated by a calculation of aggregate consequences. And remember this: a right functions as a claim against aggregate utility whether it is a legal right or
a moral right. The difference between the two is huge in the
enforcement of the right, as we will see throughout this book. But
from the standpoint of the logic of what claiming a right means,
there's no difference.

My guess is that this will come as a surprise to many who, accus-
tomed to taking a cost-benefit approach in business, nevertheless
view themselves as subscribing to the Jeffersonian (and typically
American) ideal that human beings have basic rights. Both seem like

bedrock principles. Both *are* fundamental, but, in a tough case like the one concerning Jack's behavior toward women, something's got to give.

What gives is usually consequentialism, at least in its pure, unadulterated form. Most people believe that human beings do have certain rights. A powerful example, not pertaining to business, from Richard Dawkins's controversial book *The God Delusion*, will illustrate (though I have slightly modified his hypothetical for illustrative purposes here). Suppose there are five patients suffering from serious failure of different but key internal organs, the first the heart, the second a lung, the third a kidney, the fourth the liver, and the fifth the pancreas. Suppose each would be an ideal candidate for organ transplant surgery. Suppose that all of your five organs are healthy and could be transplanted. Suppose that the six of you are all the same age, have the same family commitments, and contribute, through your jobs and elsewhere, equally to society. Suppose that the only available organs for the transplants are yours. If the transplant operations are not performed, five people will die. If they are performed, you as the donor of five key organs will die, but the other five will live.

A thoroughgoing consequentialist would have to advise you to donate your organs—or if he or she were person number six, would be prepared to make the donations. I think that almost no one would say that person number six is "obligated" to give up his or her own life to save the other five. I think nearly everyone would say, if an external force tried to force person number six to donate, that that person had a "right" not to be killed in such circumstances.

This is an extreme and highly tailored hypothetical case, I agree. But the point is important. Most people think that there are rights that should be recognized. When Congress or the legislative authority in any state or country decides to define rights, it makes identifying legal rights easy. To be sure, there can be tough borderline cases that require the expertise of lawyers and sometimes the decisions of the courts to clarify, but legal rights are in principle (and usually in practice) fairly easy to identify. But what about claims or "moral" rights, where there is no law? If problems of calculation and the inability to take account of the moral sentiments are the pitfalls of consequentialism, advocates of rights have a pair of really tough questions to answer. If there are rights, how many are there? And, by the way, where do they come from?

ARE "RIGHTS" JUST INTUITION IN DISGUISE?

We can't talk about rights very long before three questions arise.

1. Where do rights come from?
2. How many do we have?
3. How are they defined?

Consequentialists will say that these questions cannot be answered, and that talk about rights, while sounding nice and noble, is really just fluff—or worse. Jeremy Bentham (1748–1832) is probably the single most important of all consequentialist thinkers. He put it this way: "Natural rights is simple nonsense: natural and imprescriptible rights, rhetorical nonsense—nonsense upon stilts." The consequentialist sees abstract discussions of rights as a smokescreen: using high-minded rhetoric to disguise softheaded intuition. While I'm not prepared to accept that characterization, the consequentialist has identified a real problem. It turns out that identifying the source of rights, counting how many there are, and specifying their content is difficult. Many consequentialists in history have shaken their heads at such efforts and clucked, "See, we told you so."

Up to the sixteenth century (to focus on Western Europe), identifying the source and content of rights was easy—or seemed to be. The source of rights lay in the word of God. By the eighteenth century, when Adam Smith, Jeremy Bentham, and the other Philosophical Radicals flourished, some two hundred years after the Reformation, the word of God meant the word as interpreted by the church. And the church meant that which constituted the established religion in whatever country in which people lived. In France, Italy, Spain, Portugal, Poland, and much of southern Germany and Austria, this meant the Roman Catholic Church. In England it meant the Anglican Church, in Scotland the Presbyterian Church, and in much of Northern Germany, the Netherlands, Scandinavia, and Switzerland, Lutheranism, Calvinism, or some other form of Protestantism. The old unified religious worldview that had prevailed for more than a thousand years in Europe had broken down. Individuals could still profess to believe that they really knew the "word of God"—a phenomenon present in the twenty-first century in both the Western and Islamic worlds—but nobody could get around the fact that not everybody agreed.

To Adam Smith, Jeremy Bentham, and their cohorts, however, many of the purely religious ideas were outmoded. Here's an obvious example: The Biblical prohibition against charging interest was called *usury*. It sounded nice, but it was difficult to square with the needs of the new capitalist trading economy flourishing in the Atlantic world. By retiring that Biblical injunction and instead allowing capital to be "purchased" for a price—interest—the economy expanded and all measure of people benefited.

Up until the time of the Philosophical Radicals in the late eighteenth century, the common method for resolving questions about values was to appeal to an intrinsic notion of right or wrong, typically grounded in religious ideas. The consequentialism of the Philosophical Radicals, as we have seen, conflicted with the notion of "rights." But the appeal of the Declaration of Independence's endorsement of "certain unalienable rights" made it impossible for Americans to abandon the idea without trashing one of the country's founding intellectual inspirations. Most Americans think that factors other than consequences could confer rightness or wrongness to an action. Most think it makes sense to say, for instance (separate from what the law requires), that a woman has a "right" not to be sexually harassed in her place of work.

Our world shares no general agreement about God. Businesspeople today don't have the luxury of that universal certainty about rights that our forebears had three, four, or five hundred years ago. What, then, is the source of the rights about which people generally agree if it is not God's word, or the say-so of whatever established religion is in power in a particular place? Is the enterprise of people who believe that there are certain "rights" doomed if there is nothing between the "indisputable" command of God and the homilies of the leaders of our Brownie and Cub Scout troops when we were nine years old? The only suitable "in between" criterion is our ability to make a good and persuasive argument.

To those trained in engineering, mathematics, or one of the sciences where right and wrong answers seem to exist, I know this can create discomfort. But outside of such disciplines, no argument is ever going to persuade everybody. As the Greek philosopher Aristotle taught, it's a mistake to ask of a subject more precision than the subject will permit. People interested in enhancing the awareness of values in their companies won't be satisfied by saying that because arguments about values can't be as certain as mathematical proofs, there aren't any

ethical values to which we have to pay attention. Socrates, the foun-
der of Western moral philosophy, always said that he knew he knew
nothing, but that did not stop him from arguing about the difference
between good and bad. Most of us do think that some things are
right and others are wrong. And when we say "right" and "wrong,"
we mean something different from expressing our own personal
preferences, something different from saying, "you may prefer chocolate ice cream, but I prefer strawberry." We, too, can make arguments, good arguments, arguments convincing to many, about
values. We may not be able to offer mathematical proofs, but we can
persuade.

Consequentialism is useful in its place. It's potent, and general in
its application. Sometimes it's quite persuasive. But although it
worked between Linda and Andrew when it came to Tom's firing, as
we've seen, it comes up short in cases like Jack's hands-on policy
with the female support staff. So the question is, can we come up
with an equally good argument to support claims that people have
"rights"?

The answer is yes—and no. The "yes" we've already discussed.
People do have views of right and wrong that are different from tot-
ing up consequences. Enough people got together to elect a Congress that passed the Civil Rights Act. As we've discussed they felt
that discrimination on account of race and gender, the two key com-
ponents of the statute, was wrong *because* it was wrong. It might be,
indeed probably is, accurate to say that the economy is more productive because African Americans, Hispanics, and women have
greater access to jobs than it would have been if Jim Crow and its
gender analogue continued to prevail in law. Good consequences,
however, aren't *the reason* the legal right was created. The reason was
that the legal right reflected what a vast majority perceived to be a
moral right.

The "no" is the difficulty specifying the full extent of what rights
there are. There's no single criterion, or even set of criteria, that
have the same potency and generality as the one over-arching claim
of consequentialism. When James Madison was working on drafting
the Bill of Rights in 1790, he received suggestions for approximately
two hundred different rights. At one point, farmers in Pennsylvania
urged that it was a fundamental right that they should receive a
bounty for each squirrel pelt they brought in. Regarding a few rights
most can agree. Putting aside issues of violence like murder and

assault, which are not generally issues arising in business, there'd be lots of agreement. Few would disagree that a female employee has the right to be free of sexual harassment in the office. But think about Tom. Most of us would think that Tom's personal plight demands respect. The trouble is apparent when we try to say exactly what this right is. You might say that people have a general right to be well treated, but that's so vague and wide-ranging that it isn't really going to help solve hard problems in the real world. You might narrow it and say that there is a right to be well treated *as an employee*, which confines acceptable treatment to the workplace. Better, but still vague. Well treated? Does that mean you always get a raise, regardless of your performance or the company's? I don't think so.

You might want to emphasize your right not to be disrespected. This may work for the women Jack harasses, but is that really the concern that Linda has about firing Tom while his wife is dying? Tom's case seems different from that of Jack's clerical staff. So are there two different rights? Perhaps, but if different stand-alone rights exist for these two situations in business, how many are there in total? A dozen? There must be more. Two dozen? Three?

I once did an experiment in a seminar called "Law, Business, and Ethics" that I taught at the Catholic University Law School in Washington, D.C. I asked students to identify the three most important rights they thought people had in connection with business. No two lists were identical, and there was hardly any correspondence among which rights the students thought were "the most" important.

To the consequentialist, secure in his or her one-criterion ethical universe, this chaos shows the folly of talking about rights. "It sounds to me," the consequentialist might say, "that whenever you don't like the result you get from maximizing aggregate net value, you say you have a right. That's make-believe." The consequentialist's objection to rights, in other words, is that rights aren't supported by any hard and fixed principles; they are merely disguised intuitions to be conveniently trooped out to try to achieve desirable results in particular cases. They aren't guides to action; they are after-the-fact justifications for what you already want to do.

It's fine in political documents like the Declaration of Independence to speak about unalienable rights. After all, Jefferson, Adams, and the other signers of the Declaration were trying to recruit support for what, at the time, seemed a dangerous, even foolhardy adventure: rebellion against the most powerful country in Europe, if not the world. But for those of us trying to learn how to make reasonable ethical choices in the cut and thrust of business, rhetoric won't suffice. Yet, to repeat, a simple look at aggregate consequences won't be enough for Linda, nor will it satisfy Jack's victims. Many of us will say that we don't care how much good Jack does the company if he treats women this way.

Is there a way out of this morass? Must we conclude, after all, that resolving questions about values in any sort of rigorous, intelligent way is hopeless? Must we ignore all talk about business ethics on television or in the news? Should we throw all books about business ethics, including this one, into the trash, and simply call in the lawyers when trouble arises? Or is there another alternative?

VIRTUE ETHICS: AN APPEAL TO CHARACTER

To find an alternative to the apparently unresolvable tensions between the consequentialist and the person who believes that individual rights often can and should trump "the greatest good for the greatest number," let's return to Linda's story. There's almost certainly another motive for Linda's change of tactics when sending her consequentialist e-mail to Andrew. Linda has beliefs about what kind of person she thinks she is, and what kind of person she wants to be. These beliefs affect her outlook. She doesn't want to be the kind of person who fires Tom, comes home, and in response to her husband's "How was your day?" answers, "Oh, nothing much. Fired a guy whose wife is dying of cancer. No big deal. Shall we order in pizza?"

Most men and women working in business care about what their actions say about themselves. Not necessarily what other people will say about them (although this highly motivates some), but what they think about their own actions, and how they feel about themselves. Recent studies suggest that large numbers of young men and women entering the business world share this perception. Huge numbers of women and men in business, especially those with senior executive aspirations, want more out of their business lives than increased compensation and extravagant perks.

When I shared the helm of a corporation, I didn't want it to be a place where workers were humiliated, where executives lied about what they were doing, and where discrimination in hiring, promoting, and firing was practiced. My self-image demanded better than that. Of course, as a lawyer I also knew where we ran legal risks and where we did not, but beyond that basic standard, I thought about what kind of person I wanted to be. I have to look at myself in the mirror every morning when I shave. I don't want to be unhappy with the man I see.

This is an ancient idea: that a key component of making ethical choices is the effect they have on the *character* of the chooser. To be precise, it is ten times older than Adam Smith and the Declaration of Independence! It goes back 2,500 years to the Greeks, and particularly to Aristotle (384–322 B.C.), arguably the most complete genius who ever lived.

But first, a quiz. Does your company say it "puts people first"? Are you snickering? Let's face it, your company exists to make money. So does my law firm, and my corporation before that. To give Andrew his due, none of us works for the Sisters of Mercy, at least not if we toil for profit. That's fair, but despite this sensible reality, it's a remarkable and altogether encouraging phenomenon that large numbers of the best people working in America's companies—the people whom businesses most desire to attract and keep—want more than just money from their jobs. But the sheer corniness of some corporate-speak about values can still be embarrassing, even for those of us who share them. "We put people first!" "Integrity is the cornerstone of the way we do business!" Yeah, right. Window-dressing. The product of some PR consultant's billable-hour mind. These phrases are public relations fluff without content, and no one is deceived. As vapid platitudes they're so general and obligation-free that they're no help at all in solving the problems that real businesspeople confront.

If you're among the best managers and business executives, or if you aspire to be, you won't be satisfied by such glittering generalities. You and I spend long hours in a business environment, and "who we are at work" affects "who we are as people." Aristotle made this same point when he said that developing our own individual character is one of our chief responsibilities. We can characterize what he said as aiming to achieve *personal excellence*.

The focus of what Aristotle called ethics is not how to answer the question, "What *action* is right?" The chief inscription at the Oracle of Delphi was, "Know Thyself." Aristotle's brand of ethics was not about duty, but about creating excellence in ourselves. The modern, restated central issue becomes, "Who shall I strive to become in order to achieve the kind of existence that I am meant to have as a person?" Who do we want to be, and who do we want our friends and colleagues to be? What personal character traits do we care about? Honesty. Integrity. Concern for others. Sensitivity. Good judgment. This list could and should go on.

Our actions not only tell us about ourselves, they also help mold who we are. Linda doesn't want to fire Tom because *she* doesn't want to be the kind of boss who'd do that. If Elizabeth as COO decides that Jack must either shape up or ship out, the likely reason, apart from the legal consequences, is that she doesn't want to be a part of a company that tolerates such demeaning behavior. Traditionally, moral thinkers have called this approach "virtue ethics." Virtue ethics differs from consequentialism, or the ethics of rights, because it focuses not on an action—what is "done" to someone else—but its effect on you, the person taking action.

But beyond this, Aristotle and the Greeks understood the need to avoid looking at particular choices as if they were random snapshots. The choices we make are cumulative. What we have done becomes a part of us, an element of our structure, helping, guiding, and nourishing what we will do; helping, guiding, and creating ourselves as "good people." We are, in short, talking about much more than business values. We're talking about character.

I once read about a Midwestern bank that had a unique hiring process. When it set up interviews at the business schools where it recruited, it sent its top management team to meet the candidates. Management's premise was that a comparison of transcripts alone couldn't identify the candidates the bank wanted to hire. Technical skills, as evidenced by grades, were bunched together. What distinguished individual candidates was which ones the top management team viewed as most capable of operating with the honor and integrity that was the foundation of the bank's relationship with its customers.

While we can't ignore the insights of the consequentialist or the advocate of rights in resolving questions about values, acting with your eye on that face in the mirror is a helpful touchstone in business. There are increasing numbers of men and women who want more from their business lives than external marks of success, who want their business lives to be a part of coherent personal lives. People like this know that ruthless, unfeeling behavior at the office can't be left behind when they spend time at home with their families. Net worth, in short, is about more than subtracting financial liabilities from financial assets. Or, put differently, it's important not to confuse your "worth" with your "net worth."

CONSEQUENTIALISM, RIGHTS, VIRTUE—AND THE LONG ARM OF THE LAW

Consequentialism, rights, and virtue ethics constitute the three most important ways of thinking about the ethical choices you have to make. I've never been satisfied that there's a rank ordering between them. Each has a part to play. But there's one caveat. Some people argue that in business, none of them matter. So far as values or rights are concerned, these people would say, all that counts is whether there's legal risk in what you're doing. In this view, ethics is bunk, businesses exist to make a profit, and businessmen and women are justified in doing—indeed, only should be doing—whatever they can to make a profit. Questions of value or of right or wrong arise, these people say, *only* if the value or right is embodied in the law. The argument pretends to be tough-minded, but is in fact fuzzy. It typically involves a lack of understanding of how the law works, and, more fundamentally, of where the law comes from. The questions raised by this argument are sufficiently common that we'll spend the next chapter sorting them out.

CHAPTER 2

Economics, Law, and Business Choices

Not long ago, I was watching a PBS program on the origins of the universe. It was about the Big Bang and the limits of the knowable universe—real mind-bending stuff. One of the sound bites near the conclusion featured an astronomer from California. The study of the origins of the universe, she said, made her believe, as a matter of faith rather than of science, that there were other universes with completely different laws of physics from our own. Because the laws of physics are not the same in different universes, the different universes are mutually incomprehensible. There's a parallel between the astronomer's imagined other universes and the problem of how to solve the quandaries of business ethics effectively. The difficulty is that there are three universes that hardly know how to talk to one another. The first is the world of economics; the second is the world of the law; and the third is the world of ethics or, if you will, moral philosophy. If these three disciplines are not literally unknowable to one another, as are different universes with different laws of physics, its practitioners sometimes act as if they were.

If we're going to make genuine progress in figuring out how to address issues that impact others, whether we mean financially or in terms of their self-respect, we have to understand the premises of these three ways of thinking, these three universes. Then we can see how they interact. A surprisingly large number of businesspeople, and lawyers, think that law is a substitute for ethical choice, that law entirely subsumes ethics. To understand that view, however, we have to backtrack to those businesspeople who view both law and ethics as a hindrance to business. Once we dispose of that position, we'll devote most of our attention in this chapter to the law and how the advice lawyers give their business clients relates to ethical choices.

THE ECONOMIC MODEL: BUSINESS IS ABOUT MAKING A PROFIT

The way in which practitioners of one discipline seem to inhabit their own universe, and view other disciplines as equivalent to universes with different and incomprehensible laws of physics, is clear when we think about what I call the profit-driven view of business ethics. In this view, a businessperson decides whether or not to do something, or which choice among a number to accept, by making the choice that maximizes profit, or, in the more precise phrase of an advocate of this view, "long-term shareholder value."[1] Now, even with this approach, gnarly questions arise when what maximizes the company's bottom line is different from what maximizes an individual's bottom line. They're significant enough that we'll devote a whole chapter to them, under the umbrella of conflicts of interest. Let's put them aside for the moment. Our present task is simply to explore the idea that there's really no such thing as an ethical problem in business. All questions are reducible to dollars and cents. We can call this view the ethics of the marketplace. For those trained in economics or in business school with a heavy economics focus, it's appealing. As Andrew in Chapter 1 would say, "All's fair in love and war—and in business." But all is not fair in love, all is not fair in war—and all is not fair in business.

To understand this narrow way of thinking, let's return to Linda's story. We explained it in a way that Andrew, Linda's boss, could treat the decision of whether or not to fire Tom, the underperforming salesman, purely as a matter of revenue production. To allow for this pure, unimpeded focus, we deliberately chose to imagine Tom as a white male under forty. We also made Tom a regular member of the sales force, and not a high-level executive. By doing it this way, we removed all the *legal* constraints that could have hindered Andrew's bottom-line focus. Tom is white, so there's no question of racial discrimination. Tom is male, so there's no issue of gender discrimination. And Tom is under forty, so age discrimination doesn't kick in. (Yes, forty. If you haven't worked in human resources, you may not know that a person is protected by federal age discrimination legislation beginning on his or her fortieth birthday. That, incidentally, means that approximately 53 percent of the adult American workforce is protected by this legal regime.) Finally, as an "ordinary" member of the sales force, Tom would be what the law calls an "at will" employee. This means that the company can fire him at any time for pretty much any reason. (A senior executive, by contrast, likely would have an individual employment contract that would control the circumstances under which the company could fire him or her, and what it would have to pay if it did so.)

If, by contrast, Tom had been African American or over forty, or if he had an individual employment contract, or if Tom were Tamara and female, legal considerations would intrude themselves into Andrew's and Linda's decisions.

Now, there obviously are going to be many situations in which a businessperson's decision to maximize long-term shareholder value will be constrained by legal requirements. Indeed, one of the reasons that so many "economics-oriented" people favor "limited government" is because their economics outlook prompts them to think that "optimum" results are more likely to the extent government-imposed rules, that is, laws, don't inhibit their individual profit-maximizing activity. But these legal requirements are viewed entirely within the profit—or long-term—owner valuation model. Laws impose costs—nothing more, nothing less. We can readily see this if we change Tom in our story into Bob and make him a fifty-two-year-old African American.

From Linda's perspective, these changes make no difference. The guy's wife is dying—the color of his skin, or whether he's fifty-two or thirty-two, don't matter. For Andrew, at one level, the changes also make no difference. Whatever negative we can say about Andrew's cold-heartedness, we haven't seen anything to lead us to believe that he's a racist or is particularly unfeeling about people who have a little gray in their hair. What Bob's racial and age characteristics do, however, is to add to the cost of firing him. These costs are multiple, and we'll identify them separately, but their significance will be clear in the next section where we describe the lawyer's universe. First, if the company fires a fifty-two-year-old African American, without the protection of a solid paper trail documenting subpar performance, there's a real possibility that the employee will commence proceedings against the company either before the federal Equal Employment Opportunities Commission (EEOC), or similar state agency, or in federal or state court. Now, being cited before the EEOC or sued itself is a cost. This is true even if the employee has little chance of prevailing or if the company has insurance that will cover the cost of the defense. Valuable management hours will be spent working with lawyers, recovering documents, testifying and preparing to testify, and the like. It may be difficult to put a precise dollar figure on these costs, but it's certain that they are costs.

Second, of course, the company may actually have to fork out money. The case could go to trial, and the company could lose and some or all of the damages they'd owe Tom might not be covered by insurance. Or the insurance policy limits might be exhausted—insurance talk for used up—in the course of the defense, so that the company would have to pay the lawyers' fees to complete the defense.

Third, and finally, being sued for race or age discrimination can create indirect costs. These costs may be lumped together under the rubric of reputational injury. Twenty years ago, when I taught a course in strategic management in a business school, I used Wal-Mart as the poster child for how a company could be hugely profitable and super-responsive to the needs of its customers and the communities in which it was located. The protracted gender-discrimination litigation in which Wal-Mart has been involved since 2004 has tarnished its reputation beyond recognition. In a sense, this kind of cost is like the damage to morale on the sales force that, in Chapter 1, we offered as Linda's possible "bottom line" justification for delaying Tom's firing. Race or age discrimination has the potential of harming attitudes in the community at large.

ECONOMIC ETHICS: THE WORLD OF THE EIP

On the economics/market approach to business, legal costs are just like any other costs. Some costs may be more difficult to estimate correctly than others, but that is purely a technical problem. Suppose a lawyer advised the company that, based on his or her experience, there was a 60 percent likelihood that firing the fifty-two-year-old African American Bob would produce a jury award, above and beyond insurance coverage, of $100,000. In figuring out the cost of Bob's subpar performance, sales management could figure in a projected cost of $60,000 to pay the court's judgment against the company. The company could also factor in other costs we've mentioned, like lost management time to litigate the claim and the cost to pay the company's PR firm to devise and implement a damage-control strategy in the community where Bob's story might make the paper or the 11:00 news.

If we were speaking precisely we'd call this approach "economic nonethics." For simplicity's sake, though, I'll call it "economic ethics." Nothing matters except the dollars and cents on the bottom line. Its like the consequentialism we discussed in Chapter 2, but it is much narrower. Consequentialism takes into account human values and feelings. Its weakness, we saw, is the inability to assign meaningful numerical values to such nonnumeric phenomena. The economic view doesn't have this concern. If something doesn't make money or costs money, you can forget about it. Racial discrimination is neither good nor bad and the psychological consequences to a victim are irrelevant. It's just a cost. The only measure of that cost is the fine and litigation expense the law imposes.

Adherents of this view are the ethically indifferent people, or EIPs, we met in Chapter 1. EIPs live in their own universe. They can't understand why you "should" do something because it's "right." They can't understand that you should obey the law because, in general, obeying the law makes society a better place in which to live. They only can understand that *not* obeying the law is cost.

Economic ethics appeals to many. I'd bet that most readers have met at least a few people in their own or other companies who fit the model. Let's think about its appeal. First, it's simple, by which I mean not simple as in the opposite of hard, but simple as in the opposite of complex. If we return to the problem of accurately estimating the legal costs to Linda's company if it fires a fifty-two-year-old African American, we see right away that it's darn tough to come up with any realistic numbers. But tough is not the same as complex. On the economic view, there is only one criterion to consider: maximizing long-term owner value. If you adopt this view you don't have any worries about depriving a man in his fifties of his job, or of worrying that you may be acting from racial prejudice. There are no conflicts arising from other values you may hold, because, at least as far as business is concerned, you haven't got any. If you really believe that "ethics" has no place in the world of business—and we'll argue that, thankfully, few men and women think that way—you'll have no lost sleep, no pangs in your stomach, and no prickings of "conscience" about what you've done.

The second reason why economic ethics has an initial appeal is that it describes itself as the corollary of the definition of what business is, namely, an institution in our society uniquely designed to make a profit. It seems scientific, not subjective. Since the beginning of the last quarter of the twentieth century, no macrotrend has been more apparent worldwide than the global embracing of "capitalist" ideas that economies work better when individuals engage in the business of their choice with the avowed aim of making a profit. The approach seems to fit with the movement of history.

Third, economic ethics presents itself as a corollary of the discipline of economics. Economics used to be called the "dismal science." Not anymore. Now it often acts as if it were the imperial discipline. Its rise to eminence can probably be traced to the British economist and polymath John Maynard Keynes (1883–1946), whose work began the process of teaching governments how to manage aggregate demand so as to avoid catastrophes like the Great Depression that began in 1929–30. In the last third of the twentieth century, Milton Friedman of the University of Chicago and his followers exerted enormous influence on how people think about policy. Economics' successes have been manifold. Through the work of many, including Friedman, we now understand that the Great Depression was caused not by the wealthy Wall Street malefactors of FDR's rhetoric, but by a lack of knowledge and actions by central banking institutions in managing the money supply; and awareness that managing that money supply can prevent the double-digit inflation that plagued the United States in the last years of Jimmy Carter's administration, and the first years of Ronald Reagan's.

NOBODY CROWNED ECONOMICS EMPEROR

If anyone claims that "progress" is always an old-fashioned intellectual Pollyanna, point that person to economics. What we've learned in the last seventy-five years or so is astonishing and hugely beneficial to mankind. But the universe in which economic premises, economic arguments, and economic conclusions prevail is not the only universe. The legal universe, for example, doesn't march to the beat of economic arguments and purely economic considerations. The law threatens sanctions if we don't follow its strictures. While those sanctions are easily and correctly understood as "costs" that have to be accounted for, the law is not just another cost center in the economist's universe. The law tells us to do things because society, through its laws, has said we should. Unless the word is trivialized (and distorted) to mean only "seek the most cost-effective," *should* is a tough word for economics. The problem lies in the limited perspective of economic thinking, not in ideas of what we should and shouldn't do. Nobody crowned economics the imperial discipline.

Let's think back to our modified version of Linda's story, in which the nonperforming salesman, Bob, is a fifty-two-year-old African American. We've seen how firing a person who falls within two protected classes in the federal antidiscrimination laws—race and age—makes such a termination cost more than firing someone who isn't protected. Consider two possible variants on which Andrew could be basing his order to terminate Bob. In the first variant, Andrew tells Linda, "Look, I've checked with our legal department. They tell me we'd have a great case given his subpar numbers for three years. Compared with the cost of living with his performance, it's a no-brainer. As I said, fire him. Today." In a second variant, Andrew says exactly what we've just recounted, but, after he clicks the send key, he mutters to himself, "Damn those [blacks]. Can't stand having to hire 'em for sales positions. I'm so glad we can get rid of one of 'em."

If you believe that business is *just* about making a profit, you're committed to saying there's no difference between the two scenarios. Whether Andrew is simply a tough-as-nails, bottom-line-oriented guy, or a closet bigot, doesn't matter. If the numbers work, the numbers work. End of story. I don't think many of us would agree that Andrew's motivation is irrelevant. Putting it that way, however, isn't nearly strong enough. The two scenarios are quite different. The first variant, in which Andrew just talks about the cost of firing a person who is a member of two protected classes may seem callous, but there's an element of consequentialist fairness to it.

The racial innuendo in the second, however, is repulsive. Most of us don't want to live in a world where expressions of, and actions based upon, unbridled racism are perfectly OK. This isn't speculation. It's a fact. Congress, which is elected by the adult voting population, passed broad antidiscrimination legislation in the period between 1964 and 1972, and there has been no significant movement to repeal it. Thinking that racial discrimination is wrong isn't just my private view or yours; it's that of the United States, evidenced in the formal, legal way the country manifests its views. Its representatives passed laws. Now, I'm not of course saying that racism or age discrimination or gender bias has vanished from our society. It's hugely significant, however, that our legal order no longer tolerates what it passively accepted within the living memory of senior citizens, and some younger than that. Our legal order, in other words, includes a sense of right and wrong. We'll need to explore later on how legal right and wrong intersects with our sense of right and wrong not protected by law. Our task now is different. It's to show that the legal order understands itself as reflecting choices. Critically, the choices reflect values other than the economic values revealed in the cost-benefit analyses that dominate thinking in the economist's universe. The view that business is only about making a profit is not only wrong. It's an outlier.

GETTING REAL ABOUT LEGAL "COSTS"

Before turning to that part of the legal universe that the economic view neglects, let's examine the part it does consider: costs. I'm frequently astonished by how little the public really understands about how law works.

When nonlawyers think about law, they typically talk about "obeying the law." Two ideas lurk behind this. First, there's the idea that the paradigm of legal trouble is where you are *prosecuted* for a *crime*. We call such conduct "breaking the law." Second, it's easy to think the law is like a line in the sand. Cross it and you're in trouble. Don't cross it and you're not. When we think this way, we are looking at law through the prism of the *criminal* law. A TV show or a movie that has a legal plot almost always involves criminal law. The police or the FBI are trying to catch someone who committed a crime. Figuring out whether someone is guilty of murder obviously makes for a more riveting TV plot than knowing whether a corporate officer engaged in self-dealing by causing the company to purchase property he or she owned personally at an inflated price.

In most of the circumstances in which businesspeople have to address legal requirements, however, criminal law plays no part. To be sure, if you do what the juries found Ken Lay and Jeff Skilling of Enron and Bernie Ebbers of WorldCom to have done, you're going to find yourself liable to prosecution in criminal court. But criminal prosecution is the exception, not the rule.

In a criminal case, the federal or state government prosecutes an individual person, and sometimes a corporation, for violating the law. If convicted, an individual will have to pay a fine to the government or go to jail. A corporation will pay a fine. Most of the legal issues that concern businesspeople, however, are *civil*, not criminal matters. In a civil case, one person or company sues another person or company. Typically, the person suing (called the plaintiff) seeks money (called damages) from the person sued (called the defendant). In a civil case, a defendant seeks to avoid *liability*. A lawyer representing a business is typically doing his or her job if he can help the company avoid even being threatened with a lawsuit, let alone avoid one having filed or avoid one going all the way to trial.

Outside the arena of criminal prosecution, the phrase "obeying the law" doesn't work very well. We don't ordinarily say that you "disobey" the law if you fail to place adequate warnings on your product explaining how misuse can cause harm, for example, but your failure can stick you with a huge judgment on behalf of someone who is injured. You won't go to jail for any executive compensation scheme you approve as a corporate board member, but you might find yourself liable to the shareholders if your conduct is egregious. It isn't "illegal" in the criminal sense to retain a man like Jack, the sexual harasser in Chapter 1, in the ranks of your executives, but you may find your company liable for negligent supervision later if (or more likely when) his harassment activities escalate. It's no overstatement to say that the principal job of most lawyers working for businesses is to help them avoid liability. In this context, the simple notion of obeying the law won't work.

When lawyers try to avoid trouble for their clients, they focus on the borderline area between what conduct won't cause liability or punishment to arise, and what will. To think that there is a clear, unmistakable line in the sand is to oversimplify a complex reality. For a person or a company to suffer adverse legal consequences, a number of different factors have to coalesce. Lawyers call these various factors "elements." As an example, for the administrative assistants successfully to hold Jack liable in court, they'd have to prove the elements necessary to establish sexual harassment, including, for example, that he physically touched some of them and that they did not consent to the touching. When lawyers represent the plaintiff, they focus on developing evidence on the element or elements they think are going to be the toughest to prove. If they represent defendants like Jack or his company, they'll concentrate on finding the elements that will be easiest to knock down, because without all the elements, the defendant wins.

However, if your conduct lacks any element that will cause you or your company to be held liable, that does *not* mean that everything is OK, or that what you did was fine. Anybody who has ever shaken his or her head when a big-time criminal gets acquitted knows that. It's the same in a civil case. If you, or if under your guidance, the company, dances along the precipice just this side of being caught, you likely haven't escaped being entangled in the hassles and expenses of the legal system. The costs associated with defending a lawsuit are huge and not recoverable. That's true even if your insurance company pays the fees for your defense lawyers. Even if the case settles before trial, there are hard costs in terms of lawyers' fees and soft costs in terms of executive time and aggravation dealing with it. (Whatever your opinion of Bill Clinton, it's clear that, during his legal troubles in his second term, he spent a lot of time defending himself rather than doing the job of the president of the United States.) You simply can't replace the time spent working up your defense instead of doing your job; the time your staff spent gathering documents or working with lawyers; and, perhaps most important, the psychological costs and the stress of being under attack and of having some of your questionable conduct aired in public.

LEGAL RISK AND LAW'S NORMATIVE SIDE

The best way for a company to think about legal risk is not to say, "We'll obey the law." It's more helpful to say, "We want to keep out of the zone of legal danger." By the zone of legal danger, I mean not only the place where you might be held liable, but also where (even if you win in court or negotiate a favorable settlement) you've incurred the costs, monetary and psychic, of legal trouble.

Martha Stewart may have ultimately succeeded in turning her criminal conviction and jail time into a marketing ploy, but it generally doesn't work that way. Lots of people would never consider using MCI after the WorldCom scandals. Reputations are fragile and, once damaged, hard to repair. Ford Motor Company's problems with the Pinto and then the Bronco illustrate this point.

Regardless of the legal outcome, allegations that make their way into the newspapers, on to television, and now, perhaps most importantly, onto the Web persist in the public's mind.

From this it follows that what's legally safe to do isn't simply a question of pushing just up to the point of some clear line where a judge will smack you down. To avoid the risks of being caught up in the costs and hassles of the legal system, it's important to keep a safe distance between yourself and the line where your lawyers will tell you that liability or punishment begins. It's not so much a question of "obeying the law," as keeping out of legal trouble.

So far we haven't said anything that will cause a flutter in the fabric of the economist's universe. Legal requirements just make calculating costs more complex. They aren't fundamentally different from *any* cost the businessperson must address. To repeat (because this is important) on this view, the Civil Rights Act of 1964, which banned racial discrimination in hiring and firing, doesn't say to the business owner, "Hey, firing an African American or a woman or a person over forty because that person falls in one or more of those protected classes is wrong." The Act just makes it more expensive.

The advocate of economic ethics is literally an EIP—and proud of it. "Well and good," he or she might say, "I don't really care how lawyers or judges think. For me, what matters is maximizing profit." Unfortunately for the EIP—but fortunately for the quality of life in our society—most people don't think that way. It won't do, for most of us, to treat what appear to be the ethics-like commands of the law simply as costs, fundamentally no different from the cost of raw materials or employee salaries.

The variant of the story we've been working with in which Andrew wants to fire Bob *because* he's an African American shows why. Suppose instead of just mumbling his anti-black thoughts he'd shared them with Linda. At least in theory it wouldn't matter if he'd shared them on the phone or by e-mail. If Bob decided to file a race-discrimination case against the company, Bob's lawyer would have the right to take what's called discovery. The lawyer would ask for documents relevant to the case, which nowadays always include e-mails. And he or she would question witnesses under oath before the trial, in what is known as a deposition.

It doesn't take much to imagine the delight with which Tom and his lawyer would treat an e-mail in which Andrew spewed his racist sentiments. It would make the case. Just imagine the effect on a jury—which would be bound to include some African Americans—when they saw the e-mail. Probably in the real world the company's lawyer would have approached Bob with a solid settlement offer before the e-mail was produced, because, with that document in Bob's hands, the price the company would have to pay to settle would have multiplied significantly.

It's important to note that, if Andrew had just told Linda of his feelings about African Americans, rather than written them down, the trouble could be almost as bad. I often find that businesspeople think they can *say* whatever they like, so long as they don't write it down. This is wrong—provided the people to whom they tell it to don't have one of those convenient losses of memory that criminal law calls perjury.

Here's how it works. Well before the trial date, Bob's lawyer will take Linda's deposition. Linda will testify under oath, just as if she were present in court. If Bob's lawyer is doing the job properly, he or she will ask Linda a question like, "In connection with the decision to fire Bob, did Andrew ever comment on Bob's being African American?" Because she's under oath, Linda has a clear duty to tell the truth. If she doesn't, it's perjury. If Linda answers the lawyer's question "Yes," the lawyer will ask her to tell what she remembers. If Linda remembers what Andrew said, and tells the truth, the company is sunk as surely as if Andrew had sent an e-mail.

EFFICIENCY AND THE PRETENDED VALUE NEUTRALITY OF ECONOMICS

Law tells us what to do and backs up what it says with a smack: "If you don't do what you're suppose to do, you'll pay damages (and, in extreme cases, go to jail)." But that's not all it does. The law also tells us what Congress (or the state legislature or a court) says we *should* do. If the jury slams Andrew for firing Bob because he's African American, it does so because, acting on behalf of the community from which its members have been drawn, the members of the jury think that that was the wrong thing to do.

Economics pretends that this value dimension is missing. In fact, however, if you take a moment and think carefully about it, there's no way the cost of discrimination could be imposed on Andrew unless someone thought what he did was wrong. The economic ethicist's view, we can see, is a circular and hence invalid argument.

Costs are imposed only because someone—in this case, a jury acting under authority granted by Congress—expresses the sense of outrage that it's an illegitimate reason to fire an employee because of his skin color. Costs aren't imposed because costs are imposed. They're imposed because someone thinks what was done is wrong. Employment discrimination it turns out isn't at all the same as buying raw materials or supplies or paying a labor force.

Taken in its unadulterated form, the EIP rejects all the values that society has poured into its legal order, of which "it's wrong to discriminate in hiring on the basis of race, gender, or age" is particularly illustrative. If you think about it, this is a pretty bleak view of life. I don't think many people, even hard-bitten businesspeople, really subscribe to it. I think it's a ploy, and a not very subtle one, to justify all kinds of coercive and unethical business practices. There's a more obvious problem, however, with the economic ethics mentality that rejects the societal choices of right and wrong embodied in the law. That problem is this: Economic ethics advocates do not strike the word "should" from their vocabulary. To the contrary, they have a very strong sense of "should." You've probably figured out what that "should" is: maximize profits. And not only is this a very strong "should," it's the *only* "should." As women and men of business, you and I never underrate profit and increasing long-term owner value. But the *only* "should"? How could anybody come up with such a counterintuitive notion?

The answer lies in the concept of efficiency. In economics, an outcome is "efficient" when the cost of producing a given output is as low as possible. Markets, then, are "efficient" when costs are minimized as much as possible. I am not an economist, and I have no quarrel with economists creating and using concepts in whatever way they want to do their economic work. But when economics-trained, or economics-minded people use economic terms to purport to solve ethical problems, then it's time to jump in and call a halt.

If economists wanted to call the production of outputs at as low a cost as possible "abracadabra," that would be fine. It would be a value neutral term with a clear, technical meaning. The problem is that the word "efficiency" carries its own, very positive connotations in our ordinary life. In everyday life, the word means more than the technical economist's definition. Professional philosophers working on ethics would say that "efficiency" contains a "positive evaluation" or has "positive normative attributes." In plain English, this means that when I say something is efficient, in addition to the economist's descriptive meaning, I am also implicitly saying "and it's a good thing, too." In other words, efficiency isn't a neutral word; it's a word that contains an element of praise or approval.

The consequence of this for the proponent of economic ethics is devastating. The main appeal of that view is its apparent appeal to facts. Businesspeople like facts. Appeals to facts appear to avoid appeals to squishy ideas about right and wrong, about what deserves praise and what blame, which people probably always will disagree about. Yet grasping that "efficiency" contains a value assessment shows that economic ethics isn't the hard-nosed, purely factual approach many of its adherents like to say it is.

Now, it's okay that efficiency contains an element of praising what is good and that inefficiency disapproves of what's bad. What isn't okay is to pretend it doesn't do that, that it's just a value-neutral description of reality. But the problem is that once we admit that there are legitimate goals or aspirations directing us to what we *should* do, why would we select "achieving efficiency" as the *primary*, or even the *only* goal? As one writer put it, "Cost-benefit analysis ... is mistaken in thinking that a person's valuations all express the orientation of an egoistic consumer."[2]

MAXIMIZING PROFIT AND FOLLOWING THE LAW

Suppose we back off the radical economic view of ethics and say that business should be governed by *two* principles of conduct: (1) act so as to maximize long-term owner value (2) except where the law demands otherwise. Such an outlook is simple and defers to the businessperson's profit-making motivation, yet it does not pretend that the way law works is fundamentally the same as any cost-generating part of business. When your lawyer, the jury, or the judge says that you can't take race into account when you fire someone, they are telling you what you shouldn't do, that is, what you mustn't do if you want to avoid liability. That liability, of course, is a cost. But they aren't sending you a bill, like your supplier of raw materials would. They're saying that flouting society's norm, expressed in the law, is wrong, a consequence of which is the imposition of a cost.

There's a lot of appeal in this approach. While I suspect that few people really buy the radicalism of economic ethics, large numbers of businesspeople implicitly accept "maximize profit but follow the law."

Its appeal rests on an apparent solution to the problem we discussed but couldn't decisively solve in Chapter 1: there's no conclusive way to satisfy everybody about how to decide on the right thing to do. Consequentialism, rights, and an appeal to virtue all make sense. But none gives us a final answer. And there are even gray areas within each of these approaches. You and I calculate consequences differently or we disagree about the extent and context of "rights," even if we agree that those *are* rights.

So suppose we forget about trying to solve problems that some of the best minds in history have been unable to resolve for the last 2,400 years. The law provides a way out. When society has expressed its preference for a course of conduct by adopting a law, we'll use society's choice. If Congress says it's illegal to discriminate against a person on account of race, gender, or age, or to use inside information to trade in the public securities markets, Congress's decision is all we need. You and I don't need to debate about it. The law provides all the required "shoulds" and "shouldn'ts."

On the surface, this may look no different than the hard-bitten economic view that treats law as just another cost. But it's not at all the same. Because the economic view treats law as a cost, it's legitimate to try to cut the cost—just as you would try to reduce the cost of raw materials. This means that the economic view amounts to this: follow the law's dictates if, but only if, you're likely to get caught if you don't. It's like the kid and the cookie jar. Mom says, "No cookies between meals," and her shrewd child says to herself, "If I want a cookie, I just have to make sure I don't get caught. So I'll just wait until Mom goes downstairs to put the laundry in the dryer and then. . . ."

The view we now want to discuss, which maintains that a business (1) should maximize profit *and* (2) follow the law, is different. When the law says, don't fire an employee because he's a fifty-two-year old African American, it means you shouldn't fire him on that basis—regardless of whether you can hide your motive and not get caught.

We can see how this works if we consider the kind of real-life problem that never finds its way into newspaper stories or TV shows. Let's take the case of a simple contract between two companies. Suppose Alpha Heating Oil Company has a contract with Beta Company to supply its heating oil needs up to a specific quantity for a six-month period from October 1 to March 31. The contract specifies the price of $2.60 per gallon. Suppose further that during the winter the price of oil goes up. The cause could be a worsening of the political situation in the Middle East, or simply a very cold late fall that makes supplies scarce. The company will have to pay more for its oil.

One afternoon, Alpha's sales manager walks into the president's office and tells him that he can get an order to supply a large shopping mall with its needs for the Christmas season. The price: $2.95 per gallon. The only downside is that the contract with Beta gives Beta the right to request an increase in quantity of up to 20 percent for any given month at the $2.60 price, and Beta has made this request. There isn't enough product on hand to fill the salesman's orders and Beta's needs.

The president picks up the phone and calls Alpha's lawyer. He describes the situation and asks, "Have we got to pass on the new deal and honor Beta's request?"

"Technically speaking," the lawyer replies off the top of her head, "it's a no-brainer. You're bound by your contract."

"Technically speaking?" the president asks, waiting for more.

"Technically speaking, if Beta sues you, they'll win. But are they going to sue you? I doubt it. They'd have to get a lawyer, they'd have to pay the lawyer. Likely it'll be too expensive and too much of a hassle. I'd be more worried about future business with them if they find out."

After hanging up, the president turns to the sales manager. "What'll we tell Beta?"

"Leave it to me," he replies. "I'll make up some story about our supplies running out. I'll get 'em to buy it."

Let's leave for a moment the question of the sales manager telling his boss that he'll just lie to Beta about being short on product. Just focus for now on the question whether there is any reason why Alpha should not breach its contract with Beta. We know what the economic ethics guy will say. It's just a matter of adding up the costs and assigning dollar values to the benefits. If the lawyer is correct that Beta won't find out, or won't think it's worth the risk to sue Alpha for breach of contract, the law imposes no cost that can deter the president of Alpha from making a profit-maximizing decision. From the economic ethics point of view, Alpha should not honor its contract with Beta and instead reap the profits of the sales to the shopping mall. (We'll revisit this story in Chapter 7, where we discuss issues about how questionable market practices can harm a company's reputation, apart from legal costs.)

This story shows that it's a distortion to view the law simply as a cost. When someone enters into a contract with you, whether that someone is man, woman, or corporation, you understand that you've just bargained for the performance promised. Entering into a contract is not simply a matter of saying, "I promise to do this and so, unless it's cheaper (taking into account that you may sue me) not to do so." This view of legal requirements is sometimes called the *internal* view of law, in contrast to the external "costs approach." It means that *promising* to do something carries weight separate and apart from the content of the promise.

The "maximize-profit-but-follow-the-law" approach yields the opposite answer to that of economic ethics. If Alpha's president takes the view that following the law matters, he'll respond to the sales manager's suggestions by saying, "Hey, Rob. C'mon. We have a contract with Beta. End of story."

There are two important things we need to notice about this. First, the president's response is not based on some sort of a calculation that, in the long run, performing the contract rather than trying to wriggle out of it will produce more profit long-term, that is, that it will enhance long-term owner value. That outcome may very well be true. In fact, it's a premise of this book that in lots of cases it is. Good ethics generally is good business. What's important, however, is that Alpha's president isn't making the calculation.

A second point follows. What was your reaction when you read that Alpha's president said he would perform the contract with Beta simply because they, the two companies, had made an agreement? My guess is you approved of that approach. You may have thought it the right thing to do, or, if you like the old-fashioned word, that this was "honorable." All of us, especially in our roles in business, weigh costs and benefits in deciding what to do, or in criticizing or approving what our friends, colleagues, and competitors do. We do this all the time. That's what gives the consequentialist outlook we discussed in Chapter 1 its potency. But few of us think that it's the whole ballgame. We approve of the second response of Alpha's president because he's choosing to give Beta what he promised to supply even if he could make more money doing something else. The fact that he *promised* matters.

WHY MAKING A PROFIT AND FOLLOWING THE LAW ISN'T ENOUGH

We've just seen that adding "following the law" to "making a profit" is a distinct improvement over economic ethics. It takes into account a sense of playing by the rules and rejects the idea that business is just the law of the jungle. But even that doesn't go far enough.

To see this, let's recall our first Alpha scenario, in which the president decides to give no weight to the existence of a contract, and the sales manager says he'll find a way to "sell" Beta on the idea that they can't supply the additional product under the contract. There's no doubt what the sales manager is doing. He's lying. Would the sales manager be violating the law when he told his story to Beta?

The answer is no. The law contains no general prohibition against lying. If you lie when testifying under oath, say at trial, before a grand jury, or in a deposition or in an affidavit you sign, and if the lying is "material" to the matter before the court, you can be convicted of the crime of perjury. If you lie in order to induce somebody to enter into a transaction with you, the wronged party likely will be able to rescind the deal and get a court order requiring you to pay monetary damages. If you lie in a registration statement you submit to the Securities and Exchange Commission in connection with an issuance of stock you want to sell, you can be liable for fines and, at least in theory, imprisonment.

What about the sales manager's lying to Beta? If Alpha's lawyer is wrong and Beta does sue for breach of contract, and if the case doesn't settle and goes to trial, the sales manager's lie will almost certainly come out. Just as Bob's lawyer could (legitimately) inflame the jury against Andrew's company if evidence of his anti-African American sentiments came out, so too would Beta's lawyer make hay of the sales manager's lie before the jury. That's why, incidentally, if Beta does sue, Alpha should be very inclined to settle before trial. If your company's key witness is caught in a lie, don't be riding your high horse into trial. So the sales manager's lie hurts in a legal context but—provided he doesn't try to perpetuate it on the witness stand—it isn't illegal. And the company, thus, might get away with the sales manager's lie. Or it might not. Our point here is different. Although the sales manager's lie is not *per se* illegal, it's still a lie. And to say something is a "lie" is to suggest that it's somehow wrong. In this respect, what we're talking about is like what we said about efficiency, except that here the correct or, if you prefer, the implicit message of the word is negative where "efficient" is positive.

So what's the source of this negativity in "lie" or, for that matter, the positive connotation of "efficient"? It can't be the outcome of the market, because sometimes lies cost more than they gain, and sometimes they gain more than they cost. It can't be the law because, as we've just seen, the law contains no general prohibition against the sales manager's lie to Beta.

So what is it? The answer is that we have views about right and wrong which we hold separate and apart from what the law does or does not prohibit—and, of course, separate and apart from maximized market outcomes. As we said in Chapter 1, we could call such views "morals" or "values," or questions of ethics. What makes us unhappy about the sales manager's lie to Beta, I suggest, is that it's unethical.

WHY WE CAN'T DO WITHOUT A CONCEPT OF ETHICS

The discussion of the racially motivated firing of Bob in Linda and Andrew's company, and of Alpha's decision whether or not to breach its contract with Beta, vividly displays why economic ethics and economic ethics plus law come up short. Both theories fail to equip us to say things we want to say about the way we—and others—behave in the world. Put differently, economic ethics and economic ethics plus law leave us impoverished.

Our reaction to Alpha's sales manager's lie pointed out the problem. If it's "wrong" to lie where lying is not legally prohibited, there has to be some source of the "right-wrong" assessment that's external to, that is, that's not a part of, the law. Returning to the legal background of the antidiscrimination legislation that protected Bob because he's an African American makes this clear.

On July 2, 1964, President Lyndon Johnson signed the Civil Rights Act of 1964. Among other things, as we've said, the Act made it illegal to discriminate on the basis of race in hiring and firing decisions. From the moment the president lifted his pen from the official copy of the bill after signing it, it became wrong, legally wrong, to fire Bob for the reasons that the racist Andrew did. The day before the president signed the bill, it wasn't wrong. Legally speaking, that is.

You don't have to be a lawyer to know this is correct. When Congress passes a bill prohibiting certain conduct, and the president signs it (or the state legislature passes a bill and the governor signs it), what used to be legally OK suddenly becomes not OK, or *vice versa*. If you adhered to the "maximize-profit-but-follow-the-law" approach, you'd say this and no more. Law and ethics, on this view, are coextensive, that is, the boundaries of one are the boundaries of the other.

But surely there's a very important sense in which "what's okay" doesn't change with the stroke of the presidential or gubernatorial pen. Most of us think that racial (or gender) discrimination is wrong in a profound and enduring way that has nothing to do with what the law prohibits or allows. Indeed, it's impossible to explain the passage of the Civil Rights Act without recognizing that a lot of people—enough to elect a majority in the House and the Senate, and a president—had to have believed that such discrimination was wrong *so that* they wanted a law passed. If law and ethics are coextensive, if, that is, the law entirely subsumes ethics, then it's impossible to favor a change in the law on ethical grounds. There can be no sense of the "ethical" that isn't also "legal." This can't be right.

Profit maximization plus law, then, is *also* a circular argument, just like the economic ethics view. Whenever people think certain conduct should be forbidden or encouraged by law, they necessarily have views about right and wrong that aren't (yet) embodied in the law. The views they have, by definition, don't come—can't come—from what's (then) legal and what's not. You can only support a change in the law because you think something is wrong that needs to be put right if you have a view that there are *some* things that are wrong or right apart from what the law provides at any particular moment.

Was racial or gender discrimination "wrong" on July 1, 1964? I think so and I bet you agree. If, three years from now, the country leapt back to the racial and gender attitudes of 1940 and elected a Congress that repealed the Civil Rights Act, would discrimination, presto, be morally acceptable? Not to me, even if Congress's actions would, by definition, mean that it was no longer illegal. If you understand why changing the law can't change what's right or wrong, you understand why we can't do without "ethics"—in business and elsewhere.

As human beings, we believe that certain things are right and certain things are wrong. We believe it apart from the economic value of one choice or another, and we believe it apart from whether there is a law regulating certain conduct. There's no easy, clear-cut way to define what fits into this category, but the two examples we've discussed show that they range from racial discrimination at one extreme to a simple lie to a customer at the other. As we said in Chapter 1, if you're faced with a choice of doing something that will affect someone else, whether positively or adversely, questions of ethics are at least potentially present.

WORKING ETHICS

In an important way, working with ethics is tougher than working with the law. The difference I'm thinking about is this: Generally, lawyers can find the law on a particular point. After many years of practice, I can attest that the search can be painstaking and demanding. Sometimes, if finding the law means trying to piece it together from conflicting court decisions, the only correct answer may be that, though arguments can be made one way or another, there's just no clear answer. (If you went to law school, or have a spouse, sibling, or child who did, you'll know what I'm talking about. As a law professor, my responsibility is to challenge students to work out what the answer should be in the less-than-totally clear case.) While these tend to be the areas where businesspeople (and others) most need a lawyer's help, the fact remains that in principle the law exists in the objective world of cases, statutes, administrative regulations, and sometimes the Constitution. We all know, anecdotally if not first-hand, that in some countries acts that we'd call bribery or under-the-table money are a common way of doing business. In the wake of scandals where certain foreign officials demanded bribes before they were willing to give American companies lucrative contracts, Congress passed the Foreign Corrupt Practices Act (FCPA), making it illegal for U.S. businesspeople to conform to the norms of other countries that would be unacceptable here at home. (An international investment banking consultant told me that he knew of tons of orders that West European firms were able to write, instead of their U.S. competition, because nothing equivalent to the FCPA hindered them, but that's a different story.) The whole area of whether ethical values can be transcultural, and whether the FCPA is an appropriate American legal response, is a question too far removed from our business here to allow discussion.

There is a closer-to-home example of why ethics presents a difficulty that law does not. People can disagree about what the law is—lawyers do it all the time—but ultimately there's a court that will decide it. Courts have *authority* to make such decisions. In the ethical realm, there is no court. There is no ultimate authority. Most people, and I venture to say everyone who is interested in reading a book like this, think that discrimination in the workplace on account of race, religion, or gender is downright wrong. But, as a glance at specialized publications on employment discrimination law shows, people who think that such discrimination is OK are out there. The racist version of Andrew, in short, is not a figment of our imagination.

But if there is no final authority, where does this leave us? Have we come this far to find that we've arrived in never-never land? Is there no way to decide these questions that arise when simply maximizing profit leaves us uncomfortable with an outcome, and the law provides no help?

A SENSE OF DISSATISFACTION

If you've tried to read other books on business ethics, hoping that they'd help you and other managers or executives in your company establish a protocol for resolving the problems that arise day by day, you've probably been disappointed. I know I was. As mentioned in the preface, there seem to be two prominent genres. The first, commonly prepared for business ethics courses in MBA programs, is heavily laced with readings from some of the world's great moral philosophers. The writings of these thinkers are often incredibly dense and quite divorced from the reality of *any* day-to-day concerns—much less those of twenty-first century business. The second genre includes what I call anecdote books. Drawing heavily on descriptions of dilemmas that businessmen and women have faced, they specialize in making it clear that, in real-life situations, values we care about can seem to point in opposite directions. I called this the "Mary realized she had a problem" approach. They trade on an intuition that the choice a person made in a particular situation was reasonable. But they provide little guidance for solving the inevitably different problems others will face. Businesspeople know how to go about maximizing profit. They know how to use lawyers (or if they don't they can readily learn). Ethics are different. You won't get better at it by simply relying on your intuitions, though you might, by chance, achieve outcomes you'll feel good about. The morals of the clergy, or of preachy politicians, won't get you very far either.

What you need is an approach, a method. It can't be a method that will tell you absolutely and without any question what is or is not OK. What we've discussed thus far shows that. But there is a way to address ethical issues apart from law and a part from merely following the mantra to maximize profits. I call it the foursquare protocol. Before turning to the areas where the temptations of sex, money, and power cause persistent issues in companies, only some of which are addressed by the law, let's take a look at that protocol. It's the subject of the next chapter.

NOTES

1. The phrase comes from Elaine Sternberg, *Just Business: Business Ethics in Action* (Oxford: Oxford University Press, 2000).

2. Elizabeth Anderson, *Value in Ethics and Economics* (Cambridge, MA: Harvard University Press, 1995), p. 200.

CHAPTER 3

Injecting Principled Decision-Making into Managing Ethical Decisions: The Foursquare Protocol

In the previous two chapters, we've explored the assumptions of the ethical ideas that most of us have. Now it's time to talk about how men and women in business can go about intelligently translating the abstract ideas of what's right and wrong into solutions for the problematic situations they regularly confront in doing their jobs. How do we go about making choices in real-life situations?

It would be easy if there were a clear-cut hierarchy of values—if, say, one always acted to produce the optimum net quantity of good consequences over bad. As we saw in Chapter 1, most people don't operate as if there were such a hierarchy, and there are good reasons why they shouldn't. Sometimes maximizing net consequences seems to be the correct approach, sometimes we want to protect the dignity of an individual person regardless of net consequences, and other times we focus upon the kind of people we ourselves want to be. Most people, I think, resolve hierarchy issues through their intuitions. They choose what they choose and do what they do because it seems right. Don't misunderstand me; this is not only unavoidable, it's not a bad thing. Questions of right and wrong aren't like mathematics. We usually can't set out a formal proof that demonstrates one answer is superior to another. The differing responses to Linda's predicament in Chapter 1 illustrate this.

But making ethics work in organizations is difficult at a level beyond the absence of a general hierarchy of values on which everybody always (or even usually) agrees. The question is, how do we translate basic ideas of how we want people to conduct themselves into a series of intelligent and comprehensible rules or standards of conduct? And, even more difficult, how should such rules and standards be applied in practice? How, in short, can managers manage ethics so that their companies are the kinds of places that flourish ethically and where good people want to work?

In the following five chapters, as we survey the key problem areas in business ethics, we'll suggest some essential dos and don'ts. Some of these will be based on what the law requires. In others, where the law is silent or too general to provide guidance, a company's standards will have to be based on more purely ethical considerations. But that still leaves the problem of application.

No matter how good a job you do in defining the conduct your company expects, there are always going to be particular instances that raise the question: "But how do we apply our standard *here*?"

There are two circumstances in which this challenge arises. On the one hand, individual men and women working in a company will want to know with some certainty what they can do, and what they can't do. Even the clearest statement of a general rule—"don't discriminate in hiring or promotion decisions based on gender," for example—doesn't define what to do in tough, borderline cases. As students of jurisprudence put it, a rule does not prescribe its own application. (That's why there are court cases around the country every day trying to work out the meaning of the federal statute that forbids such discrimination.)

There is a second problem. When it appears to management that someone has violated a company's policy on what's appropriate ethical conduct, how do company authorities go about deciding whether there has been a violation and, if so, what should the sanction be? This process is critical. Sure, it's important to abide by company rules, and obey them in the spirit in which they are made. In an ethically sophisticated company, however, it's equally vital that the decisions management makes where there has been a violation are fair and consistent, and are *seen* to be fair and consistent. A working ethical system, in short, not only needs to tell people generally what is expected of them; it also has to have appropriate mechanisms for enforcement.

The rest of this book discusses a host of questions that arise every day—from sexual harassment through conflicts of interest, to cutting corners on product safety and to racial stereotyping. We'll talk about particular examples to illustrate the key considerations, both ethically and legally. But it's the nature of the beast that we can't discuss all the kinds of questions that come up in these areas. In a real sense there is an infinite variety—to use the lawyer's phrase—of "fact patterns." The examples we'll use likely will prompt you to think of situations that are similar, but not quite the same, as ones you've experienced. The decision protocol that we describe here will help you translate the examples we discuss into responses to those that have troubled you, are troubling you now, or will trouble you in the future.

THE FOURSQUARE PROTOCOL

Intuition isn't a reliable guide to determine the hierarchy of basic ethical norms in all cases. It's even more important to recognize that intuition won't work to help someone decide whether a company's rules do or do not ban certain behavior, or to help a decision-maker choose a course that's fair to someone who has arguably done what he or she shouldn't have. I want here to propose a method that applies to both of these situations. It's a general method, because it applies to any ethical quandary in which an employee or a manager can find himself or herself. But its focus is on the particular—how do you make the right choice in particular situations, whether they involve product safety, conflicts-of-interest, or other problem areas?

I call this method the foursquare protocol. I use "protocol" because of the word's procedural implications. Ethics in practice isn't simply or even primarily about dos and don'ts. It's also about fairness, and fairness is largely about procedural safeguards. Ethics in practice requires procedures that fairly set out what people are supposed to do, and, when someone's conduct is alleged not to have measured up, demands that they be judged fairly and squarely. And this explains the use of "foursquare." It has four key elements. The use of "square" stems from the name President Theodore Roosevelt gave his program at the beginning of the last century—the Square Deal. A company whose ethics are thriving will give its employees, and the suppliers and customers with whom it deals, a square deal.

THE FIRST ELEMENT OF THE PROTOCOL: CLOSE DESCRIPTION OF THE SITUATION

Practical, ethical decision-making begins much like when you take your child, or yourself, to the doctor. You describe the symptoms. Headache, fever, nausea, pain, whatever. The doctor mentally relates

Foursquare Protocol for Managing Ethical Decisions

1 Dig into the Facts	2 Examine Individual Reactions to Past Solutions
3 Gauge Similarities with Past Situations	4 Analyze Your Decision-making Situation

the various symptoms to the various problems that could be the cause. He or she also relates them to one another, because some problems are characterized by related symptoms. If you're an adult, and the pain you are complaining about is in your right arm, the doctor will probably think about your shoulder muscles, or the rotator cuff. But if the pain is in the left arm, the doctor will need to consider heart trouble. To find the cause of your problem, the doctor will need to get a close description of the facts.

Resolving ethical issues is much the same. If you want to resolve an ethical problem in your company, you need to treat the issue as "a patient" and get a complete account of it. This means you'll have to make sure you have noted all of the facts that give rise to the problem. Thus in the original version of Linda's story, you'd identify that Tom's on-the-job performance was not acceptable, that it had been subpar for some time, that efforts to improve his performance had failed, and that his wife had apparently been fighting a battle with cancer during the period of his poor performance. You'd also need to take note of Tom's skin color and his age, because both are legally and ethically relevant.

Note that there are many facts about Tom that his coworkers or boss would know that don't matter: his hair color, his height, personality traits, etc. This may seem pretty obvious, but don't rush by the point too quickly. The quality of your decision, like that of a doctor's diagnosis or a lawyer's opinion, can't be any better than the facts with which you start. You can't know which facts will turn out to be pertinent until you have access to as many facts as you can lay your hands on. The devil's in the details. Stick with the facts that are germane to the situation, but don't make these calls prematurely.[1]

THE SECOND PRONG OF THE PROTOCOL: GATHERING THE ACCUMULATED EXPERIENCE OF THE ORGANIZATION IN SIMILAR SITUATIONS

A few years ago Hollywood released a movie called *50 First Dates*. Not a great film, but fun and with an interesting premise. The lead character, played by Drew Barrymore, is a young woman who was in an automobile accident in which she suffered a head injury. She recovers and is OK except for one thing. Each morning when she wakes up, she has no memory of anything that happened after the accident. Thus, sleep has erased her awareness of her post-accident life. Each day is new, fresh and pristine. If history is what we remember about the past, she has no post-accident history. In typical Hollywood fashion, she meets and falls in love with a guy, played by Adam Sandler. The difficulty is she doesn't recognize him each morning. The scriptwriter solved the problem by having the Sandler character create a video that she sees when she wakes up that gives her life the continuity it lacked because of the absence of memory. Each morning she wakes up, watches the video, and discovers that she married the character Adam plays, and they have a child.

What makes the premise of the movie interesting is that the Drew Barrymore character is made without one of the fundamental attributes that human beings have—their memories. As the great English writer C. S. Lewis—played by Anthony Hopkins in the 1993 classic *Shadowlands*—put it, "Humanity does not pass through phases as a train passes through stations: being alive, it has the privilege of always moving yet never leaving anything behind. Whatever we have been, in some sort we still are."[2] Lewis was talking about the remnants of medieval ideas about romance in modern culture, but the idea is germane to organizations. An organization isn't reinvented each day. What it is, in large measure, is what it has been. The second prong of the foursquare protocol focuses upon organizational memory, organizational history.

I don't think many people in real life actually approach figuring out a solution to an ethical problem by explicitly treating the issue as something brand-new. Yet, surprisingly many talk as if that is what you are supposed to do. They say that what you should do is go "back to basics" to search for "first principles" that will tell you how to decide. What a mistake! How would you feel if your doctor's response on examining your feverish child was to say, "Let's go back to basics. Let me explain the definition of a disease"? Probably you'd be asking, "How can I get out of here and find a real doctor to tell me what's wrong with my child and get her treatment started?" What you want is a doctor who can rely on the experience he or she has had in treating patients with symptoms similar to yours. You'll want the doctor's source of treatment ideas to come not just from the basics he or she learned in his or her books and classes in medical school, and about basic principles of disease, but from the fund of accumulated knowledge about what diagnoses have worked and what haven't in practice.

In ethics, as in medicine or law and in so many other aspects of business, experience is the monarch, the sovereign to whom we owe, if not absolute obedience, substantial deference. Suppose a manager learns that one of her male employees has been engaging in low-level sexual harassment of a particular female employee. By "low-level" I mean offensive, but not extremely offensive comments, and no touching. The manager will know, or a few inquiries will make it clear, that, if the harassment doesn't get worse, the legal risk is small. But "if it doesn't get worse" is the key. Experience teaches that the conduct has got to be nipped in the bud—and in a way that doesn't make matters worse.

The second prong of the protocol asks the manager to explore other situations in which other managers, or the manager himself or herself on a previous occasion, faced a similar kind of problem. How was it resolved? How strongly did the company come down on the out-of-line employee? Performing this analysis is critical, because treating similar cases in the same way is an essential element of fairness. If one employee got reamed out last week for engaging in a particular kind of conduct, it seems unfair that someone else who does the same inappropriate thing today should escape with a minor reprimand.

There's a second reason that is also fundamental. Companies, like all organizations, can be conceived, in part, as constituting ongoing conversations. This is certainly true of a company trying continuously over time to develop, define, and live up to high ethical standards. People talk about what's going on and what's not going on; whether somebody is doing a good job or a bad one, whether the company "overreacted" to a particular situation or did not. Choices that people make when deciding whether a company disapproves of a particular practice, like not disclosing a conflict of interest, or how management responds when someone appears to have violated a standard, are parts of this ongoing intra-organizational conversation. If you want any decision you make today about what you should do to be satisfactory, you must understand how past responses have "played" in the company's ongoing conversation. That conversation—what was good, what was bad, what was really "the right way to handle a situation" and what approach stunk to high heaven—is a critical component of an organization's ethical culture.

Moreover, the conversation includes what the people who make decisions say to themselves. We frequently have a good sense of whether we approve of what others have done. But we also judge ourselves. "We sure handled that right." "It was OK, but I wish we'd tweaked what we did by doing X rather than Y." "Man, if we had that to do over again, I'd never do it that way." The second prong of the foursquare protocol, therefore, urges that reference to abstract principles of right and wrong be run in tandem with the evaluations that the ongoing conversation have ascribed to past choices. If the company's ethical culture is strong and vibrant, there's no better test.

THE THIRD PRONG OF THE PROTOCOL: RECOGNIZE THE *SIGNIFICANT* PARTICULARS BETWEEN THE PROBLEM SITUATION AND PAST SITUATIONS

No skill is more important than learning to identify the *relevant* similarities between a situation that you're facing and one you (or someone you know about) have faced before. Figuring out the relevant similarities means that you've got to understand the relevant differences. If we compare the ethical issues involved in firing Tom and in firing Bob that we discussed in Chapters 1 and 2, the differences in race and age leap out even if we imagine that their sales performances were identical. This is true, of course, because the law demands that we consider firing people who are over forty, and people who are African American, with greater care. Even if there were no applicable law, race, and perhaps age, as we've seen, would be ethically relevant because we know that men and women do get discriminated against on these bases. That, after all, is why Congress made such discrimination unlawful.

Of course, lots of distinctions make no ultimate difference. If Tom and Bob were both under forty, or if one was and one wasn't, it wouldn't matter if Tom's eyes were green and Bob's brown. Differences in skin color, on the one hand, nearly always matter, both ethically and legally in our society. The importance of skin color and the irrelevance of eye color are easy. But don't be deceived. There's probably no harder task than figuring out which differences matter and which don't. For my money, the critical difference between good doctors and average doctors, good lawyers and average lawyers, and ethically effective business executives and those who are less capable turns upon the ability to distinguish the relevant from the irrelevant. It takes training your ethical sensibilities to learn how to do this reliably. The chapters that follow on the most common problem areas are designed to help you nourish those faculties. When you think about the history of a company's ongoing, historical conversation about a certain practice, to use its success or failure to help solve a problem you face, you have to make sure you separate the wheat from the chaff, the relevant from the irrelevant.

THE FOURTH PRONG OF THE PROTOCOL: SITUATING YOURSELF TO DECIDE

Understanding the details of the situation you're facing, then, requires you to locate similar situations in your organization's history, and identify the relevant similarities between what you're facing and what people in your circumstances in the past have faced. It also requires that you be attuned to whether the organization's ongoing conversation about those choices has been favorable of unfavorable. Getting a handle on such information is like buying the ingredients and setting the table. Now it's time to cook the meal. We all know the difference between a short-order cook and a chef. Here's where your company's reputation, your conscience, and—depending upon the magnitude of the question—the welfare of other people are on the line. After you've sorted out the facts, including the company's relevant ethical memory, you still have to consider whether there is anything that compromises *your* ability to decide.

To make a choice you'll feel good about, and which your organizational superiors should applaud, and of which the ongoing company conversation will approve, you have to situate yourself in a decision-making mode. Three "self-situating" questions that you can ask yourself will get yourself oriented to do the best job you can do.

First, you need to ask if you have any self-interest in a proposed course of conduct, and if so, what it is. Obviously, if you're deciding whether *you* can make a self-interested choice, to the disadvantage of the company, in a conflict-of-interest situation, you have to be delusional not to recognize the effect of that self-interest on your decision-making process. But if you're a manager deciding how to apply company rules and standards that one of your reportees may have violated, the question is different. That person may be a valued subordinate, or even a friend. And his or her misconduct might reflect negatively on you. I call this the "don't fool yourself" question. Don't pretend, to use the old phrase, that you are purer than Caesar's wife when you're not. This is because self-interest can skew your choice.

An example will illustrate. In the 1970s and 1980s, Nancy Harris was president of the Northeast Harbor Golf Club, which owned a golf course in Mount Desert, Maine. The club's board had considered developing some of the club's real estate to raise money. Because Ms. Harris was president of the club, a real estate broker contacted her about certain noncontiguous parcels of land located among the fairways of the golf course. Ms. Harris purchased the land in her own name without informing the club's board. Subsequently she purchased additional land surrounded on three sides by the golf course. When the board found out about Ms. Harris' purchases, they were not happy, and rightfully so. Ms. Harris was asked to resign as president, and the board commenced litigation. The case went all the way to the Supreme Judicial Court of Maine, the highest court in the state. The court decided the case under a branch of corporate law called the corporate opportunity doctrine.[3] While we'll discuss generally the duties of members of a board of directors and senior management in conflict-of-interest situations in Chapter 5, it's worth emphasizing here. If you are an officer or director of a company and you learn about a business opportunity that is close to the line of the business of that company, you'd better make sure to talk to a lawyer *before* you decide to take the deal, and its profits, for yourself. Sometimes, and in some circumstances, it's OK to do so. In others it's not. But that's getting ahead of our story.

The point here is simple. If you are confronted by a choice, and your self-interest is involved, it's always relevant to pay attention to that self-interest and see how much it is influencing—or would be influencing, or could be perceived by others as influencing—your choice about what you ought to do. Our scenario about Alpha Heating's practical ability to sell its product to the new buyer at the cost of breaching its contact with Beta for its own financial advantage is clear. Yet self-interest is so pervasive that we can find it even in Linda's story. Remember that Linda is a regional sales manager. Her numbers are only as good as the combined numbers of her sales force. Whatever the cause may be, and however much we respond positively to Linda's empathy when she learns of Tom's personal situation, Tom is a drag on *her* performance. Tom's subpar numbers hinder Linda's ability to secure that promotion she's been striving for and/or the substantial bonus that she's counting on to help finance an addition to her home.

Self-interest, in short, can compromise your independence of judgment. (This is generally true. Chapter 5 will devote substantial attention to the damaging effects of self-interest in financial conflict-of-interest situations.)

The second self-situating factor is to imagine that you're on the receiving end of the course of action you're considering. Remember that we identified the subject matter of this book as actions that affect other people positively or negatively. Most of what we do has a downside for someone. That person may be you; but usually (because we're generally pretty attuned to protecting ourselves) it's someone else. Suppose you're not Alpha, but Beta, now unable to count on supplies of heating oil at a price for which you've budgeted. Or imagine how Nancy Harris would have felt if another board member of the golf club purchased individually the property that, in that situation, as president, she might have wanted to buy for its expansion.

Suppose your company is considering building a new manufacturing plant. State-of-the-art pollution-control equipment will cost an arm and a leg. Environmental counsel advises that less expensive equipment will satisfy existing Environmental Protection Agency standards. But your environmental engineers tell you that anything less than state-of-the-art equipment will lead to a certain level of pollution in the river near the proposed building site and in the underlying groundwater. The second self-situating factor requires that you orient yourself to those residents in the community whose environmental safety will be degraded if the company does the minimum the law allows. It's different being on the giving end rather than the receiving end. Think about both.

The third self-situating factor is to ask what your moral instincts tell you. Now, in Chapter 1 I said that it's a huge mistake to rely solely on your moral intuition. Doing ethics properly requires thinking, and thinking clearly. If ethics were just about doing what felt good to you, there'd be no place for reasoned argument—and the world would be even more chaotic than it is. The effort to try to come up with a sophisticated and sensitive strategy for companies would be a hopeless task.

By "moral instincts" I don't mean anything fancy. I am just referring to that basic sense of what seems right in a particular situation, and what seems wrong. I don't know whether we should say that everybody has such instincts, but that in the case of some—Bernie Ebbers and Ken Lay are obvious business examples—they are badly distorted, or whether we want to say that the Ebberses and Lays of the world are so caught up in their own egos and greed that they have none. It doesn't matter. Most people have such instincts, even if they can't fully explain or justify them or if they are sometimes pulled to ignore their promptings.

It's easy to underrate such instincts. It's also easy to overrate them. If you're caught up in some kind of cost-benefit way of thinking, you'll likely underrate them—after all, there are people out there like Andrew, whom we've described as ethically indifferent. The same is true if you have three or four or a half dozen firm principles that you believe will guide your actions. Even to yourself, your instincts maybe seem soft and squishy, unprovable, unverifiable—in short, not substantial enough to base a decision on.

If you approach from the other end, your instincts have an air of certainty about them that defy, or seem to make it unnecessary for you to engage in clear thinking or rational analysis. If you are convinced in your gut that it would be outrageous to fire Tom while his wife is on her deathbed, or if you believe that it would not be, no amount of argument, consequentialist calculation, or identification of any supposed ethical rule is likely to change your position. Unchallengeable instincts can trump hard-headed thinking.

The correct approach lies in the middle. Except in the clearest case, instincts will rarely provide, on their own, a complete answer to an ethical conundrum. On the contrary, the role that instincts play is to provide a benchmark to help determine whether the conclusions our thought processes reach are satisfactory. Instincts thus help to orient us by providing a check to rationalized or overintellectualized solutions. "You know," one might say about the golf club case, "I understand the argument that the club didn't have the money to buy the land, and that the directors were old fuddy-duddies lacking entrepreneurial zeal. But for Ms. Harris to buy the land without even telling 'em, that just wasn't right."

NEVER NEGLECT FAIR PROCEDURES IN MAKING ETHICAL DECISIONS

Knowing how to make choices about the right thing to do isn't something we're born with. Nor is it simply the application of ideas inculcated into us when we are young by parents and positive role models such as teachers, clergy, scout leaders, etc. Any particular problem will require thought. The purpose of the foursquare protocol proposed in this chapter is to provide signposts for sound decision-making. You can use it in any ethically challenging situation you come across. We'll turn now to the key areas where problems arise in business. We group them into the three primary forms of temptation we all face: sex, money, and power. In the next chapter, we'll walk through how the foursquare protocol can work to solve a situation where a company faces simultaneously two classic sexual harassment scenarios.

NOTES

1. For an important study emphasizing the importance of detailed factual descriptions in making ethical decisions, see Albert R. Jonsen and Stephen Toulmin, *The Art of Casuistry: A History of Moral Reasoning* (Berkeley and Los Angeles: University of California Press, 1988).

2. C. S. Lewis, *The Allegory of Love: A Study in Medieval Tradition* (London: Oxford University Press, 1936), p. 1.

3. Full details of the case can be found in the Supreme Judicial Court's opinion in *Northeast Harbor Golf Club, Inc. v. Harris*, 661 A.2d 1146 (1995).

PART TWO

TEMPTATIONS IN THE OFFICE

CHAPTER 4

Sexual Harassment, Gender Discrimination, and Paramour Preference

They say truth is stranger than fiction. A lawyer friend of mine told me once about a lawsuit brought by some female employees of another law firm that she had been called in to defend. The charge was a widespread pattern of sexual harassment. The lawyers and staff of the firm would frequently party together. One of the entertainments involved drinking shots of tequila. To accompany the shots, the male partners would lick salt off the cleavages of the female lawyers and staff. One of the female lawyers chose to have breast enhancement surgery. On her return to the office, there was a party. The cake was in the shape of two breasts. According to the male partners, my friend told me, the woman loved the cake. There was even some suggestion that at the annual holiday party, while human spirits were high and liquid spirits were flowing, the male partners had a little contest that consisted of measuring the size of all the women employees' breasts. Again, according to the men, the women thought this was all good fun and really liked it. Sure they did. According to my friend—who prudently settled the case early and for substantial dollars—the men seemed genuinely surprised when the women employees had enough and sued them. (This reminds me of the reports that during the Civil War, many slaveholders, who prided themselves on treating their slaves so well, were shocked when the slaves fled to the protection of the Union lines as soon as federal troops got close. "You mean they didn't like being well treated?")

Obviously, such extreme behavior is the exception, though in the eyes of most women less exceptional than in the eyes of most men.

Problems related to sex and gender differences continue to abound in the workplace. There is no reason to be surprised about this. A large part of it is that sex is one of life's great tempters. But that's not all there is to it. Many of these issues arise from old-fashioned gender roles. Let's be direct about it. Lots of men think that males are smarter and generally more competent than women. I think this way of thinking is less true than it used to be—but then, I am a man, and women may disagree. To many men, there are certain high managerial jobs that are "men's" jobs, so that it seems odd when one is assigned to a woman. I always loved Margaret Thatcher's response when a (male) reporter asked how it felt to be a female prime minister of Britain. "I've always been a woman," Mrs. Thatcher said, "and I am prime minister, so I have no idea how to answer your question."

Some of these problems are heavily and sternly regulated by the law; some are not. Sexual harassment is, of course, the subject of federal law. So is gender discrimination. But a third area, what I call paramour preference, is beyond the ken of the law, unless some form of discrimination can be shown. As such, issues regarding gender are a good place to begin our detailed discussion of the most important particular problem areas we want to consider, because some of the discussion will need to focus on legal requirements, and some on nonlegal ethical understanding.

Yet even where there are "laws on the books," they can be too heavy-handed in many situations that arise. There are two main reasons. First, the law is expensive. Even when some aggrieved women can find lawyers to handle their cases on a contingency basis—meaning they pay nothing except expenses unless they win, and, if they win, the lawyer takes a percentage, usually about one third—the case still has to be worth enough, and seem sufficiently likely to be a winner, for a lawyer to spend time on it. Most plaintiffs' discrimination cases are taken on contingent fees and lawyers accept cases only when the chance of winning is good. This does *not* mean that cases lawyers can't afford to take do not necessarily arise out of real sexual harassment or gender discrimination. It means that the harassment isn't severe enough, or the likely monetary reward high enough for the lawyer, as a practical business venture, to afford to take it on.

Second, the publicity of a legal case can deter a woman with even the most solid case from proceeding. If a woman is pressured into regular sex with her boss, she can file a claim for sexual harassment based on a hostile work environment, as happened in the *Meritor Savings Bank* case, one of the landmark U.S. Supreme Court decisions on this issue. Sometimes, however, the victim may be too embarrassed to press her claim. It's not easy to discuss these matters, much less the intimate and humiliating details, in answering questions from lawyers, while jurors, and maybe the press, look on. So even though the law is an important part of the landscape here, it's often like the tip of the iceberg floating above the surface of the North Atlantic. Most of the mass of the iceberg—like the one that sank the *Titanic*—lies below the surface. Our task in this chapter, therefore, is to examine the problems sex and gender pose in the workplace from both the legal and the purely ethical perspectives.

We're going to consider three different kinds of issues. The first, on which we'll spend the most time, is sexual harassment. This is an area where the federal courts are ready to intervene, but only if the conduct involved is egregious. Even in cases to which the reach of the law doesn't extend, there remain critical ethical issues. Second, we'll talk about sex or, as I think it more precise to call it, gender discrimination and its flipside, the prohibition against employer retaliation for complaining about such discrimination. The third, where the law is not involved, is paramour preference, giving favored treatment to one's lover or would-be lover in the workplace.

SEXUAL HARASSMENT

Sexual harassment is about humiliation and the abuse of power. Straight males can experience it, gay males certainly do experience it, but by and large it's a problem that plagues women in the workplace. That's the context to which we'll direct our attention.

Sexual Harassment and the Law

Sexual harassment victims, when they go to court, typically sue the company, rather than the individual "harasser," for damages. Why the company? It's pretty obvious. The company likely has more assets than an individual and is more likely to have an insurance policy that can be called upon to provide funds to pay the damages she may be awarded. It's the search for deep pockets that plaintiffs always engage in when they have a liability claim.

In interpreting Title VII of the Civil Rights Act of 1964 (the federal statute that provides the basis for such claims), the courts have distinguished two ways in which the company can be liable for sexual harassment. The first is that the company created a "hostile work environment" or that it allowed such an environment to flourish. The second is when the victim suffers tangible economic harm, the so-called "quid pro quo" sexual harassment. The paradigm cases of each are familiar. In a hostile work environment case, a female employee, or a group of female employees, is forced to endure a degrading atmosphere. The degrading may take the form of constantly disparaging or humiliating women, as in the law firm that I discussed at the beginning of this chapter. Or it arises when a woman is forced to suffer the unwanted sexual advances of a male employee, usually her superior in the hierarchy. In quid pro quo harassment, the male boss conditions a promotion, a pay increase, or some other work-related benefit on whether the object of his lust accepts or rejects his advances.

Now, it's outside my purpose here to dwell on the details of the legal regime regulating sexual harassment.[1] Unfortunately, some readers are likely to have to learn more about this area than they wish to know, either as victims or managers. Issues between men and women are going to arise, somewhere, sometime, because of who men are, who women are, and what our culture has taught us all about gender roles. Managers need to know that, unlike fifty years ago, the law will not stand idly by and permit some conduct to go undisturbed under the supposed justification that "boys will be boys."

But the law doesn't always apply. When it does, its influence is severe. Critical as these basic legal rules are, however, they leave a great deal untouched. We'll find this to be common as we proceed through this and the next four chapters. The law is full of a host of procedural requirements. These are often mysterious to nonlawyers but are the lifeblood of much of a lawyer's work. To the layperson, such requirements can seem artificial, inflexible, or even divorced from reality. I don't entirely disagree with such criticism, but the fact is, that's the way law works. But the basic reason the law is not a panacea for all sexual harassment victims is that the courts simply can't be bothered by lots of the small-scale, run-of-the mill, sexual byplay leading to harassment that so often occurs. However upset you may be, you can't (literally) make a federal case out of everything. As one authority on the subject puts it, "Only the most egregious conduct can support a claim of sexual harassment based on a hostile environment."[2]

The fact that the law has the ability (or the willingness) to address only the most "severe and pervasive"[3] hostile work environments doesn't mean that only such major-league hostility should be a concern for managers. Thinking that way is a critical mistake—first, because small problems have a way of morphing into large ones and, second, because a woman may be treated inappropriately even if the federal courts don't give her a legal remedy. As we saw in Chapter 2, the reach of the law is not congruent with what's right and what's wrong, even when the law—such as Title VII—was passed because it reflected a deep comprehension of the difference between ethically appropriate and inappropriate conduct.

Two Kinds of Sexual Harassment

The law against sexual harassment, as we've seen, distinguishes between whether a woman is made to feel devalued because of a hostile work environment or threatened with sanctions if she rejects unwelcome advances. That's a valid distinction, but if we want to understand what's wrong with sexual harassment, I think there's another distinction that pinpoints two different ways in which women's rights are violated. On the one hand, a woman can claim the right not to have her zone of privacy invaded, even if no third person knows about it. On the other, she has the right not to be ridiculed in public.

Invasion of Privacy

Sexual activity and even sexual thought are generally matters we keep private, out of the public eye. Indeed, we call our relationships in which sexuality is a key component *intimate* relationships. The law takes this into account by saying that there is a zone of privacy regarding a person's sexuality into which the state is barred from entering. Thus, in a classic case, the Supreme Court struck down a Connecticut law that forbade the sale of contraceptives—even to married persons.[4] The ground was that the use, or nonuse, of contraceptives was the business of people involved in an intimate relationship with one another, and not that of the state.

Each of us limits the people we allow into this zone, and even best friends typically do not discuss the details of their sex lives with each other. I get to control access to this part of my world, and so do you. It's a core part of my privacy and yours.

The first kind of sexual harassment invades this area of privacy. In its mildest form, a male employee makes lewd or sexually suggestive comments to a female. Sometimes the comments rise to the level of implicit or explicit advances. Sometimes there's an outright proposition that she have sex with him. The lewd remarks need not be made where others can hear them, and outright propositions frequently are not public. The ethical and sometimes legal objection comes from the male employee crossing the barrier into the woman's zone of privacy from which she has the right to exclude the uninvited.

In the workplace, the male frequently outranks the female in the company hierarchy, adding an element of an abuse of power to the mix. In the facts that led to the Supreme Court's landmark *Meritor Savings Bank* decision, the female, Mechelle Vinson, was hired to be a teller at the bank. The person who hired her, and then harassed her, Sidney Taylor, was the branch manager.[5] Although initially treating her in "a fatherly way," his true intentions soon became clear. He invited her out to dinner and she accepted; during the course of the meal, he suggested they go to a motel and have sex. Although Vinson initially refused, eventually, out of fear of losing her job, she consented. At the trial, she testified that, over a number of years, they met for sex between forty and fifty times.[6]

There are two crucial points we have to understand. At her trial, Vinson testified that on a number of occasions beyond the forty or fifty sexual encounters, Taylor "followed her into the women's restroom when she went there alone, exposed himself to her, and forcibly raped her."[7] Rape, of course, is a crime. Unlike sexual harassment, men go to jail for committing it. If a man has the assets to make it worthwhile, he also can get sued for big-time damages. (Remember the civil case brought against O. J. Simpson after he was acquitted in his criminal murder trial.) What's important from the standpoint of management, however, is that the use of physical force is not essential to create the problem, either in the civil courts or ethically.

Neither is it necessary that the woman fears she'll lose her job. As we'll see shortly, such pressure by a male boss aggravates the wrongfulness of what he's doing, but a male can sexually harass a female employee even if he does not outrank her and has no influence on her promotion track.

The reason why force, whether physical as in the case of rape, or psychological, when her job prospects are threatened, isn't necessary goes back to the invasion of a woman's zone of privacy surrounding her intimate life. If we think that people have rights of any kind, as we discussed in our critique of consequentialism in Chapter 1, the right to a sanctuary surrounding one's intimate life has to be near the top of the list. In the early days of sexual harassment litigation, defense lawyers came up with what was called the "boys will be boys" defense. "Coming on to women is just what men do. It's how their heads are built," the argument went. "If there's no physical violence or inappropriate pressure, there's no wrongdoing. Complaining that men shouldn't be like that is like complaining that days are short in December. It's the way the world is." Not surprisingly, courts rejected this defense. Companies that want to stay out of trouble won't countenance this kind of thinking either. A woman's zone of privacy needs to be respected.

The biggest problem companies face in the area of sexual harassment is not failing to have a policy prohibiting the conduct. Stating the policy is easy. Rather, the problem is *enforcing* the policy. Before we consider this, however, we need to look at another kind of sexual harassment, where enforcement is also the key problem. This is the problem of gender disparagement.

Humiliation and a Gender-Disparaging Environment

A work environment can be hostile to women (or, again, to gay males) on set-related grounds without even the whisper of an unwanted sexual advance. We can be clearer about this if we call such an environment "gender disparaging." Why so many people feel the need to couch their identities in feeling superior to other groups is one of the true mysteries of history and social science. You can find it all the way back to the great early civilizations of Greece and China, and it continues. From the broadest perspective, what we are talking about is an instance in which people (here, males) seek to claim superiority over others (females) not because of any personal attributes, but simply because they are males. (The same is true of some straight males who assume superiority over gay males. But, as before, we'll stick to the more common male-female situation.) The distinguishing feature is the sexual tone, but it's not the tone of a man coming on to a woman. Here, the problem isn't that a man is making unwanted sexual advances to a woman. It's that men are disparaging women as a class. The derogatory tone in instances like these is sex-specific.

Here's an example. In the 1980s, Teresa Harris worked as a manager at an equipment rental company. When her case reached the U.S. Supreme Court, the Court, speaking through Justice Sandra Day O'Connor, the first female justice, described what happened:

> ... Hardy, the president of the company, often insulted her because of her gender and often made her the target of unwanted sexual innuendos. Hardy told Harris on several occasions, in the presence of other employees, "You're a woman, what do you know" and "We need a man as the rental manager"; at least once, he told her she was "a dumb ass woman." Again in front of others, he suggested that the two of them "go to the Holiday Inn to negotiate [Harris'] raise." Hardy occasionally asked Harris and other female employees to get coins from his front pants pocket. He threw objects on the ground in front of Harris and other women, and asked them to pick the objects up. He made sexual innuendos about Harris' and other women's clothing. In mid-August, 1987, Harris complained to Hardy about his conduct. Hardy said he was surprised that Harris was offended, claimed he was only joking, and apologized. He also promised he would stop, and, based on this assurance Harris stayed on the job.[8]

The lower courts had found that Harris did not make a claim for sexual harassment based on a hostile work environment. In a unanimous decision, the Supreme Court disagreed.[9] Typically, courts give remedies only when the plaintiff can show that he or she suffered actual harm. In the Harris case, however, the Supreme Court found that what was done to Harris was wrong even though she was unable to prove tangible psychological injury. The Court unanimously found that a reasonable person would perceive the environment in which Harris worked as "hostile and abusive."[10] As Justice O'Connor put it, "Title VII comes into play before the harassing conduct leads to a nervous breakdown." What characterizes gender disparagement is the stress that "can and often will detract from employees' job performance, discourage employees from remaining on the job, or keep them from advancing their careers."[11]

What Teresa Harris endured is thus quite different from what was inflicted on Mechelle Vinson. Vinson's privacy regarding what she chose to do in her own intimate life was violated. Harris suffered public humiliation. Vinson suffered from Taylor's radically misplaced sexual desires; Harris did not. But Harris' tormentors could not escape on that ground, for, as Justice Antonin Scalia said in another case, "[H]arassing conduct need not be motivated by sexual desire."[12]

"A CODE OF WORKPLACE CIVILITY"

The lawyers for the company in the case just cited, involving harassment of a gay male, said that civil rights laws were not designed to create "a general civility code for American business." True enough. Courts have to enforce the statute that Congress passed, and that statute does not prohibit all verbal or physical harassment in the workplace. (How could it?) The statute prohibits only discrimination, meaning disadvantageous terms of employment.[13] But just because the federal courts can't get involved in a code of civility for the workplace doesn't mean that businesses shouldn't do so themselves. Unless the victim can prove that she (or he) has experienced "unreasonable interference with ... work performance,"[14] the law will not give redress. Again, this does *not* mean that comments that don't rise to the level of a civil rights violation are OK. They're not. It just means that they don't violate the Civil Rights Act of 1964. One way to look at this is to say that this is the point where law ends and ethics takes over. Another way is to note that there's a no-bright-line test that defines what crosses the line into the legally unacceptable. The more problematic the conduct, the more likely it is to land the company in legal trouble. But conduct doesn't need to violate Title VII to be unacceptable.

From what we have seen so far, we can distinguish three situations. There are outright invasions of privacy, characterized by a request—or a demand—for sexual favors. There is a culture of ridicule that humiliates individual women and individual gay men. And there is the low-level banter that inevitably goes on between good-natured, and not-so-good-natured people, as they go through their days doing their jobs. Distinguishing the first two from the third in practice can be tough.

What's even tougher is making decisions when people cross the line into inappropriate conduct not by content but by repetition. Suppose a male boss, one day out of the clear blue sky, says to his female secretary as he walks into the office after a breakfast meeting, "Hey, that's a pretty dress you're wearing today." While I know that some people say that *any* comment about the appearance of a person of the opposite sex is out of bounds in the workplace, this comment will seem innocuous to most people. Suppose, instead, that the comment is "My, you look sexy today." It's possible that some women might view the remark as a compliment, but I think most women in today's workplace would be offended, and rightfully so. Note that this comment is inappropriate for the workplace, even when it's not a part of a pattern of making advances. To say it's inappropriate, however, doesn't say that the courts can do much about it. If a woman considered bringing a suit about such a comment, any lawyer she approached would laugh her out of the office. If somehow the case got filed, any court would dismiss the case in a New York minute. It's too small, too trivial, and not the business of the busy federal courts. If you were the manager of the man who made the remark, you might let it pass, or advise him in a low-key way to avoid such comments in the future.

But suppose a boss made the same comment a couple of weeks later. Then again. Then on a regular basis. Then every day. You can see where I'm going. Frequency matters. Especially when the remarks start to look like a man is forcing his attentions on a woman, they cross the line. From the purely legal viewpoint, you can never, in advance, be precisely sure where that line is. (That's why it's a mistake to think that the law provides a bright line in the sand, on one side of which you're safe.) Because you're not going to know where, down the road, a court or jury will draw the line, the *smart* move is to make it clear that the company won't permit comments such as "you look sexy today" to continue. You won't fall down the slippery slope if you don't get on it.

I want to stress that there's another reason why repetition of such comments should be out of bounds. A pattern *itself* can give offense. When a woman finds herself gritting her teeth and wondering as she walks into the office, "What's he going to say today?" there's a real problem. In *Oncale v. Sunflower Offshore Services, Inc.*, the case about harassment of a gay male, the Supreme Court was clearly on the mark when it recognized that there are "genuine but innocuous differences in the ways men and women routinely interact with members of the same sex and of the opposite sex."[15] Comments that give offense, by definition, aren't innocuous. Comments that *might* give offense can turn out to be innocuous, but they might not. Yet a comment that, in isolation, might be on the borderline, might become unquestionably offensive if regularly repeated. One day's compliment, regularly repeated, can become, "I sure wish he'd stop checking me out every day when he walks in the office." Practical workplace civility can't tolerate isolating a single arguably inoffensive comment when it's part of an offensive pattern.

Addressing Sexual Harassment Problems

When comments cross the line from the innocuous to the offensive, whether because of their content or their repetition, there's not much that can be said in their defense. There are two sides to many questions, but not this. In a business, however, there's an additional issue. What's the company's responsibility? The usual case doesn't involve the company encouraging the harassment—though the law firm whose activities I discussed at the beginning of this chapter did so. Rather, the question is, what's the company's responsibility where it permits a hostile work environment to flourish? Let's look at two cases of sexual harassment and use the foursquare protocol outlined in Chapter 3 to see how management can compassionately but fairly go about its job of making the workplace free of sexual harassment.

Here's a variation on a true story, with names and the kind of business involved changed to preserve anonymity. Judy was a mid-level manager in a financial services/brokerage firm. Jim was her boss. One afternoon around 5:30, Judy was finishing up some paperwork and getting ready to leave. She had a dinner date for which she didn't want to be late. There was a knock on her door and Jim entered. He sat on the opposite side of the desk and talked about a couple of accounts. All of a sudden, Jim lurched around the desk and kissed her. Not a peck on the cheek, but the kind of open-mouthed kiss on the lips that Judy reserved for the special man in her life. Jim told her that he'd been trying to resist her but couldn't any longer, and he asked her to dinner. When she said she had plans, he insisted on the next evening. She wanted to refuse, but felt she couldn't.

Judy was shaken and angry. She felt violated. She hadn't been attracted to Jim before, and after this—yuk! She thought about sending him an e-mail telling him to forget the dinner, but then remembered the promotion to assistant VP that she was up for. She had worked for Jim for long enough to know that he was relentless when he wanted something, and vindictive. She worried that if she canceled dinner, Jim would torpedo her promotion, which he clearly had the power to do. She was afraid.

Judy went to dinner with Jim. She was uncomfortable, but she couldn't honestly say he was obnoxious or gross or vulgar. He came on to her, but in a gentlemanly way. The scene in her office was not repeated. Jim clearly wanted some kind of relationship; Judy didn't. She felt trapped. They began going out. They began sleeping together.

Finally, after about four months, Judy felt she couldn't take it any more. She couldn't eat properly. She lost her will to exercise. For the first time in her life she suffered from insomnia. She felt dirty. The last thing she wanted to do was to get a lawyer. She liked her job, or did before the thing with Jim started. Reluctantly, she went to senior management.

Suppose you're the person Judy approached. Doubtless you would empathize with Judy. But you'd have to have your guard up. Jim is a power in the company. You know that "he-said, she-said" stories are, well, he-said, she-said situations. And, in a case like this, there is the possibility of a lawsuit—an expensive, time-consuming, and likely embarrassing lawsuit. Judy's problem, and Jim's problem, is now your problem and the company's problem.

PUT THE FOURSQUARE PROTOCOL TO USE

The foursquare protocol outlined in Chapter 3 provides a structure that you can use. First, you need to get the facts. That sounds easy, at least in principle. It's likely, however, that this may turn out to be dicey and unpleasant. But there's no substitute. It's not just that it will be a question of he-said, she-said, where finding out the truth won't be easy. What he says and she says are likely to involve information about other people's private lives you'd just as soon not know. Unfortunately, there's no substitute for it. It's a brute fact that women largely believe that their claims of sexual harassment are disbelieved and devalued by male executives; and men frequently believe (or claim to believe) that women invent, or at least embellish, their stories. It seems almost certain that women are generally right in such cases. Indeed, there's reason to believe that lots of women don't report incidents because, on top of the humiliation of the harassment, they'll have to endure the humiliation of not being believed. But, as defense lawyers will tell you, this isn't true 100 percent of the time. Sometimes women do create stories or exaggerate what occurred. What this means for senior management is that you have to sort out what really happened. Here, even if Judy told you as the manager exactly what we've described, your job wouldn't be over. You'd have to get Jim's side of it, and, at a minimum, he would likely be quite defensive. But, as I've said, the job needs to get done. It won't be the last difficulty you'll have achieving closure in this matter.

Once you've got a clear idea of what happened, it's probably a good idea to consult your in-house counsel or the outside lawyer the company uses on employment matters. Your company, in fact, may have a protocol requiring such consultation. Sexual harassment is no longer a matter simply for the business executive. We've said that Judy doesn't want to call a lawyer and, initially, most people don't. This frequently changes where management isn't sufficiently responsive and empathetic to the woman who has endured what Judy did. Even if Judy said she hadn't called a lawyer, she could change her mind. And, to state the obvious, an *employer* can be held liable under Title VII when one of its supervisors engages in the kinds of acts that Jim committed here.

The advice counsel gives will provide you a good sense of whether you're legally exposed or not. Regardless of that advice, if Judy has come to you and the company hasn't been sued, you have to figure out how to respond to what she has suffered. The second prong of the foursquare protocol invites you to look at two things: how management has treated cases of sexual harassment before and whether employees have felt that such treatment has been fair—that is, what has been the content of what I called the employees' collective ongoing conversation about the way management has resolved ethical issues. If the company is anything but a start-up, there are likely to have been multiple incidents, some more invasive than others, some where there have been "official" decisions, and some a part of the company's collective consciousness, arising from a mountain of proverbial conversations at the watercooler. Let's play out a possible scenario.

A Company's Collective Memory

Let's assume that one of the stories in the company's collective memory involved a superstar young executive named Paul. Paul had everything going for himself. He was smart, well educated, innovative, and hardworking. He could put together complex financing arrangements whose subtlety only the most senior people could match. Like Jack in Chapter 1, Paul's only weakness was the women, or more precisely, the relatively powerless women in clerical or computer support positions whom he encountered every day. He called them "honey" or "hot stuff," or the like, and would comment on their bodies and their clothes, especially if the tops were low-cut or the skirts short. To one secretary in particular he'd say, "I bet you're something else in bed." But, at least as far as anyone knew, he never asked any of the women out and never got involved with any in the way Jim got involved with Judy.

In another instance, in the company's recent past, a male vice president named Ted became interested in an account executive named Petra. Ted was single, Petra was getting a divorce, and she was interested as well. They began having lunch and e-mailing regularly. They began seeing each other frequently in the evening and, after a time, were sleeping together. After a few months, Petra began to have doubts. She told Ted she wanted to break it off.

Ted was genuinely upset—and quite furious. When Petra wouldn't respond to his entreaties to get back together, he began to take action. Her office was moved to a smaller one, where the air conditioning didn't work very well in summer and the heat was overpowering in winter. She lost her terrific assistant and was assigned to Sylvia, well known for doing her nails and eBay, and little else. But the crisis erupted when Petra was passed over for a promotion that Ted had told her "she was in line for." After weeks of e-mail silence from Ted, she found a message, sent from his home computer to hers, saying simply, "It cost you. Now we're even."

Legal action against Paul would have been unlikely. Though his conduct was offensive, it's hard to imagine that a plaintiff's lawyer would think that a court case could generate an award of damages that would have interested him or her in taking the case. Petra's case was different. Ted's e-mail, in particular, would make a defense lawyer (and the company's insurance company) cringe, and a plaintiff's lawyer salivate. Let's suppose, however, that Petra hadn't been prepared to endure the publicity that taking her case to court would entail. So neither Paul's nor Ted's case led to litigation.

Suppose that management learned of Paul's antics from Marybeth, the secretary to whom Paul would make his comments about his fantasies about her in bed. She had told him to stop; he didn't; she told him she'd go to management if he didn't stop; he didn't; she kept her promise.

The executive VP in Paul's division was given the responsibility of talking to Paul. A kindly older man, a gentleman of the old school, the executive VP gave Paul a milquetoast version of what Marybeth had said, and what else HR had learned in its discrete investigation. Paul was apologetic. He said he hadn't realized, said he was only teasing, thought it was all in good fun, meant no harm, etc. The executive VP nodded. Paul said it wouldn't happen again. The executive VP said the matter was closed.

When it came time for year-end bonuses, the "discretionary" portion of Paul's, that is, the part not tied to achieving specific performance goals, was zero. He came up for a raise in March, and was given the lowest possible. He polished off his resume and was working for a competitor by Memorial Day.

Things went down a little differently for Ted. Ignoring her sister's advice to get a lawyer, Petra printed Ted's "now we're even" e-mail and marched into the chairman's office. She demanded to see him then and there. When making her cool her heels in the reception area outside his office for an hour or so didn't work, he agreed to see her. Petra told him the whole story. She gave him a hard copy of the e-mail.

No one in the company ever knew what actually transpired when Ted met with the chairman. It was widely known, however, that Ted was given a generous early retirement package, including a consulting contract for three years that paid him one half of his annual salary, and for which he didn't do a lick of work.

In our imaginary company, whose history included these two past incidents of sexual harassment, the take in the company's ongoing conversation on what Paul did, and what happened to him was this: Paul was out of line; nobody doubted that. Even the men who themselves were sometimes inclined to time warp to the 1950s know, in this day and age, you don't talk to a female employee about what she'd be like in bed. The women employees were predictably angrier, and some were quite outraged.

What else divided the company's employees was how Paul was treated. Paul was an extrovert, and what he was told went around the company in a matter of days. His energy in the office was common knowledge and so was the sense that nobody at Paul's level was as good at what he did. Paul made it common knowledge that he was told that, if he kept his mouth shut and his hands to himself, what he did would not be held against him. Some employees, particularly women, thought that this was not enough. Others thought it was fair; after all, he didn't pressure women into sex nor condition raises or perks upon anything.

But, everybody knew, the company *did* hold what Paul did against him. When Paul left in the way he left, it looked to everybody like management lied to him. And nobody liked that. Martha, one of the women who used to have to endure Paul commenting on her figure, summed it up when she said, "Paul was a low-life. But low-life or not, if the company makes a promise, it oughta keep it."

The treatment that Ted received also hadn't sat well, but for the opposite reason. Nobody approved of what Ted had done. How could you? Women—and a number of men—saw the sexual harassment for what it was and were angry. Even the 1950s time-warp men didn't like it, because they didn't appreciate senior executives rewarding their girlfriends. In part, they thought this was unfair; in part they objected that such practices, if not condemned, could skewer the promotion process and harm their own chances. Yet Ted was essentially handed a "get-out-of-jail-free" card—and a large chunk of cash to go with it.

Sorting Out the Relevant

You'll recall that the third element of the protocol we explained in Chapter 3 was the need to sort out the relevant from the irrelevant similarities between what happened in the past and the present problem. Before you read any farther, you might want to take a stab at doing that here.

We can start with the most obvious similarity. All three cases—Paul/Marybeth, Ted/Petra, and Jim/Judy—involve making the workplace unpleasant (or worse) for women. These aren't cases where a woman claims she has been denied a promotion simply because she's female. Petra wasn't denied her promotion because she was female; she didn't receive it because she didn't want to continue her relationship with Ted. (Although the courts call sexual harassment a form of discrimination, to come within the meaning of Title VII, straightforward denying pay or benefits to a woman on account of her sex is different. We'll talk about that situation later in this chapter.) The Ted/Petra and Jim/Judy cases, of course, are particularly close. Each involves a male supervisor forcing his attentions on a female employee. Another apparent similarity, this time between the two earlier cases, comes from how the company responded to the charges of sexual harassment: Both Paul and Ted were forced out of their jobs.

There are also major dissimilarities, as there usually are when bundles of human conduct are compared with one another. The question is whether the dissimilarities are relevant. Like Ted, Jim forced his attentions on a female employee. Unlike Ted, however, Jim did not condition a promotion on a positive response to his advances. Moreover, Jim didn't do anything as *dumb* as Ted did in writing that e-mail. While that e-mail may not change how we should assess Ted ethically, it sure changes how Title VII's prohibitions will come down in a court of law. Ted's e-mail was evidence that Petra could use against the company with overwhelming effect if she chose.

There's a second major dissimilarity, this time concerning the treatment Paul and Ted received from the company. The issue here is not what the harassing men did, but how the company responded. Paul, the junior employee, was promised a chance for continued employment, provided he mended his ways. He did so, but the company broke its promise. It sent signals through his compensation that he was no longer "desirable." Ted, on the other hand, got a sweetheart deal. Oh, to be sure, he might have lost a few years work at the likely peak of his earning power. He may have lost some honor, for instance, and perhaps a coveted seat on the board of directors. But you'd have to say he came out smelling like a rose.

If you were the senior manager with responsibility for making a recommendation about what should happen to Jim or how to respond to Judy's complaint, you couldn't just look at management's responses to the previous cases to determine relevant similarity. The third prong insists that you take into account the spin put on those responses in the company's collective memory. The company's response to past cases, in other words, isn't just what management *did*. It includes how management's choices went down in the organization's collective memory. With all of this in mind, the question is, how would you go about using what you know from these previous cases to make a decision?

The most obvious point concerns what the company's attitude toward sexual harassment must be. The short answer is that it can't be tolerated. The company's history tells us enough to know that sexual harassment is still a problem in the organization. As we've said before, organizational condemnation of sexual harassment doesn't depend upon the existence of federal statutes. Indeed, from the point of view of a woman who has an ethical right not to be harassed in the workplace, the existence of the federal law is unrelated to why she objects to such conduct. After all, Title VII was enacted because this conduct was wrong; it didn't make conduct that had been OK suddenly inappropriate. To repeat: such practices invade a woman's private space and hold her up to ridicule; in short, they compromise her dignity. She doesn't relinquish her ethical claim to this immunity by taking a job. Because we know that lots of sexual harassment fails to reach the threshold where the law can realistically intervene, the senior manager can't rely on court rulings to define the parameters. What's critical is that the company's resolution of the issues raised by Judy's complaint can't countenance—and can't be seen to countenance—Jim's conduct.

But *how* should the company implement this policy? I'm not talking about what it's going to write down in the company's ethical code. *That's* the easy part. What is the company actually going to *do* when confronted with an allegation that some kind of sexual harassment has gone on? What should it do to these males who won't, or can't, make themselves comply?

Clearly the financial services firm we've been considering has made a mess of the job in the two previous cases. Just consider the messages it sent: (1) If you're a junior employee, you're gone—and gone in an underhanded, disgraceful way; (2) If you're senior, we'll take care of you, because we're not going to let a little "sexual harassment" destroy the rewards of a valuable career; (3) If you're an employee, and you're doing something you shouldn't, you can't count on us to tell you the truth; and (4) Your treatment—your "punishment"—turns more on who you are, a top executive or a young employee, than what you've done. This means that, measured by the sanctions the company metes out, it can be worse to make inappropriate comments to female employees than to force a woman into a sexual relationship and deny her a promotion when she tries to cut it off.

Seen in light of the messages the company sent in making its previous decisions, the company has made its decisions based on an irrelevant criterion—the seniority of the offender—and not on the relevant one, the invasiveness of the harassment. And it compounded the inequity of what it did by not being honest about what it was doing. Deciding what to do with Jim, therefore, will require assessing his conduct by what (after a complete investigation of what really happened) he actually did and by making a decision that is without deception in its communication and implementation.

Situate Yourself to Make a Principled Decision

What I hope you take away from the situation I have just described is this: To decide what to do when Judy approaches you and tells you what's been going on with Jim, you can't just *deduce* your answer from some sort of provision in your ethical code (or the federal statute book) that "Sexual harassment is bad." That axiom is essential to principled decision-making, but only a part of it. What real-life decision-makers know, albeit sometimes only unconsciously, is that reaching a satisfactory solution involves engaging in a *dialogue with past practices*. You have to marry the general principle you are upholding, here, the ban on sexual harassment, with what you can learn from the past. With the benefit of hindsight, some choices will appear to right, and others will look like mistakes. To accomplish that successfully, however, there's one further task you have to perform. You'll need to remember the fourth prong of the foursquare protocol. You have to do what I call "situating yourself to decide."

First, you'll have to ask yourself if you have any self-interest. At one level, everybody in management has an interest in being seen as handling tough situations effectively. But I mean something more than that. The most obvious, if the manager is male, is whether he has any skeletons in his closet. Has he done something to or with a female employee that would open him up to some kind of discipline? Did Ted's boss let Ted off so easily because of something inappropriate he himself had done, or was doing, with another female employee? Or maybe he's aware of violating another company rule, so that his decision in Jim's case would be skewed. Don't misunderstand. I am not saying a decision-maker needs to be a candidate for canonization before he or she can make a decision. Everybody has his or her own baggage. I am saying, however, that if there is something that biases you in how to decide, you need to acknowledge that fact, at least to yourself. As we'll see when we talk about financial conflicts of interest in the next two chapters, sometimes you are "conflicted out" of making a fair decision, and you have to turn it over to others. Sometimes you can adjust for the bias yourself. But you can't simply pretend it isn't there. Acknowledging your self-interest, if only to yourself, puts you on the right road.

Second, you have to ask what it would be like if you were on the receiving end. This can be tough in a sexual harassment case. In the case we've been discussing, this means you have to put yourself in the position of Judy, whose privacy was invaded, as well as in Jim's, who may be facing at least serious embarrassment, and perhaps a blow to his career from which it will never fully recover. If you're a male, putting yourself in Judy's shoes won't be easy. I know. I've talked to lots of women about harassment issues, and I think I understand the problem as well as I can emotionally and intellectually. But I'm not a woman. I've certainly felt *invaded* by outrageous behavior in the workplace, but it's not the same thing. And if you're a woman, empathizing with Jim at all may be tough.

Putting yourself in Jim's shoes invites you to consider what happened from his point of view. I'm not justifying and I'm not excusing. However nuanced, a message about zero tolerance for sexual harassment has to get through. But if our hostility to sexual harassment is because of its affront to dignity, then we can't deny the claims of Jim's dignity as well. Most of us have had the experience of the person who's a real hardliner about office misconduct, but whose tune changes once he or she is the one charged, but that's not the point here. Judy and Jim's situation will have to be sorted out by women and men, so the decision-maker is almost certainly going to approach the situation with his or her own gender bias. To be that decision-maker, to make the kind of choice that will resonate well in the company's collective conversation, you'd have to distance yourself from your own gender bias as much as possible. This is not easy. But it's essential.

Principled decision-making, then, requires you, at one and the same time, to understand the ethical principle involved in the issue, the company's history of dealing with such problems, and anything that may skew your own ability to be fair-minded in making the choice. The process you have to go through is not the simple application of a principle like "Male employees must not harass female employees." It's about developing and operating in each case within a fully considered context.

DECIDE IN CONTEXT

Balancing these concerns, along with everything else, is the really tough job. I once had an accountant who had a poster in his office that said, "It *is* rocket science." I feel that way about making many ethics decisions. The difference with rocket science is that in ethics there's not one answer. If a rocket scientist correctly does the calculations, the vehicle will do what it is supposed to, and not fail to leave the ground or explode and fall back to Earth. In ethics, there are many different answers. Doing the best you can—which is all anyone can legitimately ask—means working carefully through all the nuances of a real-life factual situation.

In Judy and Jim's case, there are four critical considerations you have to juggle. First, you need to respond to the fact that Judy has been treated improperly—so improperly, in fact, that if she chose to file a Title VII case, your lawyers would have their hands full mounting a defense. Female employees must be certain that, if someone comes on to them the way Jim came on to Judy, the company will not turn a blind eye. Second, you need to craft the sanctions that will be imposed on Jim based on what he *did*, not who he is in the company. While what Paul did was unacceptable, it wasn't nearly as improper as what Ted did, but Ted, because of his seniority and, apparently, his clout, received less severe punishment. Third, management has a trust problem in the company's ongoing conversation about its values—perhaps quite a serious one. Whatever you decide to do, you have to make sure that the company actually *does* what you say it's going to do. At one level, starting to turn the employee distrust issue around now may be as important as how you resolved the Judy/Jim situation.

Fourth, viewed as a whole, does the solution seem fair, not only to the individuals involved, but in light of the company's shared values? Not all companies are the same. While no one with any ethical sense (or any fear of getting sued!) could condone what Jim did, it would be ridiculous to say that all companies should treat every case identically. Companies have different histories, different ways of treating people who have provided vital service in the past, different ways of treating adherence to formal policies, and so on. If you're the person to whom Judy complains, or if you are the designated decision-maker on the resolution, your choice has not only to be fair, but has to be seen as fair both now and later.

When you're looking to make a decision that you think is fair and that you believe has a good chance of surviving vetting in the collective conversation of the organization's employees, don't expect that you'll come up with a single, correct answer, with which all reasonable people will agree. Ethics simply doesn't work that way and, for that matter, neither does law. To be sure, there are choices that pretty much everyone would agree are wrong. An easy example comes from this company's history—lying to Paul about what his prospects at the company were after he cleaned up his act. You can use the foursquare protocol to frame the issues more completely. What additional facts about the interaction between Jim and Judy would you need to know? (For instance, what do we make of the fact that, whether uncomfortable or not, Judy did sleep with Jim for a number of months?) Were there nonsexual harassment situations where the company treated employees much more favorably when they were senior, for instance in a conflict-of-interest situation? (Is sexual harassment less of a problem than the existence of a more systematic pattern of management's abuse of power?) I could go on. You might wish to stop here and try to imagine how you would proceed, taking special care to put yourself (as much as you can) in Jim's shoes if you are a woman, and in Judy's if you are a man.

As you do this exercise, remember this: When you make a decision on what ethical choice to make, you aren't just making that decision, important as it is. You are helping to forge a healthy ethical culture in the company, without which long-term success will be problematic.

SEX OR GENDER DISCRIMINATION

Workplace discrimination based on gender, like discrimination based on race, has been flat-out illegal since the 1960s. The main federal statute involved, Title VII of the Civil Rights Act of 1964, uses the word "sex" to describe what we're going to talk about here. As we mentioned, the law grabs hold of sexual harassment under Title VII's prohibition against "discrimination," even though the essence of the problem isn't that women are treated more poorly than men, it is that they are treated poorly, period. Our concern here is with *differential* treatment. I like to use "gender" rather than "sex" in this context. That's because, in harassment situations, there's an explicit sexual dimension to what's going on. When the problem is unfair differential treatment on the other hand, what matters is that a woman is denied a promotion because of one of her unalterable characteristics, namely, that she's a female. In this sense, your gender is like your race. You're born with it, you can't change it, and you shouldn't be denied a job, a promotion, a perk, or a pay increase because of it.

THE RIGHT TO EQUAL PAY

A year before the passage of the Civil Rights Act, Congress passed the Equal Pay Act, requiring that women receive equal pay for equal work. Prior to its passage, women frequently received less pay on the grounds that men had families to support and women did not! Although that rationale is as dead as the "boys will be boys" defense in sexual harassment cases, gender discrimination abounds. Though there are more women in high-paying, high-prestige jobs than ever before, the latest statistics show that women's pay, on average, lags well behind that of men. According to the Bureau of Labor Statistics, in the third quarter of 2007, the median weekly salary of men was $767, while the median salary of women was $616, or only 80.3 percent of the men's.[16] Issues of equal pay are primarily issues of enforcement rather than ethics. As in the case of sexual harassment, there is nothing that can be said that supports a company's right to pay men more for doing the same job than it pays women, and federal law specifically forbids it. To say this, of course, does not mean that ethics are unimportant. As the statistics just quoted show, the problem is huge. It's just that the legal question is now pretty much open and shut. If a male now wants to discriminate against a woman regarding whether she gets hired, or what she gets paid, or about a promotion, he'd be very foolish not to keep very quiet about it. This is only partly because everyone knows that such discrimination is illegal and avoiding liability makes sense. It's also because of the growing acceptance of gender equality as part of prevailing cultural values. A man is much more likely to risk offending people by speaking of "the inferiority of women" (or, for that matter, African Americans) than his grandfather would have been in the 1950s.[17]

How Covert Discrimination Works

Men continue to discriminate against women in a host of small ways—ways that do not directly involve pay, organizational status, or promotion. A staff meeting is in progress. A host of problems are on the table. The (male) boss comes to item seven on the agenda. He explains the issue. A young woman raises her hand and explains that she dealt with the issue and has a couple of files bearing on it. Without batting an eye, the male boss turns to one of his male staffers and says, "That's great. John, will you get Melinda's file and handle it, please?"

Anyone who's been in business can picture this situation. It's conceivable that this boss has some sort of explicit thought that, "This is a major issue. I don't trust a woman on it. We need a man." But I think it's unlikely. Women readers may disagree, but as I've said, I think overt thinking that women are intellectually inferior or professionally less capable than men is much less common than it was a generation or two ago. But inchoate and unarticulated views about the inferiority of women flourish. I can hear how many men would respond to the dialogue about Melinda's files: "This is not gender discrimination. It's a question of finding the person who gets the job done. John was that person. Melinda had information. Fine. Providing it to John to get one question handled is part of her job." What would women be more likely to say? What would Melinda, who offered the experience and the information, think? Now, Melinda's attitude *might* depend on her perception of whether or not there was a pattern or practice of degrading women. But I don't think that's an inevitable part of it. "Why didn't the boss ask John to work *with* Melinda on the problem? Why, if Melinda was too junior, or too inexperienced, did the boss turn to John, a male, rather than another female? Why weren't there other females to whom he could turn?"

Let's assume that this boss is some guy who believes that key responsibilities are best entrusted to men. In such a case, of course, we'd have no trouble saying that he was explicitly discriminating, and that Melinda (and others in the room, men as well as women) would have been right to perceive it so. That's the easier case to analyze. Let's suppose, on the contrary, that his sense of male superiority is covert. He'd swear that he thinks women are as competent as men, and he wouldn't be lying, that is speaking falsely, when he said so. But he might be deceiving himself, and that's at the core of covert discrimination.

Covert discrimination is insidious. It's difficult to counter because it makes no claim to justification—indeed, if a practice is challenged as discriminatory, the charge is often denied, sometimes self-righteously so. As such, counteracting covert discrimination is generally more a matter of education than elaboration of rules. And by education I mean sensitizing people to the unconscious, prejudiced assumptions that lead to covert discrimination. Though we wish it weren't true, the fact is that people (meaning males and, in the racial context, whites) must learn to understand that their actions aren't like writing on a blank computer screen. Societal biases are inside most of our heads, whether we like it or not. We aren't going to get much help from the law here. The problem is that there is a lot of stored memory on gender (and racial) issues, and this memory influences conduct. Much of this memory, though not based on facts, operates at the level of the most basic presuppositions in the minds of those who are "on top," that is males and whites. The blank slate doesn't exist. Where gender discrimination can't be attacked in the courts, as it can be regarding equal pay, people have to be willing to challenge their own presuppositions. That's part of what having a genuinely gender-blind workplace is all about.

RETALIATION AS DISCRIMINATION

Denial of equal pay and covert discrimination are classic ways in which women are discriminated against in the workplace. There's another kind of conduct that counts as "discrimination" under Title VII that is analytically quite different but about which managers have to be particularly careful. It's when a company retaliates against an employee for complaining of sexual harassment or gender discrimination. At this stage it won't surprise you that the courts are quite unforgiving of this kind of employer misconduct.

Sheila White successfully pursued a retaliation claim against her employer, the Burlington Northern & Santa Fe Railway Company, to the U.S. Supreme Court in 2006.[18] Although Justice Samuel Alito disagreed on the reasoning, the Court voted 9–0 in White's favor. An experienced forklift operator, she was hired to work as a track operator in the railroad's Maintenance of Way Department in its Tennessee yard. When a job operating a forklift came up, her general supervisor placed her in the position. Her immediate supervisor didn't like it. According to White, he repeatedly told her that women shouldn't be working in the Maintenance of Way Department. He also made insulting and inappropriate remarks to her in front of her male colleagues. We don't know what the comments were, but, when she complained, the railroad suspended her supervisor for ten days and ordered him to attend a sexual harassment training session. So far, so good.

Then the company backtracked. The general manager proceeded to remove White from forklift operating duty and returned her to (less desirable) standard maintenance work. The general supervisor told her that this was because coworkers had complained that the forklift operator's job should go to "a more senior man." White filed a complaint with the Equal Employment Opportunities Commission (the EEOC) claiming that her reassignment was gender-based discrimination and was in retaliation.

Things went from bad to worse. Without going into details, White had a verbal altercation with another supervisor, and the company suspended *her* on the ground that she had been insubordinate. An investigation found that she had not been insubordinate, reinstated her in her laborer's position, and awarded her back pay for the thirty-seven days she was suspended. The suspension had occurred over Christmas, leaving her and her family with no money. She filed an additional retaliation charge, claiming that the suspension itself was revenge for having filed the initial charges. The case went to trial, the jury heard the evidence, and agreed with White that Burlington had retaliated against her.

Retaliation raises key issues of law and ethics. Because of the White case, law is now front and center, so we'll begin there. The law treats retaliation as a form of discrimination. At first blush, you might think that's strange. Yet "discrimination" means to treat someone differently and disadvantageously for a reason *other than* what they did. An example will make this clear. Suppose I place an ad in my local paper to sell my car for $15,000 or best offer. One person comes and, having looked over the vehicle, says, "I'll give you $13,500." Soon after, a second person comes. She says, "I'll pay $13,000 for it." No one would say I'm discriminating against the second person when I sell the car to the first person; my choice is based on maximizing my sale price. But if I made my decision on another basis—for instance, that the first person was a man, and the second person a woman—I would be discriminating against her on account of her gender. Thus, if Sheila White had been removed from her forklift operator's post, and returned to regular labor, because she couldn't do the second job for some reason—if that was *really* the reason—we wouldn't call it discrimination. But if she was removed because she is a woman, that's a different story. That's gender discrimination, and it's forbidden because Congress sought to "prevent injury to individuals based on who they are, *i.e.*, their status."[19]

Retaliation is now treated as discrimination. The Supreme Court has made it clear that this means that if you complain about gender (or race or religious or national origin) discrimination in the workplace, you can't be treated negatively *because* of your complaint. So you have a right to equal treatment, and a right not to be retaliated against if you report unequal treatment. But there's an important practical limitation. Because the Court doesn't want to open the floodgates, the result is that the employer's action must be *"materially adverse"* for retaliation to be illegal.[20] "Materially adverse" is lawyer talk for "significant."

In White's case, materially adverse impact was shown. So, if a company retaliates against a woman for challenging sexual harassment or gender discrimination, the law is equipped to hold it liable.

Before moving to the last subject we're going to take up in this chapter, let's look at what happened to Sheila White from another point of view. Though her *case* was about retaliation, let's put the retaliation aspect to the side for a moment. Speaking of her thirty-seven-day suspension, White testified about what havoc the suspension caused in her life. "That was the worst Christmas I had out of my life. No income, no money, and that made all of us feel bad.... I got very depressed."[21] Stop and think about the decision to suspend a single mother without pay just before Christmas. Do you like that decision? What does that make you think about the company that did it, or at least its decision-making process in this instance? High marks? I don't think so. Was such a decision managed in an ethically sensitive way? Suppose there was no *discrimination* involved. Suppose that Sheila White was Sheldon White, a white male single parent. The law finds it easiest to interfere in cases of discrimination because differential treatment can be readily proved to a jury. As we saw in Linda's story at the beginning of Chapter 1, not all conduct that raises our ethical hackles involves differential treatment. But while it's *discrimination* that draws the law's ire, most people's ethical sensibilities will be outraged by such an action. At the Supreme Court, the company argued that the thirty-seven-day suspension was without significance, and did not constitute retaliation, because the company reinstated White and awarded her back pay. The Supreme Court rejected this argument on legal grounds, namely, its interpretation of the federal statute. But I think we can infer what they thought about this action when Justice Stephen Breyer wrote, with seven justices concurring, "Thus, the jury's conclusion that the 37-day suspension without pay was materially adverse was a reasonable one."[22]

PARAMOUR PREFERENCE

The final issue in the realm of sex in the workplace is an area in which the law is not involved. I call this paramour preference. It's the opposite of one of the sexual harassment scenarios we've considered. In cases like our story about Ted and Petra, a male executive conditions a benefit such as a raise or a promotion on a female fellow employee's becoming, or remaining, his sexual partner. In such cases, while not rape because there is no physical violence, the woman's consent is not the result of her genuinely free choice. In the paramour preference scenario, the relationship between the man and the woman is a given. The person with power (usually but not necessarily the man) confers the benefit on his partner because of the relationship, not necessarily because she (or he) is the most qualified or most deserving.

Usually these matters are kept pretty quiet, and the only people who know about them are the man, the woman, and the people inside a company who felt they were victims of the romantically biased choice. Not so the recent scandal that forced the resignation of World Bank President Paul Wolfowitz. Mr. Wolfowitz allegedly engineered a salary increase for his female companion, Shaha Riza, of 45.9 percent in after-tax dollars (which is how World Bank employees are paid), from about $132,000 to about $193,000, when she had to leave a direct report line to Wolfowitz within the bank when he became its president.[23] The reports were that Wolfowitz engineered the raise personally—intervening outside normal channels to make it happen. If true (and Wolfowitz denied it), this is a case of what we call paramour preference.

The Wolfowitz/World Bank scandal is different from the typical paramour preference case in a couple of regards. First is the high-profile political nature of the scandal. Second, Riza worked for the bank before President George W. Bush appointed Wolfowitz to its presidency. The more common pattern is when a couple meet and become involved in the workplace, rather than when an existing relationship is brought into the organization. Finally, it's front-page news, even though no law is broken. Let's conclude this chapter by looking at a more common scenario.

"Don't Get Your Honey Where You Get Your Money"

No one thinks, in the abstract, that it's a good idea to get romantically or sexually involved with a coworker. Everyone would believe that such entanglements are likely to lead to trouble. As an employee of mine when I was in business used to say in her Texas drawl, "Don't get your honey where you get your money." But that's talking about it in the abstract. People spend more of their waking hours at work than at home. Men and women work closely with each other, get to know each other, and, inevitably, sometimes become attracted to one another. Sometimes such romantic involvements are lovely to see and entirely harmless. If both members of a couple who met in a company work in different departments, the business risk is small. If they work in the same department but are not in the same reporting hierarchy, the risk may also be minimal. But what if one is the other's boss? Here, trouble is in the wings.

The senior person controls or has influence upon salary and bonus decisions, promotions, desirability of job assignments, and various perks. Any decision the senior person makes—or any decision he or she declines to make—has a dangerous potential for trouble. Let's consider a scenario that lacks the front-page interest of the Wolfowitz/

World Bank scandal but more closely mirrors what ordinary businesses face all the time.

Let's say that Phil and Nancy work in the same company and that Phil is Nancy's boss. (This scenario can happen in the reverse, with the woman senior to the man, or in a situation where both people are gay, but higher-ranking male/lower ranking female is more common and, as we will see, creates additional difficulties in the real world that we need to address.) Now, it frequently happens in office romances that one or both parties are married, creating additional issues about secrecy. But because we want to focus on the preference issues, let's further assume that Phil and Nancy are both single and completely unattached and that they fall genuinely in love with one another.

Out of the starting gate, this is not the kind of relationship that we saw in the *Meritor Savings Bank* case or in the Judy/Jim and Ted/Petra stories. Here, we don't have an exploitative male boss seeking the sexual favors of his female employee and using his power to secure them. Of course, relationships can change over time, and in the office romance context this can create a significant risk, especially for the male. If, for whatever reason, Phil's interest in Nancy declines, Nancy may look back on the relationship and view it differently than she does now. *Now* it looks like a genuine, equal, respectful relationship; yet, if Phil has dumped Nancy, she might look at it as having been based on exploitation—and in some cases (though not here, as we have described the facts) she'd be right. Phil would be foolish if he weren't aware of this risk. If Phil and Nancy didn't work together, when Phil broke it off, Nancy would simply be unhappy. When they work together, and Phil is the boss, the risk that the breakup will turn into a sexual harassment case is real and shouldn't be underestimated.

But that's going down a different road. Paramour preference arises when the couple stays together. A promotion and a corner office and a bundle of nice perks are available. There are three principal contenders. Nancy is one and Phil is the decision-maker. Both Phil and Nancy have problems.

From Phil's point of view, he is between a rock and a hard place. His difficulties can be located in the fourth prong of the foursquare protocol, situating himself to decide. The truth is, he really can't. We all know that nobody views the person with whom he or she is involved objectively. Usually we overrate the talents, intelligence, and drive of those with whom we are involved, though like me you have probably seen the opposite. The odds are that Phil can't rate Nancy objectively, as others rate her, for the very reason of his involvement with her. Suppose, however, that he can. He may love her and have a wonderful relationship with her, but he knows that one of the other contenders for the promotion really has more of the skills necessary to be a star in that job. Can he say that to her? No matter how much they say (pretend?) that their personal life together and their business lives are kept in separate compartments, I doubt that they can. If he doesn't award her the job, Nancy will likely resent the choice, and may accuse him of bending over backward to avoid the charge of prejudice. If he chooses her, he'll be open to the charge of preferring Nancy because of their personal relationship—unless, somehow, their relationship is completely unknown to everyone else in the company, a pretty unlikely scenario so long as watercoolers, and bars, exist. Here is a classic conflict of interest if ever there were one.

Nancy's situation is no better. She too is damned if she does and damned if she doesn't. If she's denied the promotion, she may feel Phil has sacrificed her career to preserve his reputation for honesty and fair-mindedness. If she's given the promotion, people will talk. It's an index of how far society still has to come to accept complete gender equality in the workplace that women who rise high in organizations are still sometimes accused of "sleeping their way to the top." (I've never heard anyone say that a male employee slept his way to the top, though I have heard men accused of having a position above their abilities because they "married the boss's daughter.")

In a way, this is like the flip side of the fact that a man in Phil's position can't be sure that, if the relationship fails, there won't be allegations of sexual harassment. Nancy can never be sure that her promotion will be accepted throughout the company as something she deserved on its merits. This is a remnant of historic gender stereotyping, but no less a problem for Nancy because of it. If the female paramour is denied the preference because the male wants to avoid the appearance of favoritism, her career is damaged. If she gets the promotion, *regardless of whether it's justified on the merits or not*, some people are sure to gossip and accuse her of not deserving it. Ironically, the only outcome in which paramour preference would not cause a problem would be if Phil denied Nancy the promotion and Nancy believed in her heart of hearts that she didn't deserve it. While not impossible, that might be an unlikely place for her head to be.

Many companies have antinepotism rules that are designed to prevent bias in favor of spouses, children, or other relatives. Although there are legal difficulties about rules requiring one spouse to leave employment if two people working for a company marry, rules barring nepotism generally work well and do more good than harm. But, to paraphrase that discredited sexual harassment defense, so long as men and women are men and women, workplace romances will arise and questions of paramour preference will exist. The choices people will have to make aren't easy, especially as they implicate two of the central requirements for a happy life—fulfilling personal relationships and career success. What can be said with certainty is that where one has the power to confer a huge financial benefit on his or her significant other and exercises that power, and then tries to cover his tracks, he or she will be in serious ethics trouble even if, unlike with Paul Wolfowitz, the story doesn't hit the front pages.

NOTES

1. Many of the legal requirements in sexual harassment cases concern the question of who has the burden to prove what. While this is vital to a lawyer litigating a sexual harassment case, they add little to our discussion here. A good source on discrimination law in general, written by a lawyer for law students but accessible to businessmen and businesswomen is George Rutherglen, *Employment Discrimination Law: Visions of Equality in Theory and Doctrine*, 2nd ed. (New York: Foundation Press, 2007).

2. Ibid., p. 134.

3. *Meritor Savings Bank, FSB v. Vinson*, 477 U.S. 57, 65 (1986).

4. *Griswold v. Connecticut*, 381 U.S. 479 (1965).

5. *Meritor Savings Bank, FSB v. Vinson*, 477 U.S. 57 (1986).

6. The facts are summarized in the official report of the decision in 477 U.S., 60.

7. Ibid.

8. *Harris v. Forklift Systems, Inc.*, 510 U.S. 17, 19 (1983).

9. Television and newspaper reports about the Supreme Court—describing solid "liberals," "solid conservatives," and "swing voters"—while correct in some areas, are not correct in many others. Sex discrimination cases are a good example. Many of the key decisions are by substantial majorities, or are even unanimous. Wherever politics affects some of the

Supreme Court's work, there's no move toward softening sexual harassment standards by either "side."

10. The law's distinction between what the victim actually, subjectively believed, and what a "reasonable" person would believe is subtle but important, both legally and ethically. Were the inquiry into what the victim actually believed, the question for the jury would be what was actually going on in her head. The jury would have to believe, in short, that she was really upset. If she can't persuade them, she loses. The "reasonable person" standard, by contrast, asks whether an ordinary, sensible person would be upset by the environment. The law traditionally calls this an "objective" test. Its purpose is to make sure that there's something "objectively" wrong, that is, that the victim isn't a supersensitive person who's complaining about something that most people would not find seriously offensive.

In a company, the same idea is important. Ordinarily, people should be held to a standard of conduct that reasonable people will think is appropriate. The old "boys will be boys" defense is rightly in its grave; but people are people, and employees need to be able to go about their jobs acting reasonably, and without having to walk on eggshells.

11. 510 U.S. at 22.

12. *Oncale v. Sundowner Offshore Services, Inc.*, 523 U.S. 75, 80 (1998). This case forbade sexual harassment against gays. The opinion of the Court saying that such conduct was prohibited by Title VII was unanimous.

13. Ibid.

14. *Harris v. Forklift Systems, Inc.*, 510 U.S. at 25 (concurring opinion of Justice Ginsburg).

15. 523 U.S. at 81.

16. Bureau of Labor Statistics figures can be found at http://bls.gov/news.release/wkyeng.t01.htm.

17. When I say everyone knows, I mean it would be hard to imagine what kind of an ostrich wouldn't know it in the twenty-first century. And yet, in the 1990s, I remember when a senior partner in the law firm for which I worked asked a young woman interviewing for a job whether she was planning on becoming pregnant!

18. *Burlington Northern & Santa Fe Railway Co. v. White*, 548 U.S. 53, 126 S.Ct. 2405 (2006).

19. Ibid., at 63.

20. Ibid., at 68.

21. Ibid., at 72.

22. Ibid., at 73.

23. Al Kamen, "Where the Money Is," *Washington Post*, March 28, 2007, p. A13.

CHAPTER 5

The Multiple Dimensions of Conflicts of Interest

When Paul Wolfowitz allegedly used his clout as president of the World Bank to secure a huge pay raise for his companion, Shaha Riza, he was acting in spite of a conflict of interest. It wasn't a typical conflict of interest because Wolfowitz was aiming to put money in the pocket of someone close to him, not his own. But the problem is the same. Charged with responsibilities to act on an organization's behalf, a person finds his or her choices skewed because of the ability to secure a personal benefit which is not necessarily in the organization's best interest. His probable wrongdoing is a bridge into what this and the next two chapters are about: money, and the natural human desire to have more of it.

Conflicts of interest present the most pervasive ethical issue related to money that business has to face. Extreme cases implicate the law, frequently the criminal law. We aren't going to discuss the ordinary garden-variety simple embezzlement case, where, for example, an in-house accountant takes the opportunity to divert funds into his own pocket. But we will address insider trading in publicly held securities, which has figured in some of the prominent business scandals of the last few years, and which has a peculiar conflict-of-interest component. Our principal focus will be on situations that involve serious breaches of trust to a company that have to be resolved by the company's own internal mechanisms.

Conflicts of interest can be divided into two broad categories. The first is when a person's position enables him or her to make a decision on the company's behalf from which he or she personally benefits. These conflicts are the subject of the present chapter. The second kind arises where a company affirmatively *asks* employees to consider their own financial self-interest by creating incentive compensation plans. Such incentives can mold employee conduct in troublesome, sometimes criminal directions. We'll address these issues in Chapter 6.

CONFLICTS OF INTEREST AND FRONT-PAGE CORPORATE CRIME

When most people think about ethics in business, in this post-Enron, post-WorldCom era, they think about powerful corporate executives using their influence to extract vast sums of money from their companies for their own personal use. We all know the stories of Ken Lay, Jeffrey Skilling, Bernie Ebbers, and Dennis Kozlowski, and I'm not going to rehash them here. Fortunately, their actions were illegal under stringent provisions of the criminal law and, except for Lay, because of his untimely (timely?) death while the appeal of his conviction was pending, all have begun serving long jail terms.

The significance of their massive and preposterous criminal activity is twofold. First, and most obviously, there are the number of people who lost large portions of their retirement savings because of the manipulations practiced by these executives and others of their ilk. Compare the harm caused by these "trusted executives," with access to the most powerful people in Congress and the Executive Branch, with that produced by the poor teenager who walks into a 7-Eleven on a Saturday night and holds up the clerk to get the contents of the cash register. Now, a crime of violence is a crime of violence, and I am certainly not excusing it. Consider, however, the weight of the harm caused by the armed robbery of a 7-Eleven, for instance, compared with the harm to the retirement security of millions of people resulting from Ken Lay's assurances to Enron's investors that all was peachy with the company. He assured them that they should continue to dump their 401(k) funds into the company's stock, while at the same time he was unloading millions of dollars of his own stock. There's no comparison in the total social costs. Apart from a crisis in your own health, or that of a loved one, it's hard to imagine a worse nightmare than the loss of the bulk of the savings you've laboriously put aside, and counted on, for your retirement.

The front-page executive defendants were in straightforward conflicts-of-interest situations. Bernie Ebbers (somehow) sweet-talked the WorldCom board into giving him some $400 million in loans. Obviously, he had an interest in receiving that money; but it's hard to see how the company had any interest in giving it to him. What distinguishes the conflicts of interest that landed the front-pagers in jail from the more common kind is the effect on corporate outsiders—mostly members of the investing public whose retirement and other investment portfolios suffered severe losses when the companies collapsed or their stock prices plunged. In the typical case, it's the company itself that's harmed. If the shareholders are harmed, it's only indirectly. Company collapses or sharp drops in stock prices are rare.

But the harm such scandals have caused goes beyond the losses that members of the investing public have suffered. This is the second key effect of these scandals.

UNDERCUTTING TRUST IN CORPORATE AMERICA

One common way nowadays to view the entire trajectory of American history is as the chronicle of the (still incomplete) struggle for the emancipation of women and racial and ethnic minorities, in particular the African American descendants of the pre-Emancipation Proclamation slave population. That's a legitimate approach to America's story. But there is an older, different approach, one that would have been more familiar to your grandparents or great-grandparents before World War II.

A century and more ago, American history seemed more to be a battle between business and those who were suspicious of business. The conflict goes back to the early days of the Republic, to the time of the fights between Alexander Hamilton and Thomas Jefferson. The "Hamiltonian" view placed a premium on entrepreneurialism, claimed that the free market rewards innovation and enterprise and is what drives society forward, and believed that market freedom is an essential part of any valid understanding of liberty. Pitted against this idea was a "Jeffersonian" view that exhibited a fundamental distrust of business and business institutions. It expressed the fear that the power of business always needs to be monitored and regularly needs to be checked, and that the concern for "economic freedom" that the Hamiltonian business ideology proclaims is really only a disguise for greed.

The pendulum swings back and forth between these two. For more than two hundred years it has regularly done so, and there's no reason to think the ebb and flow won't continue. Typically, there is a period of spectacular business growth and widespread acclaim for the prosperity it generally brings. Then disclosures of business's excesses start to surface. Reform movements descending from Jefferson's hostility to business jump in and, with much publicity, seek a cure. Thus, in the late nineteenth century, the American economy boomed. These successes enabled the United States to begin the twentieth century as one of the world's two leading economic powers, along with Germany, far outstripping Britain, where the Industrial Revolution had begun. This was the era of John D. Rockefeller, Andrew Carnegie, J. P. Morgan, James Buchanan Duke, and others, dubbed by New Deal-era historians as the robber barons.[1] These men—and, in that era, they were all men—amassed huge fortunes by monopolizing key sectors of the economy—oil (Rockefeller), steel (Carnegie), finance (Morgan), and tobacco (Duke). Anyone who's taken Economics 101 knows that monopoly drives prices higher because there's no competition. The effect was to transfer huge quantities of wealth from the consumer to the robber barons. Popular discontent began to grow. In 1890, Congress passed the Sherman Act, the first antitrust law, and a decade and a half later President Theodore Roosevelt's attorney general used the statute to initiate proceedings that culminated in breaking up (in Supreme Court decisions on the same day in 1911) the Standard Oil and the American Tobacco trusts. In 1914, Congress passed the still tougher Clayton Act. Although vigorous enforcement of antitrust laws has declined in the last several years, these laws are still on the books—as the Microsoft antitrust case shows.

In the 1920s, business also boomed. Part of the "roar" of the Roaring Twenties came from ringing cash registers. The 1929 stock market crash, as everybody knows, ushered in the Great Depression. Business stood at its nadir in the public's opinion. Not since Jefferson in the early days of the Republic had Americans elected a so resolutely antibusiness administration as that of Franklin D. Roosevelt.

He came into office on March 4, 1933, at a time of a gigantic run on the banks. High among the concerns of those who believed that business needed another strong dose of regulation was the amount of fraud in the securities market in the 1920s. To respond, one of the first measures that Roosevelt's New Deal enacted was the Securities Act of 1933, which still provides the basic structure for regulating the issuance of new securities. The following year, Congress passed the Securities Exchange Act, which created the Securities and Exchange Commission, which still regulates, among other things, insider trading that we'll discuss later. These two statutes—which securities lawyers and other financial professionals call the '33 Act and the '34 Act—remain the core of government regulation of the securities markets. In seventy-five years, there has never been any serious effort to roll back the protections these acts provide.

Since the 1960s, the pendulum has again swung pretty heavily. An acquisitive, free-enterprise bundle of values has become mainstream. The scandals of the first years of the twenty-first century have led to a reaction against business' excesses, principally regarding financial dishonesty and overreaching. The reaction is nothing like that in the early years of the twentieth century or the 1930s, but it has been a reaction just the same. Without the scandals of the Lay/Ebbers crowd, it is hard to imagine that any Congress—let alone a Republican Congress—would have passed the Sarbanes-Oxley Act of 2002, or that a president with the views of George W. Bush would have signed it.

Unlike the antitrust acts and the two securities acts enacted at the height of the popularity of FDR's New Deal, and despite all the ink devoted to it, Sarbanes-Oxley won't have the same fundamental effect on how American business is conducted. The antitrust and securities laws addressed the way in which business was conducted—more specifically the large-scale integrity of the market. Sarbanes-Oxley certainly is designed to affect the integrity of the market by the requirements it imposes on businesses about the integrity of their financial statements. But its aim is primarily to introduce checks on individual abuses of integrity, such as those involved in Enron and WorldCom, which led to its passage.

What Sarbanes-Oxley signals is less that there are fundamental structural flaws in business or the market than there is a huge crisis in the public trust of corporate America. This is the damage the early twenty-first century scandals caused, above and beyond the harm done to the financial well-being of innocent people. They undermined the confidence of many in the integrity of American business. Think about the investor who receives a proxy solicitation which references a proposal "to conduct a study of executive compensation," accompanied by the statement "Directors Recommend AGAINST." Before the scandals, many might have read the directors' recommendation on such a proposal and said, "Right. Why waste corporate money on this?" But now? If you're like me, you wonder if the directors aren't trying to hide something about what executives are being paid, or the stock options they are receiving, and you'll vote "FOR."

Our goal here isn't to tackle the global issue of the general level of trust in American business.[2] The aim here is the more modest one of trying to understand how individual managers can make sure that conflicts of interest don't cause crises of trust within their own companies.

THE TAXONOMY OF CONFLICTS OF INTEREST

Where people with conflicts act so as to better themselves, we say they are self-dealing. Such self-dealing typically doesn't bring down companies. But it does destroy careers. And where conflicts of interest are rife within an organization, the company can suffer a blow to its reputation for integrity that can harm its position with its customers and suppliers and, critically, with its employees and potential employees.

Let's start with a simple working definition we're going to need: aggregate compensation package, or ACP. An ACP is the total aggregate benefits a person receives from his or her employer, including total formal compensation (salary and bonus), prizes, perks (including benefits to family members), and status enhancements. Generically, conflicts of interest arise when a company employee, including, of course, a top executive, has a chance to make a decision on behalf of the company that will enhance the employee's own ACP. When an employee is encouraged to make a choice to enhance his or her own ACP because the company *wants* that decision made, there is no conflict problem. That's the theory behind incentive compensation. But where the benefits to the company and to the employee pull in opposite directions, there's a conflict of interest.

Conflicts of interest, then, arise from the *structure* of a certain class of choices facing a decision-maker. As we'll see, the default position in such situations is either that one pass the decision to someone else who does not have the conflict or, if that's not possible, at least to disclose the conflict. It usually spells trouble when a person makes a decision without disclosing a conflict, regardless of the choice made. The structure of the tempting choice is always the same: Do I benefit the company or myself?

If we are going to understand the taxonomy of conflicts themselves, therefore, we have to distinguish them based on the content of the choices made. It makes sense to identify three categories. Category one conflicts of interest are conflicts where the choice the conflicted decision-maker adopts is illegal. In such cases, the criminality overshadows the fact that, for example, a Bernie Ebbers or a Ken Lay was in a conflict-of-interest situation. Was it in WorldCom's interest to provide Ebbers with $400 million in loans? Did Ebbers enhance his ACP by strong-arming the board into approving them? Sure, he made money, and lots of it. Did it harm the company? Yes, again. It transferred assets that could have been invested in the company's business to Ebbers' pocket. People like Ebbers clearly have conflicts of interest, and their "disloyalty" to their companies is one of the defining characteristics of what they do wrong. But because of the criminality, and civil liability of these cases, attention doesn't focus on the "conflict" piece of it.

I call category two conflicts those in which a person chooses the option that enhances his or her own ACP, but the conduct isn't so egregious that the choice causes the decision-maker to land in jail or even to get sued. At an abstract level, category one and category two overlap with one another. You might say it's a difference of degree and not of kind. I can't argue with that. But it's a good idea to treat them separately, because it's category two conflicts of interest that management has to deal with most often, including designing rules and practices that minimize their occurrence.

Category three is the really seductive one. This is where the decision-maker can defend the self-interested choice by pointing to the benefit the company received. There's a phrase that's attached to this scenario. "Hey," says the person who's just enhanced his own ACP, "what's the problem? It's a win-win." We'll see why this is a dangerous situation—even though people justify their conduct by uttering this mantra, and companies and courts sometimes allow them to get away with it. In fact, because of its insidious character, this is the *most* dangerous problem in the conflicts-of-interest universe apart from blatant criminal conduct.

But first let's consider the category two outcomes—the kind that day in and day out worry (or should worry) management. These are cases where somebody wins and somebody loses. Nobody calls these "win-win."

ZERO-SUM GAMES AND CATEGORY TWO OUTCOMES

There's a branch of applied mathematics and economics called game theory. It studies the logic of situations in which participants attempt to maximize their individual returns. Game theorists use the term "zero-sum game" to describe choice scenarios where, if you add up all the gains of all the participants who benefit, and then subtract the losses of those who lose, the sum will be zero. They are, in short, situations "in which a participant's gain or loss is exactly balanced by the losses or gains of the other participant(s)."[3] A category two conflict of interest works like a zero-sum game. The person who acts successfully to augment his or her own ACP makes those gains at the expense of the company.

Let's look at two generic situations where this is the outcome.

Suppose that Jane works in the real estate department for a retailer that has stores in a number of states. Her department's task is to identify locations in areas that management has targeted for expansion and then, when a go-ahead to acquire is given, to work with real estate agents and lawyers to finalize the purchase transactions. Because the company is in an aggressive expansion mode, Jane and her department have been working to find sites in a number of different states.

Now let's suppose that Jane has been told that the company is interested in opening up in a particular part of the Chicago suburbs. There's nothing exceptional about her working on this deal. The north central region has been her territory for a couple of years.

Unknown to anyone else in the company, Jane's father owns land in a particular suburb that appears to fit the bill. Jane's dad has been holding onto the land for some time because he isn't the type of guy who'd get rid of an investment for a song, and he hasn't yet heard the right price. Jane knows her company. When it really wants something, it's prepared to pay top dollar. It's part of the company's style; it's part of the reputation it consciously wants to cultivate in the real estate market so that, when it wants a parcel of land, it can get it.

Jane's department has developed criteria for determining whether a target site for a store in a location that has been chosen for expansion is an "A" (definitely try to acquire it); "B" (good, acceptable, get it if you can't find anything better); and "C" (not what the company wants, pass on it). The evaluation process is thorough. It takes into account everything from real estate taxes through the proximity to other retail stores that will enhance a walk-in trade, to the demographic and income level of the surrounding area. Jane has performed this analysis countless times since she has been in her present job. Using the same methodology she's used before, Jane rates her father's property. It receives a score of A-. Two other properties in the target area rate much worse. One got a B- and the other a C. But a fourth really appeared to be a match for the company. When Jane performed the analysis, it came up a straight A. The demographics of its immediately adjacent area were slightly better than the area around her dad's tract for projected company sales, and the price was somewhat less than her dad hoped to get.

This was not the outcome of the evaluation Jane desired. She wanted the company to buy her dad's parcel of land. She redid the calculations. The results were unchanged. She considered what to do over and over in her mind. The company had bought many parcels of land like her father's, some even with lower ratings. If the fourth parcel were suddenly off the market, purchasing her dad's would be easy. She knew that her dad simply had not been able to find a buyer. Moreover, she knew that he faced some large medical bills for her stepmother that insurance hadn't covered. Jane had worked at the company for a while and was well respected. The company had confidence in her ability and her boss was unlikely to second-guess her choice—provided that she made the numbers conform to the company criteria. It was a Friday. She decided to sleep on it over the weekend. She'd make her decision. When she came in on Monday her head was clear. She fixed the records so that her father's parcel of land had the higher score, did the paperwork supporting her recommendation for the purchase, and submitted it. In due course, just as she suspected, her recommendation was approved and an offer made. The deal closed a month later.

Let's look at a second scenario, with a similar outcome but a different fact pattern.

Jane's colleague, Harry, is a senior purchasing agent in the corporate purchasing department, specializing in home furnishings and DIY (do-it-yourself) products. Among the items he purchases is outdoor house paint. At present, Harry has the responsibility to make a recommendation about which of the competitive lines of paint it carries the company should choose for a "featured value" marketing campaign at its many locations next summer. Because of the amount of walk-in trade in the stores Jane and Harry's company operates, there's fierce competition among the industry's paint suppliers for the designation. No manufacturer could doubt that partnering in the promotion would increase sales.

One morning, a sales representative from one of the competitors for the "featured-value" promotion, let's call him Jess, telephoned Harry. He told Harry he'd be in town next week and would like to take Harry to lunch to discuss the business the two companies were doing together. As Harry's company had no rule against accepting such invitations, Harry did so.

"Where would you like to go," asked Jess.

"It doesn't matter to me," replied Harry. "I'm easy."

Jess then proposed they go to one of the best restaurants in town. When Harry said, "Are you sure?" Jess replied. "Of course I'm sure. You and your company are important to us and I want to make sure you know it."

While chatting over lunch, Harry mentioned that he had been putting off having his own house painted. Without batting an eyelash, Jess immediately offered to take care of supplying all the paint that would be necessary to do the job. Harry had priced the job himself. Even with his employee discount, to buy all the product he'd need would set him back about $3,000. Harry paused. "That's awfully nice of you," he said in a friendly way, "but I can't accept. Things have been a little tight, and I really can't afford to hire someone to do the job. And with this bad back of mine, I don't dare try it myself."

"Not a problem," said Jess. "We value our relationship with your company and with you personally. Suppose we offered to pick up the cost of the labor as well. We'll arrange everything. Just give us some dates that are good."

Harry smiled and thanked Jess. He mentioned a few weeks that were good for the painting to be done and then moved on to other subjects.

On his return to work he set aside the folder he was keeping on the contenders for the featured value promotion partner. He'd made up his mind. About ten days later, he submitted his recommendation that Jess's company be the featured-value partner for the summer in the outdoor paint line. As was his custom, Harry's boss accepted the recommendation without comment or question.

"THIS COMPANY WON'T PUT UP WITH THIS"

How would you react if you were Jane or Harry's boss and you found out about these two deals? I know what I'd do. I'd hit the ceiling. Jane and Harry each had the chance to augment their own ACPs. In Jane's case, she had the opportunity to put money in her father's pocket, and she chose to do it. The cost to the company was that it did not acquire the optimal parcel of land for its expansion in the Chicago area. Here's where the zero-sum game model comes in. Either the company or Jane (through her father) was going to benefit. Jane picked herself.

Harry did something different. Offered an initial bribe, he worked to solicit a larger one. In exchange for getting his house painted, he awarded what amounted to a contract to the company that gave him the bribe without so much as going through the pretense of determining whether the company deserved it. He picked a benefit to himself without worrying about whether it was the optimal choice for the company. If Jess's company deserved to be the featured-value partner, it was only a coincidence. Harry's focus was on himself—and his own ACP.

It's a no-brainer to say that no company could put up with what Jane and Harry did. Although the precise sanction in each case would require careful case analysis under the foursquare protocol, any company would need to have a rule forbidding what these employees did.

But what is it that bothers us about what Jane and Harry did? Is it the outcome in the two cases, or the ways in which they went about making their decisions? Do we locate the problem in the result or in the process? We can tell, if we change the facts in our stories to make the results different.

"BUT IT'S A WIN-WIN"

Suppose that Joan works in the same retailer's real estate department as Jane. To make it clear, let's keep the baseline facts parallel. Joan's job is to find a location for the site of a new store in another city, let's say Charlotte. Again, a member of her family is the owner of one of the key target sites. Following company procedures, Joan runs her rating test, just as Jane did. But here there's a difference. Here the property owned by her relative—let's call it her sister—comes out a definite and unmistakable number one. It gets a clear A; the next best is no better than a low B+. To be sure of her results, Joan runs the analysis a second time. Same outcome. Her choice seems easy. Why, it isn't even really a choice at all. "If this property were owned by a perfect stranger," Joan says to herself, "I'd have to pick it. To make any other choice would not be doing my job. Should I not make the best choice for the company simply because my sister will also benefit? Sounds silly to me."

Now suppose that, instead of Harry deciding which manufacturer of outdoor paint the company will select to partner with in its featured-value promotion, that task falls to his colleague, Hal. Let's substitute Hal for Harry and keep the story the same down to the discussion of Hal's need to get his house painted.

Let's suppose that when Jess offered to give Hal enough paint to do the job, Hal hesitated and said he didn't think he should, but that Jess said he wouldn't take "no" for an answer. Hal said OK, but said to Jess, "No strings attached." "Sure," said Jess, "understood."

When he got back to his office, Hal dug into the files of Jess's company and its competitors. He really wanted to get his house painted, and not having to shell out $3,000 for paint would be a big help. But he wasn't going to give Jess the business if his company didn't deserve it. He did a careful analysis and concluded that Jess's company deserved the nod for the featured-value promotion. Soon thereafter, Hal placed a substantial order for Jess's brand of house paint for the retailer's stores nationwide. He also recommended that the salesman's brand be dubbed for the featured-value promotion. Just to make sure we get the issue clearly in focus, let's suppose that

Jess's company *genuinely* is the best—Hal's analysis was completely accurate. None of the competitors can match the entire package Jess's company can offer in exchange for the award of the featured-value slot, such as better promotional help, a favorable pricing policy, extended payment terms, and so on.

ARE "WIN-WIN" CONFLICTS OF INTEREST OK?

Joan and Hal's respective situations are what we earlier called category three conflicts of interest. They differ from category two conflicts, like those of Jane and Harry, most obviously, in results or, to use the word we've used before, in consequences. Jane and Harry took benefits for themselves *at the expense* of their employer. To their employer, their motives would be quite unacceptable. What Jane and Harry received wasn't an accident. They achieved their personal profits intentionally. Jane fudged the results in her company's acquisition suitability protocol to make her father's property come out at the top of the list. Without her manipulating the results, the company would not have chosen to purchase her dad's parcel of land for its suburban Chicago location. As to Harry, not content with an offer of a small bribe, he held out for a larger one, the cost of the labor to do the house-painting job, and then did no comparative analysis of Jess's company's merits and that of its competitors.

A category two conflict of interest, then, raises red flags about both *consequences* and *motives*, about enhancing one's personal ACP at the expense of the company's bottom line and intending to do so.

Category three conflicts, on the other hand, differ from category two conflicts because category three *consequences* don't present a problem. They are the "win-win" cases. Now, in the real world, the facts may not always be clear about whether a self-interested choice turns out to have genuine win-win consequences—though the people who have made decisions to justify the enhancement of their own ACPs frequently try to defend their choices by *saying* the result was a win-win. We don't have to worry about such an argument in the case of Joan and Hal. To bring the unvarnished issue into focus, we stipulated that their self-interested choices did provide optimal benefits to their employer.

Category two cases present problems, whether we look at consequences or motives. Category three situations are fine on consequences, because the results really are win-win. But what about motives? Do we care, if the consequences are OK? Let's consider the difference between Jane and Joan's cases.

Were both Jane and Joan self-dealing? There isn't any doubt about Jane. Having decided that she was going to try to get the company to purchase her father's land for the new Chicago location, Jane did her best to make it happen. Trading on her good reputation in the company, she assumed nobody would double-check her results when she falsified data. Her deception worked.

Joan didn't falsify data, which is good, but did she self-deal? A straight-up, aboveboard analysis selected her sister's land for the Charlotte acquisition. If it hadn't, would she have fiddled the results or not? We don't know. But the temptation would have been there.

A consequentialist would say that a hypothetical question like this is pointless. What matters, *all* that matters, are results, and the results of Joan's choice weren't tainted by self-interest. This produced, as we said, a "win-win." We don't care what Joan thought, or what she might have done. We care about what she did or, more precisely, the consequences of what she did.

Such an answer makes me uncomfortable and I think it would make most managers uncomfortable. The consequentialist effectively says to employees "If you self-deal, just make sure the company doesn't come out on the short end of the stick." This amounts to saying that acting on a motive to self-deal *can* be OK. To put it differently, if that is OK with Joan's and Hal's choices, when asked if self-dealing is permitted in a company, management is basically saying, "It depends." This is the fatal flaw in the consequentialist approval of category three conflicts. People are effectively encouraged to self-deal, provided they think they can justify a win-win outcome if they are found out. In the real world, outcomes will rarely be as unequivocal as we described them here for illustrative purposes. An approach *encourages* self-dealing if the self-dealer can persuade herself or himself that the outcome is a win-win. The result is an ethical environment that few managers would want to advertise to their boards of directors or their shareholders.

To help understand a workable approach for management, let's see how the law treats business conflicts of interest. Remarkably, the law treats conflicts of interest differently depending upon the kind of action involved. We're going to look at two of the most important areas. The first is "insider trading," where the law is unflinching in its prohibition against buying and selling publicly traded securities when one has confidential inside information. The second is a self-interested transaction by corporate officers and directors. Astonishingly, the law here permits exactly the kind of after-the-fact validation of self-dealing that we just suspected managers would be well-advised to avoid publicizing—or permitting.

INSIDER TRADING—BANNING CONFLICTS OF INTEREST IN THE PUBLIC SECURITIES MARKET

When we talked about the public's periodic, almost cyclic reaction against business abuses, we mentioned the two statutes passed in 1933 and 1934, in the first two years of FDR's New Deal. As noted earlier, the second of these, the Securities Exchange Act of 1934, created the Securities and Exchange Commission, commonly known as the SEC. Under authority granted in the act, the SEC has promulgated rules banning insider trading.

Insider trading, in a nutshell, is when men and women with confidential "inside" information trade in the stock of a company whose shares are available to anyone on one of the public securities markets, such as the New York Stock Exchange, the American Stock Exchange, or the so-called over-the-counter market. Insider trading is not usually called a conflict of interest. Probably the main reason is that the SEC's independent and robust regulation of the problem makes it unnecessary. But it frequently fits the definitional criteria for a conflict of interest, because the person trading with the benefit of the inside information is an employee of the company who, thereby, owes duties of confidentiality to the company.[4] The SEC's rule, which the courts routinely enforce, is simple. If a person has inside information about a company whose securities are publicly traded (and thus subject to SEC regulation), he or she may buy or sell the company's stock *only if* the insider first discloses the information to the public. The rule thus presents a simple alternative: disclose or refrain from trading. In theory, the purpose of the disclosure requirement is to eliminate the unfair advantage the insider has from his or her inside information and to protect the company from disclosure of its confidential information. When the insider is an employee of the company in whose stock he or she wishes to trade, the insider, as an employee or even a senior manager, owes a duty to the company to keep quiet about its confidential and frequently proprietary information. This means that, practically speaking, the insider can't disclose, making insider trading forbidden unless and until the information becomes public.

One of the early classic cases defining this rule comes from the 1960s and illustrates the issue. A group of insiders at the Texas Gulf Sulfur Company became aware that the company's geologists had discovered a valuable mineral strike on the Canadian Shield. The company acquired the property. Before the finding was made public, meaning before the market price of the company's stock reflected the anticipated profit from the new acquisition, the insiders bought shares. In proceedings instituted by the SEC, the insiders were held liable.[5]

You can see why the opportunity to engage in insider trading is like the ability Jane, Harry, Joan, and Hal had to influence a business decision in a way that put money in their pockets. In each case, their possession of nonpublic information is the vehicle to enhancing their own ACPs. Simple conflicts of interest differ from insider trading in that, in conflict situations, the "person" harmed is the company that does not get the best deal it could. In the insider trading case, by contrast, the harm runs generally not to the company itself, but to anyone who purchased or sold company stock in ignorance of the information—the so-called "fraud on the market" theory.[6] Still, when the insider trades, he or she violates the obligation owed to the company—what lawyers call a "fiduciary duty," meaning a duty based on trust and confidence and requiring deference to the well-being of the party to whom the duty is owed. In such a case, as in the typical conflict scenarios, the person is acting in his or her own interest, and not that of the company.

The SEC's prohibition of insider trading isn't anything to mess around with. Driven by the lure of huge stock market profits, however, a few people do. The SEC can institute civil proceedings, like it did against Texas Gulf Sulfur, and it can force inside traders to disgorge their earnings. The SEC can also file criminal charges. For example, in the spring of 2007, a jury in my home state of Colorado heard a criminal case brought against billionaire Joseph P. Nacchio, once the head of Qwest, one of the "Baby Bell" descendants of the old Bell Telephone Company. Although the jury did not convict him on all counts in the indictment, it found him guilty of nineteen counts of insider trading. Nacchio had sold stock in the company totaling some $52 million at a time when, based on insider information, he knew that Qwest's dire financial straits made it unlikely that it would achieve its publicly announced earnings targets. When a publicly traded company fails to meet its earnings targets, its stock price usually falls. By selling before the bad news became public, he made a huge sum of money. The result? Nacchio looks like he is on his way to jail.[7] The court sentenced him to six years in prison and fined him $19 million. He was also ordered to forfeit $52 million in stock-trading profits.

The insider trading rules do not allow violations to be classified like category three conflicts of interest. The government doesn't have to show that the insider's trades actually harmed others. The policy enacted by Congress, administered by the SEC, and not challenged by administrations of either political party since inception is that the public securities markets need to be fair to all. "Fairness" means that every investor who wishes to buy or sell securities has access to the same public information as every other. Fairness resides in the procedure. That's why the accused inside trader can't try to escape civil liability or a criminal conviction by saying, in a variation of the win-win theme, "I won and you (at least) didn't lose," for example, "because my trades were too small to affect the market price at which other people traded."

Because disclosure is generally impractical, it's easiest to understand the SEC's insider trading rules as forbidding the practice. Before we look at the need for internal conflict-of-interest disclosure requirements within a company, we need to look at a counterexample to the idea that win-win outcomes can justify self-dealing. This can be found in the law governing self-interested transactions by corporate officers and directors.

SELF-INTERESTED TRANSACTIONS AND THE DOCTRINE OF "ENTIRE FAIRNESS"

"Probably the longest standing concern of corporate law," write two scholars of the subject, "has been that corporate officials may cause the corporation to enter into overly generous transactions with themselves."[8] Corporate law is not just the field of law that governs large multinational behemoths. It's the branch of law that regulates businesses, large and small, which are incorporated, and its doctrines are similar to those in partnerships and other forms of business organization as well. One of its key principles is what's called the "duty of loyalty." The central requirement of the duty of loyalty is that a director or an officer must act in a way to benefit the corporation, and not himself or herself personally. There's no mystery why this is a major problem: a corporation, obviously, can act only through its officials, and when officials have the power to act, temptation is present. Historically, and today, many have found it difficult to resist. As Klein and Coffee put it, a corporate official can sell property to the company "at an inflated price or buy assets from the corporation at a bargain price."[9]

In the early days of American business, such self-dealing transactions were simply forbidden. If the corporation came into court and showed that an officer or director had self-dealt, the court would rule that the transaction was void *"without regard to fairness or unfairness of the transaction."*[10] That's changed. Although the law varies from state to state,[11] the self-interested transactions of officers and directors can be OK'd if either or both of two conditions are satisfied: (1) a disinterested majority of the board of directors (or sometimes shareholders) ratify the transaction; and/or (2) the court, at a trial, determines that the transaction was "entirely fair" to the company. The unspoken premises of these rules, and cases under these rules, is that persons acting in conflict-of-interest situations can get away with enhancing their own ACPs if they can persuade the board of directors to ratify what they did and (usually) if, through their attorneys, they can persuade a court to pronounce it "fair to the company." After-the-fact category three conflict justifications, absent insider trading, are alive and well in straight-out cases of managerial self-dealing!

To illustrate, let's look at the facts of a case that I regularly discuss with my law students in a class on corporations. It involves a food products company well known in the Midwest, called Cookies, which makes not cookies but barbeque sauce.[12] (Its name comes not from its product but from the fact that it was originally founded by a Mr. Cook.) The company's initial start-up was rocky. The turn-around into a successful business came after Duane "Speed" Herrig acquired control, but not complete ownership, of the company. Cookies boomed. Minority shareholders became upset, however, because Mr. Herrig engaged in a few transactions that unquestionably enhanced his own ACP. On Cookies's behalf, he extended an exclusive distributorship agreement with a company he personally owned, Lakes Warehouse. He entered personally into a royalty agreement with Cookies for a taco sauce recipe he developed. From his point of view, it was a good deal. Finally, Cookies's board of directors, which consisted entirely of people that Herrig selected because he was the controlling shareholder, increased his compensation. Minority shareholders sued the company, complaining about Herrig's self-dealing.

Nobody could deny that Herrig had made Cookies a profitable company. He was obviously a hard-working and talented businessman. Where self-interested transactions are concerned, however, that really isn't the issue. Rather, the question is, do we think it wise to allow someone who is running a company, of which he or she is not the sole owner, to self-deal, and then say it's OK if the deal turned out to be a good one or a fair one to the company? More precisely, are we going to say that a self-interested transaction should be allowed to stand where a self-dealing officer or director is able to hire good enough lawyers to persuade a court that, to use our terminology, the self-dealing is a category three and not a category two transaction? Wouldn't that require us to say, returning to our examples of Jane and Harry, that the only thing they did wrong was the result they achieved?

The problem with this approach is that it puts us right back in the consequentialist mess from which we've tried to extract ourselves earlier. Good outcomes shouldn't be allowed to cure the defects of questionable motives. If they could, the improper, self-dealing motives don't matter at all. Self-dealing is a problem only if the results turn out—or a court can be persuaded that they turn out—not to harm the company that thought it could claim the loyalty of its employee. Yet that is what the law of self-interested transactions by officers and directors provides. In the Cookies case, that's exactly what happened. The majority of the Supreme Court of Iowa ruled against the minority shareholders and upheld what Herrig had done on the ground that it was fair and reasonable to the company. The dissenting justice thought that the majority had "been so enthralled by the success of the company"[13] that it didn't analyze carefully enough whether Herrig's action had been fair to the minority shareholders. The only barrier that the self-dealing officer or director has to surmount, then, is to carry the burden of proof on the fairness question. The dissenting justice disagreed with the majority on the working of that technical legal requirement. He did *not* disagree that proof of fairness to the company would allow the self-interested transactions to stand. If the transaction is "win-win," the self-dealing motive gets a pass.

SHOULD GOOD RESULTS IMMUNIZE SELF-INTERESTED TRANSACTIONS?

Some people say that there are good arguments to justify this approach to self-dealing.[14] I don't think any of them work. I think that the law became more lax in permitting this kind of self-dealing because, in the twentieth century, the climate of opinion about business persuaded corporate leaders and their lawyers to take a shot at limiting the prohibition on self-dealing, and they got courts to buy it. But our question is this: Can companies that want to maintain high ethical standards afford to say that self-dealing is OK provided that the result is "fair" to the company? Should companies tailor their conflicts-of-interest rules to validate transactions if, when all is said and done, the outcomes are win-win? I don't think so.

Let's return to thinking about Joan and Hal, our retailer employees whose self-interested transactions wound up benefiting the company as well. If you're Joan's boss, or Hal's, or the company's senior management or board of directors, is what they did perfectly OK? Is it really true that no one would care about conflicts of interests if they always, on after-the-fact study, are shown to have produced the benign results?

I believe that the answer to all of these questions is no.

MANDATING DISCLOSURE

What's wrong with what Joan and Hal did is that they acted without *disclosing* what they were doing. They acted in secret. Like Jane and Harry, they had every opportunity to enhance their own ACPs at the company. As we've stipulated with the facts, they didn't do so. But they had the chance, and it's the opportunity that's critical.

There are two basic reasons why disclosure should be required. First, most people are neither saints nor sinners. Most won't blatantly ignore the duties they owe the companies that employ them, but a number—a substantial enough number to make conflicts of interest a pressing problem—are capable of succumbing to temptation. Second, in the real world, there will nearly always be doubt about whether the self-interested choice was *really* the choice that was best for the company as well. This means you ordinarily can't know whether self-dealing will fall into category two or category three until all of the chips have fallen and you've conducted a thorough investigation. Or, in the right kind of case, until a court has made its decision.

No company should signal that it condones employee self-dealing. To do so fatally compromises the commitment to integrity that has to be at the base of any meaningful, and realistic, set of ethical standards within a company. After-the-fact validation of self-dealing as win-win subordinates integrity to a financial outcome. That can't be right. It also can't be safe. Look at what it invites.

Jane or Harry's conduct would get them immediately fired in many companies, particularly if either had a record of previous integrity violations.[15] The same is less likely to be the fate of Joan or Hal. You don't have to be a consequentialist, unconcerned about people's motives, to reach this conclusion. Joan and Hal acted only when they had established to their own satisfaction and in good faith that the outcomes that benefited themselves personally also were optimal outcomes for the company. They could say, and their bosses might well believe, that they would *not* have chosen the course that enhanced their own ACPs. And it might be true. No outsider will ever know for sure. Perhaps Joan and Hal don't really know themselves. The human capacity for self-delusion is substantial.

That is exactly why a company's ethical standards must emphasize disclosure. Upfront disclosure is the best antidote there is to self-dealing that harms the company, just as the disclosure requirement serves to inhibit most insider trading. If you've had to disclose your self-interest, the chance vanishes that you'll "fiddle the numbers," as Jane did in our example. A disclosure requirement, in short, functions as a gentle nudge to push you in the direction your conscience recommends.

Are there going to be men and women who ignore a requirement to disclose before the self-dealing as easily as they ignore a bar against the self-dealing itself? Of course. But explicitly requiring disclosure counsels a course of action that can avoid the wiles of temptation before they have fully taken hold. Moreover, requiring disclosure can ease the task of managers and other decision-makers when they are faced with assessing employee self-dealing. "Did you tell somebody about your personal interest in a proposed transaction?" leaves a lot less wiggle room than "Was the company harmed by your self-dealing?"

A company, then, asks for trouble if it doesn't prohibit self-dealing in the clearest terms. I've never heard of a company that, at least implicitly, doesn't do so. Implementing a disclosure requirement, as we've just seen, can be a valuable tool to prevent people from thinking they can justify their self-dealing by pleading win-win. We're not going to eliminate conflicts of interest. But it's "taking care of business" to require disclosure when employees find themselves in conflicts-of-interest predicaments.

Yet that's not the whole conflicts story. A basic part of implementing business strategy nowadays is incentive compensation, which implicitly invites people to enhance their own ACPs. We'll turn to the peculiar conflicts of interest problems this presents in the next chapter.

NOTES

1. The phrase was popularized by Matthew Josephson, *The Robber Barons* (New York: Harcourt, 1934).

2. For a more detailed analysis of this problem, in the context of the corporate law of Delaware, where a large number of publicly traded American corporations are incorporated, see Sarah Helene Duggin and Stephen M. Goldman, "Restoring Trust in Corporate Directors: The Disney Standard and the 'New' Good Faith," *American University Law Review*, vol. 56, no. 2 (December 2006), pp. 211–274.

3. Wikipedia, the online encyclopedia. See entries for "game theory" and "zero-sum games."

4. Not all insider trading is a conflict of interest. Sometimes corporate "outsiders" receive "inside" information and trade on it. When they do, they may be charged by the SEC as "tippees," that is, traders on information received by way of a tip. The government initially investigated Martha Stewart for illegal insider trading as a tippee, but she was ultimately charged and convicted on other, easier to prove charges.

5. *Securities and Exchange Commission v. Texas Gulf Sulfur Co.*, 401 F.2d 833 (1968). The case was decided by one of the eleven (now twelve) U.S. Circuit Courts of Appeals, this one sitting in New York City and known as the Second Circuit. The case did not go to the Supreme Court.

6. The Supreme Court embraced this concept in *Basic, Inc. v. Levinson*, 485 U.S. 224 (1988).

7. At this writing, an appeal is pending.

8. William A. Klein and John C. Coffee, Jr., *Business Organization and Finance*, 10th ed. (New York: Foundation Press, 2007), p. 163.

9. Ibid.

10. Harold Marsh, "Are Directors Corporate Trustees?—Conflicts of Interest and Corporate Morality," 22 *Business Lawyer* 35, 36 (1966).

11. Because the power of Congress under the Constitution was, once upon a time, limited, corporate law has historically been a creature of state law. As such, the details vary from state to state, unlike the provisions of federal securities law that are in principle applicable nationwide.

12. The decision of the Supreme Court of Iowa can be found at *Cookies Food Products v. Lakes Warehouse*, 430 N.W.2d 447 (Iowa 1988).

13. 430 N.W. at 456.

14. See *Business Organization and Finance*, p. 163. Here is how Klein and Coffee articulate the arguments that allow self-interested transactions, in the circumstances we have been discussing, to stand: "Those who believe the prophylactic rule of the nineteenth century was too strict can argue that often a corporation, in its start-up years, must turn to its directors for financing or specific assets. Also, directors frequently represent various constituencies with which the corporation does business: customers, suppliers, creditors—each of whom may want a representative on the board to monitor the corporation. These representatives may provide useful advice and expertise for the corporation. Finally, with the emergence in recent decades of independent boards of directors, staffed by outside directors, it may be that the need for judicial monitoring has declined." These arguments seem specious to me, particularly the last. The presence of so-called independent directors has reduced the need for judicial monitoring the self-interested transactions? Tell that to ex-WorldCom shareholders.

15. Managers must remember that, even in the case of an egregious ethical violation such as Jane's or Harry's, there may be legal considerations that should prompt you to think twice before firing them immediately, unless there is absolute and uncontradicted evidence of wrongdoing, such as catching Jane red-handed fudging the numbers on her property evaluation. For instance, Jane, as a female, is a member of a protected class under employment discrimination laws, and either might be a member of a racial minority, over forty (the age at which age discrimination protection kicks in), or disabled. While members of protected classes aren't immunized from ethical violations, the astute manager must be aware that firing such a person could buy the company a lawsuit which, though ultimately successful, would likely prove time-consuming and expensive. As we've said in discussing prong one of the foursquare protocol, the facts will be decisive.

CHAPTER 6

Incentive Compensation: Honesty, Greed, and Fraud

Conflicts of interest pit individual interests against company interests. That's why, as we saw in the last chapter, they have to be watched so carefully. This chapter considers a situation that seems, at first blush, to lie at the opposite end of the spectrum—incentive compensation. The point of incentive compensation, after all, is to align the company's desire to achieve certain goals with employees' objectives to make themselves better off, that is, to enhance their personal ACPs. The most common available reward is money—whether by way of a bonus or a higher commission rate on sales. In a number of notable instances, and at the higher echelons, rewards frequently are stock options—the right to buy the company's stock at a particular price. If the market price goes up, the option holder exercises the option at the lower price, resells at the market price, and sweeps in the gain—like winning at a roulette table. Stock options, at least as initially conceived, were themselves a kind of valuable incentive compensation. If top executives owned stock in the company, so the theory went, their "piece of the action" would motivate profit-maximizing choices that, in turn, would benefit all stockholders.

The reality has been different. Efforts to achieve the benchmarks that trigger incentive rewards have led to some of the most flagrant breaches of trust in recent memory. I wish it were true that abuses are simply the result of a few bad actors. Then the solution would be straightforward—do your best not to hire 'em, and if by mistake you do, fire 'em. But it's not that simple. Incentive compensation by its very nature incentivizes conduct no company interested in the quality of its ethics can afford to tolerate. The problem is made worse when incentives are supported by a cutthroat culture of "winning."

Incentive compensation and motivational programs are at the core of modern American business. Incentive compensation (comp) plans and exhortations to "win" are as much a part of the workplace landscape as is the presence of both men and women. Taking on the working of incentive compensation is going to raise some eyebrows. So let me be very clear: I am not going to argue that incentive compensation plans and success-oriented motivational programs should be eliminated. They are valuable, and in some cases, essential. But their unquestioned value must not be permitted to obscure the negative side. Incentives inevitably create certain kinds of problems. "Boys will be boys" is not an adequate defense of a sexual harassment lawsuit; but because boys *will* be boys, there are going to be sexual harassment problems. By the same token, greed is going to prompt abuses of even the most carefully designed incentive comp plans. Managers must be equipped to deal with this reality.

INCENTIVE COMPENSATION AND THE INCENTIVE TO LIE

To see how and why greed is a persistent problem, let's step back for a moment and think about incentives. Incentives, as we all know, are a key tool for management to secure the performance it wants. Say you have an objective you wish to reach. You can tell the people who work for you that you really hope they'll accomplish it. Or you can tell them that if they fulfill your goal, you'll pay them for the success. Which is likely to be more effective? Generals, admirals, and other high-ranking military officers may be able to get their subordinates to do what they want simply by giving orders. Military institutions, after all, are characterized by their command structures. Successful business organizations, except in isolated cases, are not. People react more favorably to the carrot than to the stick. Businesses prosper when employees are motivated—and, of course, even military commanders need to worry about morale. As Jack Welch, the acclaimed retired chairman of General Electric (GE) put it, "If you want people to live and breathe the [company's] vision, 'show

them the money' when they do it, be it with salary, bonus, or significant recognition of some sort."[1]

Incentives can be separated into two categories. One is general
and, in a sense, backward looking. You anticipate that if you do a
great job at something you've been asked to do, come the time for
your review, your boss will say, "Hey, you did a great job! This bonus reflects that." Most of us have worked hard at an assignment,
hoping to receive a pat on the back and perhaps something additional in the form of a bonus check. Generalized incentives, with
discretionary after-the-fact rewards, don't present the kind of issues
we're concerned about here. Indeed, they're not what we usually
mean when we talk about incentive compensation.

Our concern is with incentive comp programs that promise specific rewards for the achievement of distinct objectives. In theory, at
least, they're not discretionary. They're mandatory, an obligation the
company has undertaken to perform. "Achieve a specified level of
performance (sales, profitability, reduction of debt, or stock price on
a certain date)," the company says, "and you will be paid 'X' dollars," or "receive stock options calibrated in such and such a way,"
or "get a weekend at a posh resort." You can see why such programs
are so appealing to management. The company specifies exactly
what it wants. Employees aren't forced to guess about what will
prompt the pat on the back at review time. Numbers—clear, unchallengeable, and objective numbers—drive the plan from both ends.
Right? Unfortunately, not always.

Think for a minute about what incentive comp plans actually reward.
Performance? You want to say yes. Certainly that's what such plans are
designed to reward: performance and only performance—not a boss's
subjective evaluation of those who work for him or her. And, of course,
that's what usually happens. But, in fact, "performance" is not the answer. The basis for the reward the employee receives is not his or her
actual performance, but the company's record of the performance,
which may be accurate or inaccurate. It can't be otherwise.

To take the simplest of examples: If, under an incentive comp plan,
a salesperson is entitled to an additional 15 percent commission on
units of a product he or she sold over a specified base, the reward is
paid—and can only be paid—on the sales attributed to the salesperson
as reflected in the company's records. The assumption, of course, is
that the records do accurately reflect the salesperson's actual sales. But
they may not. A mistake may have been made. Or, here's what

concerns us in this chapter: The records may have been tampered with and falsified. More significantly, false data may have been fed into the computer that make it *appear* that a specified level of sales, a target stock price, or whatever triggers the reward has been achieved. Whether true or false, or correct or incorrect, the triggering event for the payment of the bonus is what the records say happened, whether or not that accords with reality. You only see what's in the mirror. If the mirror gives a distorted image, there's no way to detect it. Business records in short are a reflection of the reality, not the reality itself, but it's the records not the reality that count.

Fiddling accounts probably goes back to the first written records in China, Babylonia, and Egypt several millennia ago. Computer technology simply makes the task more sophisticated, but not necessarily harder. Temptation provides the motive, and opportunity the impetus to act. As we'll see, fiddling the data encourages practices that are much more than simply entering a different number into the computer. But the underlying problem is breach of trust and the dishonesty involved.

THE CORE REQUIREMENT: PLACING A PREMIUM ON A CULTURE OF TRUST AND HONESTY

Sometimes I'm asked to sum up the single most important task for a company that wants to be committed to the highest ethical standards. You'd think there might be a lot of competitors, but there aren't. A company needs to establish a culture of trust and honesty. If it does, all kinds of things fall into place. If it doesn't try, or fails in its efforts, the company is likely to face a host of ethical problems, low employee morale and consistently high legal costs.

Karl Marx is distinctly out of fashion these days, both in politics and philosophy. One of his key ideas, however, continues to resonate. When you're examining any social institution, you need to know what undergirds it to understand its essence. Marx called this the infrastructure. What sits above the infrastructure is the superstructure. The superstructure isn't unimportant or somehow ephemeral. It's just not what the institutional structure rests on.

A company's ethical infrastructure isn't a set of rules or a nicely stated (and elaborately reproduced) corporate code of ethical conduct. It's a real-life, we-really-mean-it commitment to trust and honesty. There can be no "ifs" or "buts." Cutting corners and engaging in "sharp" practices can't be acceptable *ever* and, with particular relevance for the subject matter of this chapter, it can never be rewarded.

An organization simply must place a premium on trustworthiness and honesty. Sexual harassment and gender discrimination, which we discussed in a previous chapter, are endemic because a number of men seem incapable of seeing women other than as sex objects and as fully equal members of the workforce. But these problems are often compounded by cover-ups, where management can't be trusted to place responsibility where it belongs. Honesty regarding such matters is often hard to come by.

As far as putting hands metaphorically in the corporate cash register and removing a portion of the contents is concerned, however, untrustworthiness and dishonesty is not the byproduct of another problem, like the way some men relate to women. It *is* the problem.

It would be impossible to attempt to catalogue all of the small ways in which people can and do cheat their employers about money. The important point is what to do about it. I think the answer is simple. A company should be ruthless in is its intolerance of financial dishonesty. There should be no requirement that a person has to exhibit a pattern of financial deceit before the company will come down hard upon him. Allowing a pass for a first offense, in fact, is entirely inconsistent with the notion that "Dishonesty will not be tolerated!" If an employee sees that he can get away with defrauding his employer without having to answer for it, the signal he receives is not, "Each dog is entitled to one bite, so we'll overlook it here." Rather, the loud and clear message is, "Hmm. The boss doesn't know, or the boss doesn't care." This is a license to proceed. When management doesn't treat dishonesty as absolutely unacceptable, some interpret their laxity as an incentive to cheat.

Take a case in point. A company hired a new marketing executive from out of town. The company's sales performance had been dwindling, and the new marketing guy looked like the answer. In addition to a lucrative salary, his employment arrangement provided that the company would pay for a round-trip ticket once a month to his original home while his children finished out the school year. When his boss reviewed the marketing executive's first couple of monthly expense reports, she noted that he had charged two trips the first month and three the second. Additionally, the reports contained airport parking fees, meals, and mileage to and from the airport on these trips. The marketing executive's boss pulled the employment agreement to check her memory. She was right. It contained no provision to cover incidental expenses in connection with the return to his previous home and only one trip a month.

The marketing executive was off to a good start, and, goodness knows, the company needed improvement in this area. That's the reason it hired him. Moreover, the boss didn't like confrontations with employees, particularly senior ones. She let her concern go, initialed the expense forms, and submitted them for payment.

Now, it might have turned out that this was just a single blip on the radar screen. Once the marketing executive's kids had finished the school year and moved to their new home, everything might have functioned smoothly. It might have been that the marketing executive misunderstood his agreement with his new employer, or that he was under stress from the new job, the new city, and his family living elsewhere. It might have been. But it wasn't.

In the actual situation from which this story is drawn, the marketing executive not only treated his boss's payment of personal expenses in excess of what his employment agreement authorized as a license to take opportunities. He viewed it as an invitation to enrich himself, and he did. The most remarkable, although not the most important, was when he was observed leaving the office carrying a pack of a half dozen rolls of toilet paper—presumably so that he would not have to spend his own money on that necessity.

A company asks for trouble when it pulls its punches in response to employee dishonesty—and that definitely and specifically includes dishonesty on the part of management. Had the company simply made a mistake in hiring the marketing executive, or was he the kind of guy who saw an opportunity in the company's lack of real commitment to trust and honesty, and took it? Temptation is always going to be present, and opportunities will abound. When circumstances appear unencumbered by risk, because the company does not articulate and act upon a policy of ruthless intolerance of dishonesty, the result is predictable.

But the key point here isn't intolerance of personal dishonesty. It's that companies frequently incentivize dishonesty. On one level, the company we just talked about incentivized the marketing executive's dishonesty by allowing him to believe that he could get away with small-scale theft. At another level, the incentivized stakes can be much higher.

A POWDER KEG

An incentive compensation plan in a company in which a culture of trust and honesty doesn't flourish is like throwing a lighted match into a powder keg. The harsh truth is this: Incentive compensation plans motivate employees to mold their performances to achieve company objectives. But, equally, they incentivize people to falsify what they've achieved in order to receive the promised rewards. I'm not saying that most people cheat. They don't. But the structure of incentive comp plans is unable to distinguish between fair play and cheating. If you just look at the incentive comp plan itself and in isolation, there is no difference between the incentive to perform and the incentive to make it appear that you have performed!

The difference between incentivizing real performance and the mere pretense of such performance has to do with integrity, the culture of trust, and honesty. The incentive plan itself rewards what the records show, whether they are based on reality or fiction.

If creating a culture of trust and honesty is going to be effective, it has to start at the top. Books on leadership routinely trumpet the necessity that leaders govern by example. There's no sphere in which this is more powerfully true. Unfortunately, however, members of senior management, because of their status and power, are often likely to be in a position to avoid adhering to the standards and obeying the rules they impose on others. Senior managers make the rules and enforce them. As we saw in discussing self-interested transactions by officers and directors in the previous chapter, many of them have the practical ability to use lawyers help to design rules, or ways to get around them, that allow senior managers to accomplish what ordinary employees can't get away with.

To see how incentive plans can allow expectations to run amok where a culture of truth and honesty does not flourish, lets take a look at a scandal that rocked one of the giants in the software industry, Computer Associates, now known as CA.

STOCK OPTIONS, OUT-SIZED BONUSES, AND THE "THIRTY-FIVE-DAY" MONTH

Remember the famous line from the 1987 movie *Wall Street*? Addressing the shareholders of a fictionalized company called Teldar

Paper, of which he is the largest shareholder, Gordon Gekko, the unscrupulous corporate raider played by Michael Douglas, brashly tells the audience:

> The point is, ladies and gentleman, that greed, for lack of a better word, is good. Greed is right, greed works. Greed clarifies, cuts through, and captures the essence of the evolutionary spirit.

Now, of course, greed is not good, and you're not supposed to come away from *Wall Street* thinking it is. But where do you draw the line between "greed" and the "profit motive"? The great early-twentieth-century British macroeconomist John Maynard Keynes famously said it was the profit motive, rather than the old-fashioned value of "thrift," that was the engine that drove the economy.[2] Nowadays there's a lot less condemnation of the profit motive than there was in the post-Victorian, anti-business, upper-crust British society from which Keynes sprung, which looked down its collective nose at "trade" (regardless of the original source of the inherited incomes on which they lived). We view bettering ourselves financially—enhancing our ACPs—as a normal and perfectly acceptable part of being human. So where does (illegitimate) "greed" start and the (legitimate) desire to make a profit stop? The answer is the line between trust and honesty and breaches of trust and an absence of integrity. That's the line between genuinely achieving what's incentivized and manipulating the data so that it *appears* that you did.

The Computer Associates scandal wasn't like Enron or World-Com, where millions of investors lost substantial portions of the nest eggs they had put away for retirement, though, of course, large numbers of people did lose money. What makes it relevant here is that the scam that led to the scandal turned upon falsified numbers. Now, the numbers weren't simply falsely entered into the computer. It was not as simple as that. Rather, it was that the basis of the numbers was false. The aim was to achieve the rewards promised by the incentive compensation system.

Here's how it worked. For a number of years, CA had a practice of recognizing revenue it had not yet earned. Why? The company's incentive compensation plan tied gigantic bonuses for senior executives to the price of the company's stock. Stock price depended on earnings or, to be precise, CA's *published* earnings, what it told the investing public its earnings were. The problem was that the company's earnings weren't what it had led the market to expect. The solution, dishonest though it was, was to recognize revenue not yet earned in a period to boost the period's earnings numbers. Of course, this produced a snowball effect, for each period robbed at the beginning, had to rob at the end merely to make up the shortfall, and then to rob further to meet Wall Street's expectations of earnings. "Recognizing" revenue not yet earned made it *appear* to investors that earnings targets had been met or exceeded. Ergo, the stock price rose. And the executives received their bonuses.

According to a press release issued by the Securities and Exchange Commission (SEC) in fiscal years 2000 and 2001, CA prematurely recognized $2.2 billion in revenue, after having prematurely recognized more than $1.1 billion in revenue in prior quarters. More particularly, over the reporting periods involved, the company recognized profits from at least 363 software contracts that the company and/or its customers had not yet executed. The mechanism was called the "thirty-five-day month" because calendar months were "kept open" in order to receive, or backdate contracts, to fall in the reporting period. The higher revenue led to a higher stock price. When the company appeared to be meeting or exceeding Wall Street's performance expectations, the stock price remained high and so did executive bonus compensation. In the words of the director of the SEC's northeast regional office, "Like a team that plays on after the final whistle has blown, Computer Associates kept scoring until it had all the points it needed to make every quarter look like a win." When the company stopped recognizing unearned revenue as earned, it was a disaster. Again, according to the SEC press release, when the company failed to keep its books open during the first quarter of its 2001 fiscal year, the company's stock price dropped 43 percent in a single day.[3]

The SEC got involved in CA's accounting irregularities because the company's overstatement of revenue—25 percent, 53 percent, 46 percent, and 22 percent in the four quarters of fiscal 2000—constituted false and deceptive practices in the public securities market.[4] Such practices were made illegal under the Securities Exchange Act of 1934, whose enactment in the wake of the 1929 stock market crash we mentioned in the previous chapter. The purpose of that act was to establish and maintain integrity in the public securities markets.

The bonuses that top CA executives received were enormous. The total amount of stock option bonuses senior executives got amounted to approximately $1.1 *billion*. Former CEO Sanjay Kumar, who is now serving a twelve-year sentence in federal prison, netted $330 million in 1998 alone.[5] Other perpetrators of the fraud, too, are now behind bars.

We can't just dismiss the CA scandal as just another example of greed run amok. If the salesperson we discussed above who would receive an extra 15 percent bonus on sales of a certain product was able, either through his own skill as a hacker or through the connivance of someone in information systems, to manipulate the record of his performance, he likely would be fired rather than prosecuted. CA's executives went to jail because their wrongdoing affected the public securities market. From the standpoint of examining what incentive comp plans actually incentivize, however, the cases are the same. If you're not driven by a commitment to integrity, your only reason not to falsify the records that will trigger your incentive comp reward is the fear of getting caught.

You might say, of course, that jail time, disgorging ill-gotten gains, and, if you engage in securities fraud, a permanent SEC-imposed ban on working in the industry will deter misconduct. Maybe yes, and maybe no. Depending on the amount of money at stake, well— you understand that as well as I do. Some people will always be prepared to take the risk if there's enough money involved. But let's not, as a society, be overly proud that the CA fraudsters were apprehended. We don't know who, in other companies, did not get caught.

If you studied a lot of economics in college, you might be inclined to say abuse of incentive plans is simply a cost that must be charged against the benefits such plans undoubtedly confer in motivating employees, and senior managers, to achieve performance goals that will benefit the company and its stockholders in the long run. We've considered this argument before and seen the problems with it. Sure, identifying trust and honesty as the backbone of a company's ethical culture is a good thing, you might say, but ultimately abuse is simply a cost of doing business. It's kind of like the retail business. There is always a certain amount of employee theft. The point is to keep it as small as possible—and punish the thieves when you catch them.

It's not this simple. The fact is that, however much many companies say and really do think they mean it when they say that trust and honesty are not negotiable. Many of these same companies build into their value systems powerful incentives that cut in the opposite direction. This is especially true when the amount of the reward can make a real difference in the recipient's financial well-being.

There's something else that's built into contemporary business culture that compounds the problem. Above and beyond the simple quantity of the dollars, there's the problem of what I call the winning paradigm.

THE PERILS OF THE "WINNING" PARADIGM

At least since the early 1980s, when Jack Welch began his phenomenal run as CEO of GE, discussion about success and achievement in American businesses has been dominated by sports and military metaphors. Five years after his retirement, Welch told a *Fortune* reporter, "You want to be No. 1. There's nothing wrong with that. You don't want to be a loser."[6] In 2005, Welch published a wide-ranging and compelling management book titled simply *Winning*.

This outlook has spread far and wide. How many television commercials have you seen recently where members of a "team" in an office exchange high fives, like a team that has just scored the winning touchdown in the Super Bowl, because some overnight carrier got a package delivered in time for a meeting? It's hard to pick up any book in the management or leadership section of your local bookstore that doesn't assume that the object of business is "winning."

What's the origin of this? It's hard to say for sure, but a good candidate is a reaction to the anti-business counterculture of the 1960s and early 1970s. Although the mainstream reaction against the excesses of that period has been strong and long-lasting, I think there remained in the early days a lingering sense that there was something not quite OK about talking too openly and too directly about squeezing every possible ounce of profit out of the market. Brashly talking about making money for money's own sake wasn't cool or (although the phrase had yet to be invented) politically correct. It sounded greedy. To speak of traditional but technical measures of business success, such as return on equity, on the other hand, was worse. To put it mildly, goals like this lack emotional fire.

The language of "winning," of "being number one," is altogether different. It casts succeeding in business like succeeding in a big game or even in a life-and-death battle. It equates business success with that of the champion, or a conquering hero.

Not everyone buys it. A high-powered woman I know complains that this attitude gives the organization the feel of a men's locker room. Regardless, talking this way is embedded in the thinking of many business leaders. For the foreseeable future, it's here to stay.

Now, I am going to say something unpopular, something that runs against the grain of so much writing about management, and much practical management in last couple of decades. The ideology of winning has a dark side—indeed, a very dark side. We have to be wary of putting too much weight on winning.

The ideology of winning frequently provides a motive to cut ethical corners. Oh, I know every writer and company *says* that this isn't so, but where paying lip service to a mantra is just that, we have to say so. While writing this chapter, I happened to pick up *The Samurai Leader* by Bill Diffenderffer, a former vice president of both IBM and Continental Airlines. This passage in the introduction leapt off the page:

> Somebody has to win. Maybe it will be you—or at least some derivative of you ten years from now after you've experienced a lifetime of stress and frustration, conflicted personal priorities, and compromised ethics and values. (OUCH! That even hurts to write!)[7]

We can hide from reality, but self-delusion is a dangerous strategy, particularly where ethics is concerned. Given our subject, I'm not going to dwell on "conflicted personal priorities," though no reader of this book who has worked a demanding job has any doubt about what these are and the real costs they impose. But compromising ethics and values demands to achieve the goal of winning demands our serious attention.

INCENTIVES AND RULES

It's all well and good to say, as Jack Welch does in *Winning*, that a company should hire or promote only people with integrity, those "who play to win the right way, by the rules." By "the rules," Welch means people who "know the laws of their country, industry, and company—both in letter and spirit—and abide by them."[8] I agree.

How could anyone disagree? But behind this nice talk, there's a problem. The problem is incentive compensation plans and how they work.

We generally think of rules as telling us what not to do: do not record unearned profits as earned in a particular period; do not engage in a self-interested transaction without disclosing your conflict to management; do not fail to pay your federal income taxes on time, etc. We can call these *prohibitory* rules. But rules don't just forbid or prohibit. Sometimes they are designed to enable. The rules that tell your lawyer what formalities have to be observed to make sure that the will she drafts for you will be effective to pass your property as you desire on your death is a perfect example. There's no rule that says you must have a will if you don't want one. But if you do, here's what you have to do. If you think about it, you'll see that an enabling rule is a device that allows you to get something you want by doing certain things. Take your desires about what you want done with your property on your death, have it put in writing, sign it, and get it witnessed in whatever way the law of the state in which you live requires, and, presto, on your death your wishes will be carried out.

Incentive comp plans function like enabling rules. You don't have to have your compensation increased or receive a cash or stock option bonus. But if you want to, here are the performance objectives you've got to meet. If you are a salesperson in the company introducing a new product into the market, as we talked about a few pages ago, and you want to achieve a higher commission in your next pay envelope, devote your efforts to selling the new product. If you are a senior executive whose compensation is determined by achieving a certain stock price, manage the company so that its performance will encourage investors to continue buying your stock, thus increasing its price. The incentive compensation arrangement is the rule that enables you to achieve increased compensation or other forms of "goods." You don't have to wring your hands and hope that, come Christmastime, your boss will remember what a great job you did last April and reward you with a handsome year-end bonus. If you achieve the goals, you are entitled to the reward, just like the person making a will or entering into a contract will achieve his or her preferred property distribution at death or a valid enforceable contract with someone else. The enabling rule entitles you to get a certain result. That's what incentive compensation plans are supposed to accomplish.

In this context, what does abiding by the rules, both in letter and spirit, mean? Not using a thirty-five-day month to record revenue—that's easy. But what if you can "win" by bending the rules?

"WINNING" AS PSYCHIC COVER

Few people will ever acknowledge that acting honestly and honorably is unimportant, at least in public. I can't conceive of a senior executive ever explicitly and verbally trivializing the requirement to act honestly—although what he or she actually is prepared to do to receive a huge reward may be another story. No one ever says, "It's OK to break the rule about integrity."

The primacy of winning has justified wartime conduct that would otherwise be unacceptable from the earliest times until today. This isn't the place to discuss whether President Truman was right to drop atomic bombs on Hiroshima and Nagasaki, or whether President Bush was right to institute certain domestic surveillance plans after September 11. My point is that national leaders have used "winning a war" not simply as a justification for conduct that many question on ethical grounds. They have treated the winning mantra as so self-evident that they have deemed repeating the phrase as enough to remove all other questions from the table. Uttering the mantra substitutes for formulating an argument about what's right.

The same goes on in the world of business. Sometimes achieving the results that incentives are designed to help meet have the effect of putting the demands of trust and honesty to one side. The reason—or should I say the culprit?—is the cult of winning. Winning gets so much favorable press inside an organization that achieving it seems to trump all other goals.

The goal of winning functions like psychic cover for employees, managers, and senior executives. It provides an excuse to put aside other concerns because of the supreme importance of winning. Trying to win is its own justification. Achieving what an incentive comp plan encourages outweighs the prohibition against compromising trust, honesty, and integrity. For, as Bill Diffenderffer says, "Somebody has to win."

The psychic cover that the ideology of winning provides can be used to justify an array of unethical practices. The highly successful performer may be excused for his regular inappropriate comments to women. Or his matchstick temper, or his racial prejudice, may excuse behavior that humiliates and dehumanizes subordinate employees (see Chapter 8). Ruthless, self-centered go-getters may get promoted because "they win." But the winning ideology has a particular bite in connection with incentive compensation. One of the most celebrated stories of the perils of the "winning" paradigm is the 1994 Joseph Jett scandal at the now-defunct brokerage firm of Kidder, Peabody & Co., at the time owned by GE.

"YOU MAKE MONEY AT ALL COSTS"

Kidder, Peabody was an old company, founded in April 1865, the month the Civil War ended. One hundred thirty years later it was brought down by an ethical scandal of monumental proportions. In a manner all too familiar a decade later, Kidder, Peabody was found to have reported false profits in the bond-trading market in an amount ranging, depending on which source you read, from $210 million to $350 million.[9] Although he has always denied his guilt, the chief culprit was alleged to be a young, high-flying bond trader with degrees from MIT and Harvard Business School named Joseph Jett.

Jett claimed that he was simply implementing a scheme concocted by higher-ups, a variant on the "superior orders" defense that the Nazi war crimes defendants used (unsuccessfully) at Nuremburg after World War II. Whether or not you believe Jett, the fact is that the United States Attorney's Office did not pursue criminal charges against him, the National Association of Securities Dealers (NASD) rejected Kidder's allegations that he committed fraud, and an SEC administrative law judge found that the Commission had failed to prove that he committed securities fraud.[10] To complicate the matter further, Jett also consistently maintained that he was made the fall guy for the scam because he is African American, a claim he defends in his 1998 book, *Black and White on Wall Street*. Jett's exoneration was not complete. The same SEC administrative law judge who found that he did *not* commit securities fraud found that he *intended* to do so—perhaps a judicial compromise when the government's evidence wasn't quite enough. Jett was fined $200,000 for this offense and ordered to repay $8.2 million in bonus money he had received for his share in the falsely recorded profits.[11]

My interest here in Jett and Kidder and, yes, GE, doesn't go to trying to sort out the truth in this lurid financial version of a "he-said, she-said" tale. What matters here is what we know about Jett's attitude before the scandal. What did Jett think when he was singled out for praise within the company and given the prestigious chairman's award for his (apparently) stupendous performance in 1993 as Kidder's top money-maker, and awarded a bonus in excess of $8 million for his efforts?

Because of the magnitude of his success, Jett was invited to speak to a gathering of 130 company executives at a Kidder conference held in Florida. Here's what Jett said to motivate has colleagues: "You do anything to win. You make money at all costs."[12]

Anything to win? Make money *at all costs*? Really?

Now, I don't for a moment think that doing "anything to win" was actually GE's policy. I admit I have a soft spot for the company, because its lamps division kept my grandfather's electrical supply business supplied with product during the darkest days of the Depression. But, with the exception of renegade outfits like Enron, I don't think that would be the policy of any reputable company.

I'm not, however, talking about company policy. I'm talking about attitudes and motivations.

Achievement, meeting or exceeding profit expectations, in short, winning—these were the stuff of GE's core culture. After all, Jack Welch defined the "galvanizing mantra" at GE to be that each business unit had to be either first or second in its market, or it would have to be fixed or sold.[13] Welch scoffed at the idea that a culture focused on winning encouraged employees "to cheat or cut corners to meet corporate goals." "Joe Jett was thinking about GE's quarterly earnings sitting down there?" he asked rhetorically in an interview. "Anybody with an IQ over 70 would know that Joe Jett didn't care about GE's earnings. He never thought about GE. He had a game going for himself."[14]

WHAT WAS JETT SUPPOSED TO BE THINKING ABOUT?

Of course, Jett had a game going for himself, and that's equally true if he was guilty of doing what he was alleged to have done, or innocent as he protests. Isn't that the very point of incentive compensation? The public record doesn't disclose precisely how much of Jett's huge bonus was for appearing to achieve or surpass specific, incentivized objectives. But it doesn't matter. The whole point about incentive comp plans is to invite employees to think about themselves, or more particularly, about augmenting their own ACPs. Incentive compensation invites you, even encourages you, to have a game going for yourself. That's why it's supposed to work.

Welch may have been right about what Jett thought of GE's quarterly earnings goals. He may have been wrong. My guess is that he was right. But with all due respect to the "Manager of the Century," Welch's attempt to distance GE from Jett's alleged wrongdoings is a giant disconnect. Jett wasn't lavishly compensated and ballyhooed as Kidder's "Man of the Year" before his fall because he cared about GE's earnings. He got his $8-plus million bonus and his chairman's award not because of what he thought about GE's goals but because of what his work did to enhance those earnings, or would have done had they been legitimate. Isn't the theory of incentive compensation to put an employee's self-interest in the service of company goals? "Your job isn't to decide the company's goals," the company effectively says. "Your job is to do what we tell you. And, incidentally, just to make sure you understand what we're after, we'll pay you big time if you translate that understanding into performance."

You might even say that, in such a world, most will understand that their goal is to make money for themselves. It applies the reverse of the famous, or should I say, infamous, trickle-down theory of economics to enhance their own ACPs. That's the theory that says if the highest echelons on the salary totem poll make money, their wealth will trickle down to benefit even the lowest ranks. The strategy behind incentive compensation is to create trickle-up benefits. If all employees look after their own ACPs by doing what management incentivizes, then the company will achieve what it wants to achieve. Employees—even the high-flyers like the Joe Jett's of the world— aren't supposed to decide on goals. That's above their pay grade. That's management's job.

"YOU DO ANYTHING TO WIN"

The ideology of winning adds an important and, as Jett's case shows, disturbing element. Reaching incentivized goals is an individual, almost private experience. It's about enhancing your own ACP. But working to enhance your own well-being lacks a component that binds you to the company and its aspirations. Welch's criticism of Jett for not having "GE's quarterly earnings" on his mind seems to fault him for not doing so. As I've said, that's a disconnect, inconsistent with the way incentive compensation is designed to achieve company goals. But, whether Jett was guilty of the criminal and fraudulent activity of which he was accused or not, he unquestionably had bought into GE's central business aspiration: winning. Winning is the glue that is supposed to bind individual, incentive-driven ACP maximizers together. The idea, however, trades on a confusion—the difference between the company succeeding in the market and an individual succeeding in the internal quest for status, power and money.

WINNING AND COMPETITION

You don't have to be a rocket scientist to wonder about a corporate environment that praises a person who says that you do anything to win and that you make money at all costs. Isn't a company that permits this asking for trouble? Can a company that pays out huge bonuses to employees in an environment that features such talk be surprised when ethical problems—huge ethical problems sometimes—arise? Incentive compensation appeals to what we have called enhancing one's own ACP, but which Gordon Gekko more abrasively called greed. It attempts to motivate by concretely telling the individual what he or she can do for himself or herself, not what good it does for the enterprise as a whole. The ideology of winning, by contrast, cloaks self-interest in working for something larger than yourself. For all their praise of individualism, Americans love to feel a part of something bigger, something that transcends their own personal concerns. The ideology of winning accomplishes that goal, but does so at a cost, or maybe I should say a risk. It transforms looking out for your own self-interest into more than mere greed.

But it can't be a surprise when a huge emphasis on winning can lead some to conclude that "winning" means "winning at any cost." Playing by the rules, unfortunately, can fall by the wayside. Thus, a company that makes winning the trademark of its operations can turn out to resemble the guy who, though he doesn't commit the murder or the robbery, drives the getaway car. And, as readers of thrillers or viewers of TV crime shows know, the person who drives the getaway car can be prosecuted as an accessory after the fact.

The ideology of winning is dangerous in another way as well. Where there are winners, there are losers. Someone winning implies that someone is losing. It's a fact that ours is a competitive world. Whether it could be otherwise is a question for theologians and philosophers. It starts in the competition for food or water or light among the plants and tiny creatures that inhabit your backyard. It extends throughout life. Remember high school? The competition to be starting quarterback on the football team? Or first violin in the orchestra? Or the lead in the school musical? Then there's getting in to college, doing well in college, perhaps repeating the same in graduate school, then getting a job, getting promoted, getting a better job. Remember the story a couple of years ago about the second-string punter on a college football team who slashed the leg of the number-one punter so he would have the chance to do the kicking? Competition is with us perpetually. But that doesn't mean its results are entirely beneficial.

Competition exists because resources are scarce. There's only one starting quarterback. In the competitive environment of the natural world, we speak of a species' survival as "success." In business, nowadays, we often call it "winning."

When a company is struggling in a tough market environment, trying to induce customers to buy its product rather than that of the competition, there's clearly a winner and loser, and actually a series of winners and losers. There isn't any other way. For about a hundred years or so before the 1980s, socialists thought there was an alternative. Nothing is final in history, of course, but from the perspective of the early twenty-first century, socialism did not prove a viable alternative to create a strong, growth-oriented economy even to its would-be adherents. Competition between companies is a benchmark not just of the American economic system but, increasingly, of the entire world economic order. To be sure, competition between companies can create ethical problems, as we'll see in Chapter 7. If you adopt a "do anything to win attitude" in the marketplace, you stand an excellent chance of finding yourself and your company a defendant in a lawsuit for damages, if not in a criminal prosecution.

What about competition *within* a company? Sure we want employees, top to bottom, to improve themselves and their productivity. And we want to reward those that do. But do we want to encourage those who succeed to regard themselves as "winners," and those who fall short as "losers"? Do we want the visible marks of success—huge compensation and companywide acclaim—to be so important that the ambitious say, "You do anything to win"?

It isn't good enough to say that you never compromise your integrity or violate the rules and leave it at that—because there's too much evidence that a significant minority of people will add under their breaths, "Unless the payoff is sufficiently large." Simplistic assertions about never compromising integrity give a bad name to real, tough-minded efforts to arrive at solutions to real-world problems. They subject ethics to the charge of being irrelevant! In 2004, Citigroup CEO Chuck Prince, in the wake of scandals in Japan and Britain, told *Fortune* that in the eighteen years he'd worked for retired kingpin Sandy Weill, "I never thought ... that you had to say to people, 'We want to grow aggressively, and don't forget you can't do things that break the law.'"[15] If solving ethical problems were easy, I'd be spending my time teaching my students to be good, effective, and honorable lawyers, and representing my clients, rather than writing this book. And you'd be doing something other than reading it. But it isn't easy.

The problem is simple to state but dreadfully hard to solve. How do you encourage and reward success without putting those who don't quite make it in a negative space and without creating incentives to deceive?

DISTINGUISHING BETWEEN AGGRESSIVE MARKET BEHAVIOR AND AGGRESSIVE CORPORATE CULTURE

The ideology of winning is well established in American business, as we've noted. So far as competition in the market is concerned, its value is hard to challenge. As we'll see in Chapter 7, legal standards that impose civil liabilities for improper market conduct abound. In this area, the law does a good job of constraining the most egregious conduct. Given human nature, there are simply going to be people who try to win the competitive struggle illegitimately. It's not surprising that the legal regime regulating fraudulent or otherwise inappropriate market conduct has to be extensive and finely tuned, with many ins and outs and careful distinctions. Seeking to win in the marketplace without paying attention to the rules is more than problematic. It's very risky indeed.

Viewing a company from the inside, however, gives an entirely different picture. The formula for trouble is simple: Incentives (I) + an Ideology of Winning (IW) = a High-Risk Ethical Environment (HREE). Except in extreme cases like CA's and Jett's—where, for example, the integrity of the public securities market is compromised— excessive zeal to win internally will create ethical, not legal, issues.

"WE WIN AS A TEAM"

How can excessive zeal be curbed? How do you control the consequences of I + IW = HREE? Start with statements like, "You do anything to win," or "You make money at all costs." Recognize them for what they are: literally they are equivalent to saying, "I think I'll just help myself to what's in the cash register (provided I think I can get away with it)." This simply won't do. The commands of ethics must infuse strategy and the implementation of strategy. They can't be a subject separate and distinct, like one of the four courses you took during a particular semester in college or business school. You can't say, "this company is dedicated to the highest ethical standards" and then reward, or turn a blind eye to, unscrupulous or dishonest conduct.

Alongside "winning," one of today's key organizational (and motivational) themes is "team building." When the focus is on the company's position in the competitive market, they work in tandem. Capturing key customers and winning an increasing market share generally requires that a number of men and women pull in the same direction. From an intracompany perspective, however, "team building" is a powerful ingredient in creating a humane corporate culture, in which people are more likely to want to work, and in which ethical problems are less likely to emerge. I think the two go hand in hand, and I believe that an ideology of winning cuts the other way.

I remember many years ago, when the University of Michigan, my law school alma mater, lost (as usual) its annual season-ending football game to Ohio State, this time because the Wolverine placekicker missed a last-second field goal that would have won the game. To fans like me, the errant kicker was the culprit. But I've never forgotten the postgame comment of the late Michigan coach Bo Schembechler: "We win as a team, we lose as a team."

Beating the competition—fairly and under the law—that's the excitement of business. Beating your fellow employees to win plaudits and cash—that's quite another. When people see a company's success as a triumph of effective team play and not as the result of the extraordinary talents of an individual star, they are more likely to take ownership of the company's goals. But more importantly, they aren't going to view their individual success as a triumph earned at the expense of other employees. And a lot of the poison in the air that such stiff intracompany competition creates will simply not make it into the building's heating and cooling system.

Bad actors, people in it for themselves and how much money and prestige they can grab, aren't very likely to want to work in an atmosphere like this. "Oh," they may say, on the way out the door after what has (hopefully) been a short stint, "this place doesn't care about rewarding achievement." But generally that's just not right. The "achievements" that need to be rewarded are the company's legitimate goals of achieving success in the market. If you want to diminish the concept that "we win as a team," set up and nurture a culture where employees compete with each other like the company competes with the competition. If you invite hungry wolves into a pasture, you can guess what's going to happen to the sheep. Being part of a winning team doesn't seem to have been a part of Joseph Jett's mindset. Everything we've said in this chapter shows this isn't easy. Incentives *do* incentivize honest and dishonest conduct alike. Checks, balances, and controls are obviously vital. But a culture that privileges teamwork rather than one employee "winning" at the expense of another is a critical start. This is where leadership comes into play.

HOW CAN A HUMANE CORPORATE CULTURE "WIN" IN COMPETITIVE MARKETS?

There are two styles of leadership sharing a common devotion to the bottom line but differing dramatically in form and style. I call them the "survival-of-the-fittest" style and the "captain-of-the-first-team" style. Both want to win in the market. Both understand that well-articulated, performance-based incentives can contribute. That's about as far as the similarities go.

The survival-of-the-fittest style of leadership presupposes that all life is a competition and that the "best" or "fittest" prevail in the struggle. The concept is a bastardization of the ideas that Charles Darwin expounded to explain the existence of different life-forms over time, and their multitudinous changes during the eons of geologic time. It's called social Darwinism. It entirely fails to differentiate between beating the competition in the marketplace for leading market share, a good thing, and advancing one's own position or compensation level within the company as against, and, if necessary, to the detriment of, fellow employees. If you achieve market preeminence, it's because your product or service is better. That's a core value of our economic system. But if you get the largest bonus or the most attractive bundle of perks, is that because you're better? Competition is the order of the day everywhere and the winners get fat—but the losers? Well, who cares about them anyway? They're losers. The leader who views his employees like this treats them like interchangeable parts.

Fortunately, there is another model. It's where the leader views himself or herself as the head of a team striving to accomplish a goal. Because teams like this can "win" in the market, I call such people not the captain of the team, but the captain of the first team. The captain of the first team wants to win in the marketplace just as much as the survival-of-the-fittest manager, and both understand that they can't do it alone. They require help. It's how they view the helpers that's different, and it's huge.

I've been a boss, but I've also worked for others. One of my bosses knew how to operate as the captain of the team to perfection. She was the boss; no one ever doubted that. When she wanted something done, there was no doubt that you'd received a directive. If you didn't perform up to her expectations, you'd hear about it—calmly, professionally, but in no uncertain terms. If you succeeded, you were certain to receive kudos—and thanks. It felt like a team. The striving to get better—to win—made it feel like the first team.

Many bosses are quite different. You could sum up their management styles—you can't call it a "leadership" style—with the expression, "It's all about them." If the group succeeds in anything, the boss takes all the credit. If it failed in an objective, this kind of boss regularly searches for someone else to blame. If you've ever been in this situation, you know the emptiness it engendered. If a crucial element in testing the worthiness of an action from an ethical point of view is how a proposed action feels if you're on the receiving end (recall the fourth prong of the foursquare protocol in Chapter 3), then the actions of this manager receive a failing grade.

But the survival-of-the-fittest leadership style has a more specific lesson to teach. What such a boss is interested in is his own compensation—and not just the absolute amount but where it puts him relative to others. In Chapter 8 we'll discuss such people, whom I dub Napoleons of the workplace. When winning means beating the competition, that's one thing. But when the competition includes every person within their own organization whom they view as a competitor to their own preeminence, it is quite another.

The aggressiveness that is a vital attribute in the marketplace doesn't stop at the boundaries of the company. It spills into the intracompany world, with devastating effects on morale. Sometimes the effort to rise to the top and get paid the most can produce stunning fraud and illegality. Although Joe Jett continues to deny it, such allegations were the widespread appraisal of his conduct at the time the $350 million charge against earnings was taken because of the bond shenanigans at Kidder, Peabody. But even when the numbers aren't as big or the prosecutor isn't on the scene, when the mantra is "win at all costs," trouble is brewing.

By their very nature, incentives provide people with reasons to achieve their financial or power goals. In and of themselves, incentives are neutral—you can reach the objectives by abiding by the rules or by skirting them if you can do so without getting caught. Whether employees will bend the rules or not, therefore, depends on factors external to the incentives themselves. Two factors are critical to preventing incentives from swallowing ethics. The first, as we saw in the previous chapter, focuses upon whom you hire, and, if you make an ethical mistake in whom you hire, rectifying the situation promptly. There's no substitute for good people.

The second is what we've dwelt upon in this chapter, the tone of the corporate culture and the management style that this tone promotes. If a company's dominant ideology is one of winning, and rising executives engage in cutthroat competition to achieve preeminence, there will be little, beyond good luck, to protect the company from incentive rewards overwhelming abiding by the rules. But if trust and honesty is the order of the day—I mean *really* the order of the day—that doesn't have to happen. Managers who view their roles as captains of a team trying to win in a tough market by all pulling together can create a climate where ethical standards aren't subordinated to receiving the rewards that are incentivized. Sustaining a culture of trust and honesty, and adopting a captain-of-the-first-team management style go hand in hand.

This style of management deserves to be called "ethical leadership." It creates a team prepared to achieve market success, but not at the expense of undermining the importance of trust and honesty within the company. In such an environment, management can create incentives that prompt people to act so as to achieve legitimately the company's business goals. They aren't foolproof, because people are people and temptations are real. But they aren't simply window dressing either. Replacing the concept of winning against fellow employees with playing on the first team is the strategy most likely to make incentives achieve what they were originally designed to accomplish. We know what that is—business success in a tough, competitive market. "Winning," then, is an idea appropriately directed outward, toward the competition. In the next chapter we turn to the ethical, and here largely legal, rules, which establish the matrix in which a company can legitimately pursue that objective.

NOTES

1. Jack Welch and Suzy Welch, *Winning* (New York: Harper Collins, 2005), p. 69.

2. "The engine which drives enterprise is not thrift, but profit." John Maynard Keynes, *A Treatise on Money*, vol. 2 (New York: Harcourt Brace and Company, 1930), p. 149.

3. SEC Press Release No. 2004-134, SEC Files Securities Fraud Charges Against Computer Associates International, Inc., Former CEO Sanjay Kumar, and Two Other Former Company Executives (September 22, 2004), available at http://www.sec.gov/news/press/2004-134.htm.

4. Ibid.

5. Alex Berenson, "Software Chief Admits to Guilt in Fraud Case," *New York Times*, April 25, 2006, p. A1.

6. Betsy Morris and Patricia Neering, "The New Rules," *Fortune*, July 24, 2006, p. 74.

7. Bill Diffenderffer, *Samurai Leader* (Naperville, IL: Sourcebooks, 2005).

8. Welch, *Winning*, p. 83.

9. *Business Week*, May 10, 1999, p. 19 ($210 million); "Jett-Lagged," *The Economist*, vol. 331, no. 7680, April 23, 1994, p. 75.

10. *Business Week*, ibid.

11. Ibid.

12. "Jett-Lagged," *The Economist*, April 23, 1994, p. 75.

13. Welch, *Winning*, p. 169.

14. *Time*, October 3, 1994, vol. 44, no. 14, p. 56.

15. *Fortune*, November 29, 2004, vol. 150, no. 11, pp. 114–122.

CHAPTER 7
Money: Cutting Corners with Your Customers

Henry Ford, a century ago, and Bill Gates in our own time, became billionaires by coming up with ways to mass-market products that, a few years before, nobody had imagined but which soon nearly everyone wanted. Increasing profit in most companies is more prosaic. You do things, singly or in combination, that increase the bottom line: sell more goods or services, sell what you sell at greater margin (higher price, lower cost, or some combination), or decrease expenses, both fixed and variable. A couple of points on margin here, a couple of points of market share there, a cut of expenses for office supplies—all add up to a higher profit.

In this chapter we address issues that arise as companies try to pick up that little bit extra in questionable ways.

It's often said that a successful company has to be devoted to its bottom line. Yet the "bottom line" can mean two different things. It can mean a commitment to the long-term health and profitability of the company, of which its reputation for candor is a critical component. Or it can mean a preoccupation with the next quarter's earnings. The latter is our focus here, for that kind of devotion can unearth numerous temptations that appear to promise a quick fix.

INTO THE MOUTHS OF BABES

Can you imagine thinking it would be a good idea to sell adulterated apple juice for consumption by infants because the adulterated product was cheaper to produce and thus the bottom line would be increased? It's hard to believe. Putting aside the legal and ethical issues of such a venture, how could any company decide to do something as dumb as this? It's a public relations disaster waiting to happen. But someone did.

The company that blundered into this mess was Beech-Nut. It's an old story, but one that's not out of date.

In the late 1970s and early 1980s, the company marketed and sold apple juice. The target market was infants and very young children. The problem was this: As senior executives knew, in order to save on the cost-end, millions of bottles of the so-called "apple juice" contained little or no apple juice at all. The product the company was selling was sugar water that tasted like apple juice.[1]

The cause behind this blunder was the simple problem that managers face day in and day out. Try to reduce the cost of goods so that the gross margin on sales will be larger. Pressed by cash shortages, the company abandoned its traditional suppliers of pure apple juice concentrate and began dealing with another, lower-cost supplier. Though the savings amounted to only about one half of 1 percent of the manufacturing budget, the company was in a cash crunch so that, in the words of the *New York Times Magazine* postmortem in the scandal, "the pressure was on."[2] The new "apple juice concentrate" was essentially sugar water. Eventually, the supplier's price dropped to 25 percent below market, but this seems not to have alerted Beech-Nut executives that something fishy was going on. Or if they figured out what was going on, like good ostriches, or executives who didn't care, they did nothing to inquire.

After the purchases from the new supplier had begun, Beech-Nut was acquired by the Swiss giant Nestlé. (At the time Nestlé itself had just been embroiled in a worldwide scandal for deceptive marketing practices in the selling of infant formula to Third World mothers.) Nestlé appointed Niels Hoyvald as president of Beech-Nut. In his 1979 resume, the Danish-born Hoyvald had bragged that his special talent was "aggressively marketing top quality products."[3] At Hoyvald's criminal trial for violating provisions of federal food and drug laws, there was some dispute about how early he knew about the problem, and hence how long he concealed it. By June 1982, however, it was clear that he knew what was going on.

Rather than accepting advice to recall the product, which would have had the effect of disclosing to the public what the company had been selling since 1978, Hoyvald launched a cover-up. The climax looks like a scene from a bad movie. Because of fear that the product would be seized by the New York State Department of Agriculture, Hoyvald authorized a nine tractor-trailer caravan to take 26,000 cases of juice across the Hudson River to Secaucus, New Jersey, out of New York's jurisdiction, under the cover of night. Moreover, Hoyvald used his self-touted aggressive marketing skills to ship 23,000 cases from San Jose, California, to Galveston, Texas, for shipment to the Dominican Republic, where they were unloaded on the public (not, apparently, in violation of U.S. food and drug laws) at a 50 percent discount. In a phrase that became all too familiar in the early years of the twenty-first century, one of the prosecutors summed up Beech-Nut's behavior as "a classic picture of corporate greed and irresponsibility."[4]

IF IT LOOKS TOO GOOD TO BE TRUE, IT PROBABLY IS

The Beech-Nut apple juice story helps us to identify three issues that arise when the pressures to improve the (short-term) bottom line conflict with, and are allowed to prevail over, legal and ethical requirements. First, the company was cash-strapped. It was looking for *anything* that could reduce costs so as to increase the profit margin. Where the bottom line is concerned—unless you're Henry Ford or Bill Gates with a really new and big idea—the devil's often in the details, and even small decreases in costs can make a difference. But even small decreases can sometimes be too good to be true. The price of the concentrate Beech-Nut was buying, as we've noted, eventually fell to 25 percent below market. After the fact, which is where, after all, federal prosecutors operate, one of the government team said that that such a substantial decrease "should have been enough in itself to tip anyone off" that the concentrate was diluted or adulterated.[5] We don't know if the Beech-Nut management was clueless—or willfully blind. Probably the latter. If something looks too good to be true, it probably is. And people, especially those hard-bitten people who earn their livings as prosecutors, are unlikely to be fooled.

THE ALTERNATIVE TO A COVER-UP:
TIME TO CALL YOUR LAWYER

Second was the cover-up. Although the instinct to hide wrong-doing is a powerful motive, doing so almost always multiplies the risk you've already got several-fold. Richard Nixon, the only president in American history forced to resign the office, was brought down not by his involvement in the small-fry burglary of the Democratic National Committee headquarters in the Watergate complex, but by the bungled efforts to cover up the crime. Whenever it actually was that Beech-Nut's top management learned that they were under investigation for selling apple juice that contained nothing from apples, they knew they were in trouble. None could realistically have doubted that the authorities were going to come after them, and, even to the extent that effective lawyers could minimize the harm, the effect on the company's reputation in their target market—mothers caring for their babies—had to be huge. The temptation to cover up, to make the whole story go away like a bad dream, is great. It simply must be resisted.

People make mistakes. They do things they shouldn't. If you realize that you, or the people you supervise, have done something wrong, you have to play damage control expert. *Here* is where a genuine devotion to the company's long-term health, its bottom line over time, should kick in. Now, I'm not going to be so naïve as to say that cover-ups always fail and that they usually make bad things worse. Frequently, yes. Always, no. If management's interest is genuinely in the long-term well-being of the company, as it should be, it's not smart to guess that your case will be special, your cover-up will succeed, and no one will ever know the difference. If you're in charge, don't bet that those responsible will escape unscathed, and the company's reputation will be untarnished. The odds are against it. It's not the prudent course.

Here, the likelihood of escaping detection was minimal. So, when New York state authorities were honing in on the adulteration of the apple juice, executives loaded the nine tractor-trailers with juice and drove them to New Jersey. Does no one in the New York State Department of Agriculture have a counterpart in the New Jersey department? Do state lines affect the ability of federal food and drug officials to pursue their investigations? What the Beech-Nut executives did was not only dishonest, it wasn't very smart.

We've talked about many instances in which what we ought to do is affected by the law and the desire to avoid liability or, in extreme cases, criminal prosecution. We haven't said much about lawyers—when you should call them and how you should use them. Where management has discovered serious wrongdoing, there are really only two alternatives: orchestrate a cover-up or get counsel involved *now*. About the only thing that can be said in favor of the first choice is that it saves on lawyers' fees. That, however, is short-term thinking of the most potentially disastrous kind. You save if, and only if, the cover-up succeeds and there are no administrative investigations, criminal charges, or hostile class-action suits. Remember, your discussions with your lawyers are completely confidential, under the cloak of what's called "attorney-client privilege." Unless you're asking your lawyer to help you commit a *future* crime or fraud—which a lawyer is ethically forbidden to provide by the Rules of Professional Conduct adopted in each state—your attorney is bound to keep what you discuss confidential. Armed with full knowledge, lawyers frequently can minimize the consequences of what's been done wrong. That's one of their jobs.

If you've been selling sugar water to mothers to feed to their babies, and if you've done this for a long time, even the best lawyers aren't going to make it all go away. Good attorneys know what is the most problematic part of the company's case. Now, this is important, so as they used to say in school, listen up. *What lawyers know to be the greatest risk may not be what company executives identify.* A good lawyer will not operate in a vacuum when issues of the company's market reputation are at stake. Frequently, the most dangerous point of the legal minefield simply isn't where the layperson thinks it is. Second, lawyers know or can acquire information about how courts and various administrative and enforcement agencies will react—what their policies are, and how the personalities of the decision-makers can affect outcomes. Lawyers are criticized in the media and, of course, by politicians, for using their skills to divert the worst from coming down against their clients. People who make such criticisms, of course, advance their claims when *other people* are in the crosshairs. It's a little different when *you* are in trouble. When things are falling apart because of something you or your company did, everybody I've ever heard about is very glad that there's a profession that's not only trained to help, but has an ethical obligation to act, within the law of course, zealously to represent their clients.

For management, the lesson is a simple one. Better to spend money on good lawyers than on hiring tractor-trailers to get your adulterated goods across the state line in the black of night.[6]

CORPORATE PATRIOTISM AND GOING TO JAIL

The third lesson follows closely from the second. According to James Traub in his *New York Times Magazine* piece on the subject, John F. Lavery, a second key Beech-Nut executive, rejected his lawyer's advice to plead guilty. Both Lavery and Hoyvald insisted on standing trial. As Traub put it, "[B]oth men, by most reports, are still convinced that they committed nothing graver than a mistake in judgment. Hoyvald and Lavery seem to think of themselves as corporate patriots. Asked by one of the prosecutors why the entire inventory of concentrate was not destroyed once it came under suspicion, Hoyvald shot back testily: 'And I could have called up [Nestlé headquarters in] Switzerland and told them I had just closed the company down. Because that would have been the result of it.'"[7]

Loyalty is a cardinal value—in one's family, with one's friends, and to one's company. We praise and admire people who exhibit it. But it's only one value among many we care about. It's difficult to justify the old jingoist patriotic cant, "My country, right or wrong." It's downright impossible to do it with one's company—at least without jettisoning all other moral values and ignoring the law of the land.

Companies expect their employees to be loyal—and in the case of senior management, the law makes that duty quite stringent and labels it a "fiduciary duty," akin to the duty the administrator of an estate owes to a beneficiary. But blind, unthinking devotion to the company simply won't do. When you've worked for a company for some time, you become enmeshed in its outlook, its way of doing things, its values—in short, its corporate culture. If you are in senior management, you may have even played a key role in shaping it. When that culture privileges bottom-line success above everything else, people within the company are at risk of losing sight of the fact that the rest of the world doesn't much care about a company's bottom line. Other things matter more. Now, businesses can't be run by public opinion polls, but if a cross section of the public were asked about which was more important, the profitability of Beech-Nut or selling pure and honestly labeled goods to parents to feed to their children, there can't be much doubt about the outcome. Executives who think that the public will buy into their corporate goals as a defense to corporate wrongdoing are time and again proved wrong. Hoyvald and Lavery didn't win huge profits for themselves, as did their descendants in scandal in the Enron-WorldCom-Tyco era. But they went to jail.

Beech-Nut's sugar-water-disguised-as-apple-juice scam was deceptive. It was misleading. It was, if you want, a shoddy product masquerading as something else. Mothers aren't likely to buy sugar water for their infants, but, if they were, they wouldn't pay what they'd pay for apple juice. The Beech-Nut apple juice story is an example of cutting corners on the production side of something to be sold to the public. The purpose of the masquerade, of course, was to make a profit. It was certainly unethical and, because of the century-old regime of regulating pure food and drugs, it was illegal. Only one thing can be said in mitigation of Beech-Nut's conduct. Although the apple juice was "adulterated" within the meaning of the law, it wasn't dangerous. Some products are dangerous. Sometimes cost-cutting is the culprit. That's an even worse story.

CUTTING CORNERS ON PRODUCT SAFETY

The poster child for corporate greed prevailing over the safety of the public is the Ford Pinto case from the 1970s. Preproduction engineering reports on the car showed that the placement of the fuel tank made it liable to explode in even minor rear-end collisions. Once the model was released to the market, about fifty people died. Internal Ford documents, which lawyers for the deceased victims eventually got in pretrial discovery, showed that it would have cost $15.60 to fix the problem; Ford considered this too high. In one 1981 case, Ford was held liable for punitive damages in the amount of $125 million.[8]

The Ford Pinto is to cases about dangerous products what Enron is to conflicts of interest. Its total outlandishness makes it a favorite of business-bashers. It's pretty obvious that deciding that it's too expensive to fix a problem that's a danger to human life or safety won't cut it—ever. But you know that. Unfortunately for Ford, some of its

executives didn't know it. Problems with dangerous products typically start with the less overtly unacceptable practice of cost-cutting:
trying to add a couple of points to the net profit number by shaving
costs ever so slightly. . . .

Cutting corners on product safety can be dangerous to consumers.
It is also risky to the company. To understand why cutting corners
on safety is a risky company practice, we have to look at the legal
environment of modern product liability litigation. This is one of
those areas where legal regulation is so pervasive that avoiding getting smacked by the law provides all the reason you need to do the
right thing. No subject that we discuss in this book is more likely to
yield severe legal sanctions to those who cause harm than product
liability.

A PRIMER ON PRODUCT LIABILITY

Product liability law is one of the main targets when business people, and liability insurance companies, vent their hostility to lawyers.
One of the media's favorites for this charge is the McDonald's hot
coffee case, *Liebeck v. McDonald's Restaurants*,[9] in which a jury awarded
a McDonald's customer $2.9 million for damages sustained when she
spilled a cup of hot coffee on herself. A verdict like this makes good
newspaper copy and a compelling thirty-second sound bite on the
nightly news. As is often the case when the media report about legal
developments, the facts are little more complicated, and less clearly
outrageous. We'll come back to this case shortly, but what's essential
to understand at the outset is that courts do render large damage
awards when defective products harm people. We call this "product
liability law" and it's here to stay. Though there are abuses, I wouldn't
want to live in a world where manufacturing and marketing dangerous products was something companies could get away with. As we'll
see, that used to be what the world was like.

This legal regime is so pervasive that, as a practical matter, the
legal duties to sell safe products subsume pure questions of ethics.
One particular aspect of product liability law is so important that I
want to emphasize it up front. In nearly all states, the law imposes
liability for harm caused by dangerous products on a basis that lawyers call "strict liability." This means that, if a person is injured by a
product, he or she may recover against the product's manufacturer

without having to prove that the manufacturer was "at fault," that is, that it was negligent. To simplify, the injured person need only prove that he or she was using the product as it was supposed to be used, and that the manufacturer failed to give adequate warnings. This approach makes life a whole lot easier for injured people trying to recover damages, and a whole lot riskier for companies that don't pay enough attention to product safety, than proving fault would be.

It may come as a surprise to many, but until well into the twentieth century, manufacturers generally were able to escape liability to people injured by their products. They had two formidable defenses. First, under an ancient and arcane doctrine called "privity of contract," the injured party could sue the manufacturer only if he or she had purchased the product *directly* from the manufacturer. (When you purchase something from somebody, in the eyes of the law, you have entered into a contract with the seller. "Privity" simply means that there is a bond of union between both parties to a contract arising out of the contract.) Second, until the 1970s, manufacturers generally could be held liable only if the injured person could prove that the company had been negligent. Proving negligence involved showing either that the product was carelessly designed, or that the particular unit that harmed the injured person had been carelessly manufactured. Good defense lawyers can make proving such a case difficult—and expensive.

Abandoning both the need for privity and the requirement to show negligence drives the modern legal machine. Let's look at each.

HOLDING A PRODUCT'S MAKER RESPONSIBLE

The regime that flourished up until after the mid-century made it a condition of success in court that the person seeking recovery for damages sustained from a product had himself or herself purchased the product from the manufacturer. This meant that if you and I had both been injured by a malfunction of a Model T Ford that *you* had purchased directly from the Ford Motor Company, you could recover compensation for injuries but I could not. And if (as would have been likely) you had purchased it from a dealer, neither could you. As we've just mentioned, the basis for this anomalous rule lies deep in the compartments of the old-fashioned lawyer's mind. If you bought a Model T from Ford itself, your purchase made both you and the company parties to a sales contract, putting you and Ford in what's called "privity of contract." The rule actually makes sense if we're talking about who can sue someone for breach of contract—obviously, a party to the contract, and not a nonparty. But here we're talking about injuries. It's not difficult to understand why manufacturers who sold their products through a distribution chain rather than directly to the end user would love this rule. They didn't care much about what lawyers and judges in England were thinking when they originally articulated this rule; it meant they got a pass on the harm caused by their products.

In 1916, future U.S. Supreme Court Justice Benjamin Cardozo, then a judge on the highest court in New York state, issued a seminal ruling that began the long process of changing this outlook. The purchaser of a Buick wanted to sue the manufacturer, Buick Motor Company—this was before the creation of General Motors—because the wood its wheels were made of crumbled into fragments as he was driving it, causing him serious injury. The problem was that the injured would-be plaintiff had bought the car from a dealer. Most of us, unconcerned about privity of contract, would probably think that if Buick made the wheels, if the wheels were defective, and if the defective wheels caused harm to the injured person, Buick should be the party held responsible. That's what Judge Cardozo ruled.[10]

It took nearly a half a century to make Cardozo's ruling nationwide. When the law changes through judicial decisions, the shift is almost always gradual. (The law changes quickly when Congress passes a statute. That's what happened when it enacted the Civil Rights Act of 1964.) Nobody ever proposed changing the privity requirement by federal statute, so change came through decisions of supreme courts in the various states.[11] But eventually the law got rid of the requirement that the victim of injury caused by a product needed himself or herself to have been the purchaser. And good riddance. It simply doesn't make sense that a company should be liable to a person injured by its products if, and only if, the company directly sold the product to the victim. What matters is the defect in the product, not who, in the chain of distribution, sold it.

STRICT LIABILITY

The second major pillar of modern product liability law is of more recent vintage. It's the rule that allows plaintiffs to prevail without showing negligence on the part of the manufacturer. Whereas the old rule on privity of contract from our point of view (if not that of a lawyer ninety years ago) functioned as a lucky "get-out-of-jail-free" card, the abolition of negligence cuts deeply into the thought processes required of manufacturing executives.

In the Buick case, the plaintiff was prepared to prove that the company was negligent in installing the defective wood in the car's wheels. We use the word "negligence" in ordinary speech, but in law it has a precise meaning. A person, or a company, that fails to exercise as much care in a particular circumstance as a reasonable person would exercise in the same circumstance is "negligent." It's the way the law says someone was at fault, not intentionally, but through carelessness. This is not a difficult concept. What's tough is proving it. You have to determine who did what and when. It's the rare case in which there will be documents, or a witness who is prepared to testify, that will straightforwardly establish negligence. Juries spend a lot of their time deliberating on this in cases in which the plaintiff must show negligence to recover. Moreover, the plaintiff—as the person seeking recovery for injuries—has the burden of proof. It can be a pretty formidable hurdle. This began to change just before the middle of the twentieth century.

In a case that began to mark the change, during World War II, a waitress in California was injured when a bottle of Coke exploded in her hand, breaking into two pieces and inflicting a deep, five-inch cut severing blood vessels, nerves, and muscles in the palm of her hand. The case went to the Supreme Court of California. The majority of the court said that the negligence of the Coca-Cola Bottling Company could be inferred. The plaintiff won. A concurring justice, Justice (later Chief Justice) Roger Traynor, advanced a different and seminal argument. He said that "it should now be recognized that a manufacturer incurs an absolute liability when an article that he has placed on the market, knowing that it is to be used without inspection, proves to have a defect that causes the injury."[12] Justice Traynor's phrase "absolute liability" didn't get picked up by the law. But the concept did. We now call it "strict liability." It's critical to understand how strict liability differs from negligence. Negligence, as we've seen, requires proof of fault—namely, carelessness. So, were negligence to be the standard, the injured person would have to prove *both* that the injury was caused by the defective product and that the manufacturer's negligence was responsible for the injury the product caused. When the standard is strict liability, the injured plaintiff has a much easier task. He or she has to prove only the first. The injured victim has to show that there was something wrong with the product, its defect. The victim does not have to show why or how the manufacturer caused the defect.

In 1963, a California man was injured by a "Shopsmith," a combination power tool that could be used as a saw, drill, and wood lathe. Chief Justice Traynor now had a unanimous California Supreme Court behind him. Here is how he defined the strict liability standard:

> To establish the manufacturer's liability it was sufficient that the plaintiff proved that he was injured while using the Shopsmith in a way it was intended to be used as a result of a defect in design or manufacture of which plaintiff was not aware that made the Shopsmith unsafe for its intended use.[13]

Chief Justice Traynor made it clear that the basis for this rule was a choice to allocate the financial burden of losses to manufacturers, and not to their customers. According to Traynor, "The purpose of such liability is to insure that the costs of injuries resulting from defective products are borne by the manufacturers that put such products on the market rather than by the injured persons who are powerless to protect themselves."[14]

Under this regime, to repeat, if the plaintiff can prove that he or she was injured by a product, and that the product had a defect, the plaintiff wins. The manufacturer could have been unbelievably careful in designing and manufacturing the product. No matter. The monetary risk of injury, under strict liability, belongs to the manufacturer (and its insurer). As a practical matter, unless the manufacturer can show that the injured plaintiff misused the product or ignored warning labels, the manufacturer generally will have to pay.

The responsibility that strict liability imposes upon manufacturers is thus very great. It's not enough to be careful. It's not enough to act with as much care as would a reasonable person under the circumstances—the standard, for instance, that governs whether (in most states) you're liable for a car accident and someone is injured. Although it's not a recognized legal term, I think the best way to describe what a company has to do regarding its products is to act with extraordinary—that is, much more than ordinary—care.

The law's practical requirement of extraordinary care makes manufacturers sit up and take notice, both on the design and manufacture of products. A design defect is potentially more important, for if there's a defect in the design of a product, it means that there's something wrong with every unit of the product. If this is the case, the likelihood is that there will be a number of injuries. Design defects, as we'll see shortly, also present important ethical issues for companies.

Manufacturing defects mean that something went wrong in the way *some* of the units of the product were made. The defective wood in the wooden spokes in the 1911 Buick in the *MacPherson* case is an example of a manufacturing defect. From the point of view of the injured victim, it doesn't make a difference whether his injury was caused by a design defect or a manufacturing defect. From the point of view of the manufacturer, the difference is huge. If, so far as the company knows, the defect occurred in only one unit of the product, there's nothing to do. Good product liability insurance coverage will probably cover the loss, including the attorneys' fees incurred defending and, frequently, settling the claim before trial. If it appears that a particular lot of the product contains the manufacturing defect, the company can institute a recall and take steps to prevent the recurrence of similar injuries.

LISTENING TO YOUR CUSTOMERS
(EVEN WHEN THEY COMPLAIN)

The strict liability standard in product liability cases sends out a loud and clear message to manufacturers: the burden is on the company that puts a product on the market to ensure that it's safe. If a consumer uses a product as the maker intended, and the consumer is hurt, the company will have to pay. To use the language of economists and specialists in this branch of the law, the legal system allocates the risk of loss to the company that could have done something to make the product safer, and not to the consumer.

With these ideas in mind, let's take another look at the supposedly outrageous McDonald's hot coffee spill case.

Let me begin with a word of caution. Press reports about what happens in legal cases are generally unreliable. It's not that television and newspaper reporters aren't smart or that legal cases are more complicated than anything else. It's just that many reporters tend to live in a world of thirty- or forty-five-second capsules. Sometimes, if the story is really important, a network news show might give it a minute or a minute and a half. Try to explain a complicated development in your business to someone in that time frame. You don't get past the surface. Newspapers tend to have more in-depth reporting. But legal nuances often get lost.

So the surface story was that a woman burned herself with hot coffee she'd bought from a McDonald's and received a jury award of $2.9 million, of which $2.7 million was for punitive damages. Now, since most of us at one time or another have spilled coffee or hot tea, this seems pretty outrageous. Good copy for the media. A thirty-second firecracker.

What really happened is a little different. To understand, we have to clarify two kinds of damages that American law awards that were mentioned briefly before. The first are called "compensatory" or "actual damages." The second, as we saw in the Ford Pinto case, are called "punitive damages." Compensatory damages are those that are awarded whenever a plaintiff wins a monetary award. In an accident case, compensatory damages include hospital and medical bills, anticipated costs of long-term care (if any), and lost wages. It's generally pretty easy to calculate these damages. The other kind of compensatory awards are for "pain and suffering." By their very nature, they can't be calculated with precision. But the law is right to treat them as compensation. If you are lying in a hospital bed because a faulty crane fell on you while you were visiting a construction site, you're probably hurting badly. If you got compensated only for your out-of-pocket medical expenses, and your lost salary, I think you'd feel that the wrongdoer hadn't paid for everything you suffered. In our legal system, juries decide this number based on evidence presented. It's imprecise, but no less "actual" compensation for that. In the McDonald's case, the jury awarded Ms. Liebeck $200,000 in compensatory damages (which the court reduced to $160,000 because it concluded that Ms. Liebeck had been 20 percent at fault).

The big number was the punitive damages award. As we've seen, punitive damages can be awarded *only* when the wrongdoer acted deliberately, recklessly, or the like. The jury awarded $2.9 million, which the court reduced to $480,000. What had McDonald's done wrong?

The evidence at trial revealed that McDonald's had a corporate policy of serving coffee at a temperature of 180 to 190 degrees

Fahrenheit, while the industry average was less than 148 degrees. The plaintiff also showed that a liquid at McDonald's temperature would immediately burn the skin, and that she had suffered third degree burns and was hospitalized for eight days. Finally, and most important for our purposes, McDonald's admitted that, in the previous decade, they had received 700 reports of coffee scalds, but had refused to consult a burn doctor about the risks.[15]

Viewed in this way, the jury did not tag McDonald's for $2.7 million in punitive damages for selling coffee that was too hot. It tagged McDonald's for management's failure to respond to customer complaints—lots of customer complaints—that there really was a problem with the temperature at which they served their coffee. These complaints came at a rate of more than one a week for ten years. Does that sound like reckless management indifference to a problem to you? It sounds like it to me.

We don't know why McDonald's ignored these complaints. It may have been that most un-retail of mindsets, "We know better than our customers." Or it may have been the costs involved in gathering the necessary information. It doesn't really matter.

Some people say that the McDonald's hot coffee case shows that America's product liability system is in need of drastic overhaul. Reasonable minds can differ on that, but the McDonald's case doesn't prove it. It shows that a company can get in trouble if it ignores complaints about a dangerous product—and scalding hot coffee, while not deadly, is certainly dangerous. The legal result is aligned with what most people would say is the proper ethical result. Who, after all, is better placed to remedy a product defect, the product's maker or the consumer? Who's in a better position to know if a consumer's complaint is an isolated example, the whining of crank, or an indication that there's a real problem?

The answer is obvious. It also reveals why product liability law developed as it did. It took nearly half a century to get there, but, with a few exceptions, most American state courts have come to the realization that product safety should be made the responsibility of the makers and distributors of products, not the customers who purchase and use them. You've all heard the old saying, "caveat emptor," let the buyer beware. As far as the sale of potentially dangerous products is concerned, the situation is now just the opposite. Cutting corners on the safety of products doesn't simply raise ethical problems, as it would have done many years ago. It creates severe legal risks.

"SHARP" MARKET PRACTICES
AND LEVERAGING LAWYERS' FEES

Ethically problematic conduct in the market isn't limited to deceptive marketing or selling dangerous products. It goes by lots of names—cheating, sharp practices, and dishonesty are three of them. Some of it is petty—you get short-changed in a store and vow never to shop there again. When it's more serious, the law is usually there to help. Indeed, along with remedies for personal injury, the most active parts of the civil justice system (that is, apart from criminal cases) are those addressing the various allegations that go back and forth between companies and the businesspeople who work for them. If you took a business law course in college or graduate school, you probably remember that the law divides this universe into two parts: "wrongs," which the law, because of its French origin, calls "torts," and "breaches of contract." When someone induces you to participate in a deal by misrepresenting material facts, depending on the details, you probably can sue for fraud, a tort. When you have a contract with another company and it fails to perform, you can sue for breach of contract and, at least in theory, get the "benefit of your bargain," that is, what you would have earned if there had been no breach, or at least you can recover the gross amount, before the payment of lawyers' fees. As in the world of product liability, this is an area in which the law is the most potent source of guidance about what companies can and should do.

But not entirely. Sometimes the law provides only the backdrop. This is because of the rules about paying lawyers' fees. Generally speaking, you have to pay your own lawyers, even if you win. It doesn't have to be this way. In England, from whose legal system ours descends, the loser typically pays after a court case. In the United States, however, with rare exceptions, each party typically bears its own legal costs. Lawyers call it the "American rule" on fees. Let's return to an example we used earlier to show what kind of issue can arise.

Recall our example of Alpha Heating Oil Company's contract with Beta Company to supply its heating oil needs for a six-month period from October 1 to March 31, which we considered in Chapter 2. The contract specifies the price, $2.60 per gallon. So that you don't have to flip back, remember that we supposed further that during the winter the price of oil goes up. The cause, as we said, could be a worsening of the political situation in the Middle East, or simply a very cold late fall that makes supplies scarce. It doesn't matter. Alpha company will have to pay more for the product it sells, and Beta, under the contract, will pay less than market price.

One afternoon, Alpha's sales manager walks into the president's office, and tells him that he can get an order to supply a large shopping mall with its needs for the Christmas season. The price: $2.95 per gallon. The problem is that Alpha's contract with Beta gives Beta a right to request an increase in quantity of up to 20 percent for any given month, and Beta has made the request. Alpha doesn't have enough product on hand to fill both the sales manager's potential order from the shopping mall and Beta's request.

The president tells the sales manager he'll get back to him. As soon as he's alone, he calls Alpha's lawyer. He describes the issue and asks, "Have we got to pass on the new deal and honor Beta's request?"

"Technically speaking," the lawyer replies, "it's a no-brainer. You're bound by your contract."

"Technically speaking?" the president asks, waiting for more.

"Technically speaking, if Beta sued you, they'd win. But are they going to sue you? I doubt it. They'd have to get a lawyer, they'd have to pay the lawyer. Likely it'll be too expensive and too much of a hassle. I'd be more worried about future business with them if they find out."

We used this illustration in Chapter 2 to show that there can be ethical reasons to act even when the law itself provides no practical remedy. "We *ought* to perform the promises we make in contracts." Our point here is that engaging in sharp market practices is a way of getting into *reputational* trouble.

It's one thing to "puff up" in negotiations to try to achieve a contract. People not only do it all the time, it is hard to imagine how the genuine give-and-take of negotiations could proceed without it. But it's quite another thing to choose not to perform an agreement you improvidently, or unluckily, made. The fact that you can leverage the other side's legal costs doesn't change the analysis.

Not honoring a contract is, in its own way, akin to lying. It's breaking a promise. After all, the best simple definition of a contract is "a legally enforceable promise." Supreme Court Justice Oliver Wendell Holmes Jr. (1902–1932), probably one of the two most honored judges in U.S. Supreme Court history,[16] once said that having a contract means that party has a right to perform or pay damages.[17] I don't agree. Taken literally, this means that making a promise in a contract is not a promise—in the sense of a genuine undertaking to do something—at all. The moral "obligation" of having said you'll do something is missing. To most of us, entering into a contract is not simply equivalent to saying, "I promise to do thus and so, unless it's cheaper (taking into account that you may sue me) not to do so."

Two conclusions follow from this. Business is a world of give and take. If you want to depend on receiving the favorable benefits of the bargains you've made, like Alpha, you'd better be prepared to perform your promises. At the height of the Cold War, in discussing dealing with the Soviets, President Kennedy said that you couldn't negotiate with people whose posture was "What's mine is mine and what's yours is negotiable." What you expect to receive from those with whom you deal, you'd better be prepared to give when it's your turn.

The second point involves reputation. If you renege on your contracts, or deliberately short your customer on quantity or substitute lower-quality goods because of lower costs, you risk blows to your reputation. The fact that it may be too expensive for the other side to sue you doesn't eliminate the reputational injury. There are companies, and individuals, with whom we all prefer to deal. The common denominator is that we trust them. Companies and people who are as good as their word are worth continuing relationships. Those that aren't, aren't. A company that succumbs to the temptation of a short-term profit, like Alpha Heating in our example, risks a negative, long-term effect that outweighs the short-term gain. This is especially true where the law imposes sanctions. Think of the Ford Pinto. Think of Beech-Nut's apple juice taste-alike sugar water.

The plain fact is that performing a contract frequently is *more* expensive than not performing, because you can make money by not performing, and the costs of litigation will deter the other side from taking you to court. That doesn't make it OK, and it doesn't make it prudent in the long run.

Leveraging off the fact that you have more ability to play chicken with someone else, because that company can't afford the legal fees and other costs of litigation is, I suppose, what people call "playing hardball." I don't much like the phrase. It drips a little too much of testosterone run amok for my taste. That's not, however, what principally disturbs me. When you leverage your power not to perform your legal obligations because of your relative economic strength against your opponent, you're acting unethically. Remember the fourth prong of the foursquare protocol we described in Chapter 3: when you act, imagine what it would be like to be on the receiving end of what you're doing. It's like cutting corners on product safety in the hope that no one will be injured and you'll make a little more profit. In the Alpha/Beta case, the risk is that Beta will find out what Alpha did. Alpha's reputation for honest and fair dealing is bound to plummet.

As we've seen in this chapter, legal rights exist to challenge much of what we'd call unethical market practices. Cutting corners in this area generally means exposing yourself to substantial legal risks. In product liability cases, in which injured victims' lawyers typically work on contingent fees, those risks are likely to hit home if you haven't exercised what I've called extraordinary care in the safety of your products. The toughest ethical dilemmas are those in which you can leverage your economic power to stave off legal risks, as where not performing your contractual promises looks like a good way to augment the bottom line. In cases like that, what's at stake is your reputation for honesty and trustworthiness in the market in which you operate. It's certainly an issue of right and wrong. It's equally an issue of protecting your most valuable commodity, your reputation.

NOTES

1. For a full account of the scandal, see James Traub, "Into the Mouths of Babes," *New York Times Magazine*, July 24, 1988, at SM18.

2. Ibid., at SM37.

3. Ibid.

4. Quoted in Traub, *supra* note 1, at SM18.

5. Ibid., at SM20.

6. Companies in trouble sometimes turn to public relations professionals to help them try to avert reputation disaster. PR people certainly have their roles to play, but they typically can't abide what is frequently the lawyer's advice to keep quiet: the proverbial "no comment." I agree, saying nothing is often bad publicity; but saying something that counts as an admission against the company and its executives when they're prosecuted or sued for millions of dollars generally creates bad publicity that is much more long-lasting and far worse.

7. Traub, *supra* note 1, at SM53.

8. *Grimshaw v. Ford Motor Co.*, 174 Cal. Rptr. 348 (Cal. App. 4th Dist. 1981). Punitive damages, also called exemplary damages, are awarded above and beyond what is thought to be necessary to compensate an injured person for his or her losses. Punitive damages can be awarded only when a defendant has engaged in intentional wrongdoing, reckless disregard of human life, or the like. They bite especially hard on business because, in most states, as a matter of public policy, liability insurance policies do not cover punitive awards.

9. *Liebeck v. McDonald's Restaurants, P.T.S., Inc.*, No. CV-93-62419, 1995 WL 360309 (Bernalillo County, N. M. Dist. Ct. August 18, 1994).

10. *MacPherson v. Buick Motor Co.*, 111 N.E. 1050 (N.Y. 1916).

11. For reasons that are both historical and related to text of Article I of the Constitution, product liability questions are matters of state law. That meant that change in the rules had to occur state by state, often through the laborious process of decision by state supreme courts. During the first half of the twentieth century, most constitutional experts would have agreed that Congress had no power under the Constitution to make such a change to apply nationwide at once, as happened with the Civil Right Act of 1964. Today many experts would probably say that the Constitution does give Congress that power, should Congress choose to exercise it.

12. *Escola v. Coca-Cola Bottling Company of Fresno*, 150 P.2d 436, 440 (Cal. 1944) (Traynor, J., concurring).

13. *Greenman v. Yuba Power Products, Inc.*, 377 P.2d 897, 901 (Cal. 1962).

14. Ibid.

15. Mark A. Geistfeld, *Principles of Products Liability* (New York: Foundation Press, 2006), pp. 223–226. Professor Geistfeld's discussion of products liability issues is illuminating, but the figures he provides on the damages awarded in *Liebeck* are not correct.

16. The other is Chief Justice John Marshall (1801–1835), the author of a number of decisions defining the basic structure of American government.

17. "The Path of the Law," 10 *Harvard Law Review* 457, 462 (1897).

CHAPTER 8

Power and Abuse of Power: Challenging the Culture of Humiliation

DREADING MONDAY

Imagine it's Sunday night. How do you feel about the prospect of getting up Monday morning and going to work?

Although it's fashionable in some circles to complain about "having to go to work," most managers and executives in challenging, high-powered, and highly interesting jobs either don't complain, or don't really mean it when they do. Work isn't just their source of income. It's where such people derive an important part of their sense of their self-worth, and where they readily feel a true sense of accomplishment. That's a feeling that's hard to duplicate elsewhere. If you've got a job you love, you probably find yourself sometimes saying, "I can't believe I get paid to do this." I've had that feeling. It's great.

Not everybody is that fortunate. Some people simply don't have the skill set, or the temperament, to find interesting, challenging work to perform. People like this usually dread Monday mornings.

But there's another class of people who dread Monday mornings, and it's these people who demand our attention. If you're in this group, you know that there's nothing wrong with the job on paper, or the kind of work you do. The problem is the people you work with or for, most frequently your boss. Now bosses, too, can be divided into different categories. There's the procrastinator or the plain incompetent. People like these can make life frustrating, maybe worse. But our focus here is on another kind: people who use their positions of power to make the lives of their employees living hell. They may be genuinely malevolent, or people with outsized egos who forget that others inhabit the planet, and the workplace, but they needn't necessarily fall into either of those categories. They need to feel important and have found they can accomplish this by humiliating you. They make you dread coming to work. I've had that feeling, too. It's awful. I call it the Monday dread.

POWER AND WORKPLACE HORRORS

You can experience a bad case of the Monday dreads because you simply can't stand someone you work with. You and your coworker may simply have a personality clash, or he or she is a particularly difficult person. Or she's going through a divorce, or he's afflicted with a health problem that makes him crabby. I don't want to minimize situations like this, but they're not my focus.

The Monday dread that's relevant here comes because your boss is so impressed with his or her own power that he or she feels entitled to treat you entirely inappropriately, to make you *feel* that you are powerless and subordinate—in short, to humiliate you. Our focus is on understanding the feelings of those who endure, or maybe I should say suffer, such humiliation. It's the most common kind of workplace wrongdoing arising from abuse of power.

Abuse (other than sexual abuse) in the workplace has received increased attention in recent years. According to recent statistics, legislation has been introduced in thirteen states to combat workplace bullying. One of the most compelling business reads I've had for years is Stanford Professor Robert Sutton's 2007 book, *The No-Asshole Rule: Building a Civilized Workplace and Surviving One That Isn't*. A couple of years ago, it was the theme of a very funny best-selling book, and subsequent movie, *The Devil Wears Prada*.

Still, nonracial, non-gender-based abuse is not a subject that typically figures in the discussions of business ethics. It should. Controlling abuses of power within a company is critical for any business that genuinely wants to create an up-to-date and genuinely appropriate work environment. Parallel to the last prong of the foursquare protocol—reminding you to imagine yourself on the receiving end of conduct—I want to focus on what it feels like to be the subject of abuses of power. As I've said, the best umbrella to encompass such feelings is humiliation. We'll look at two distinct kinds of humiliation. First, we'll discuss humiliation that is the felt consequence of the naked abuse of power by one's superior and the employee's inability—apart from quitting—to do anything about it. This is a kind of inappropriate, demeaning, and unethical behavior that all too many employees have to put up with day in and day out. Second, we'll take a look at how humiliation can be experienced as a manifestation of that particularly ugly phenomenon, racial or ethnic prejudice. We'll close the discussion by emphasizing that management cannot allow itself to be an enabler of conduct that allows humiliation to flourish.

THE NEGLECTED STEPCHILD

Abuse of power is the single most neglected subject in the discussions about proper conduct in business. At first blush, this seems very strange. If, as we've seen, ethics is fundamentally about treating others in ways that do not harm or disadvantage them, abuses of power are paradigm cases of ill treatment. What could more obviously be "the wrong thing to do" than to mistreat an employee who works directly for you or whom you outrank in the company hierarchy? Only the downright financial dishonesty discussed in Chapters 5 and 6 seem as blatantly unacceptable.

The reason for the different treatment lies in the fact that it's so much easier—or should I say so much more common?—to draft rules about financial wrongdoing than about the subject of this chapter, "power wrongdoing." In fact, we frequently excuse power wrongdoing in a way that we would never excuse financial chicanery or sexual harassment. It's almost like we expect people with power to abuse it. We say, "It goes with the territory." No one could seriously think that it's OK for a corporate executive to buy or sell his company's stock the day before the release of its quarterly earnings reports because having such information "goes with the territory" of being a corporate executive. Nor—at least since the 1980s—will anybody seriously maintain that female employees have to put up with requests for sexual favors from their male bosses because such behavior "goes with a male boss's territory."

We haven't ended insider trading or sexual harassment. But at least they're no longer regarded as OK. We criticize people for doing either and, when legally competent proof is available, courts hold the culprits liable. Although this isn't the kind of claim that can be proven, I'm sure there are fewer of these abuses then there'd be if the wrongfulness of insider trading and sexual harassment hadn't become part of mainstream American business values. I look forward to the day when power wrongdoing within a company will fall in the same category.

Management can and should recognize abuses of power for what they are. Dealing with such abuses is an obligation that falls on any manager who has a senior subordinate who abuses his or her subordinates. Sometimes addressing a problem reaches all the way to the highest authority in a corporation, the board of directors. As everyone knows, some of the worst offenders in American business are CEOs and their closest advisors—men and women over whom only the board has authority. Let me say it plainly. Any company that puts up with frequent or systematic abuses of its employees by bosses (at whatever level) has no right to claim that it's "a good company to work for" or, in that overused tagline, "we put people first."

Although there are different ways to slice the pie, I find it useful to divide people who abuse their power within an organization into three categories. I call them the bad people, the Napoleons of the workplace, and the humiliators.

BAD PEOPLE

I know that some will think it old-fashioned to use the word "bad" to describe some people. Oh, it's OK to use the phrase for the great tyrants of history, like Hitler, Stalin, or Mao, whose lists of murder victims extend into the millions. But in business, it's not politically correct to put it this way. It's "judgmental." It's "over the top."

If that's what you think, that's fine. You won't have any trouble recognizing the worst offenders in the other two categories. But while I don't think that Skilling, Ebbers, and Lay are the moral equivalents of Hitler, Stalin, and Mao, I do think that there is a malevolence in their perfect willingness to harm others that defies any other description.

If you remember Charles Dickens' classic *A Christmas Carol*, you'll recall the mean old boss Mr. Scrooge. One Christmas, Scrooge received nighttime visits from three ghosts, Christmas Past, Christmas

Present, and Christmas Yet to Come. The horrifying spirits caused Scrooge to change completely and become a kindly old man and, presumably, a courteous, generous, and considerate boss. Now, I'm not saying that a transformation like Scrooge experienced can never happen. I think some people recognize the errors of their ways and *genuinely* repent what they've done. (I mean really repent, not simply utter the *mea culpas* white-collar criminal defense lawyers advise their clients to make to try to get judges to lessen their sentences when they got caught.) But such change is exceedingly rare. If you have the misfortune to come across someone who would lie, cheat, and steal from his own family, and whom you don't believe will change even if awakened by three ghostly visitors, you've got a genuine bad person. If you're the boss, fire him. If he or she's the boss, update that resume and look for another job. It's as simple as that.

NAPOLEONS OF THE WORKPLACE

There's another class of people who resemble bad people but who are different in an important regard. I call them Napoleons of the workplace. It's not that they're bad. It's that the power of their positions goes to their heads. The frequent result is abuse. But, because they're not utterly devoid of ethical sense, a company devoted to fostering a humane place to work can sometimes turn them around. Kirke Snyder, a long-time professor of business ethics at Regis College in Denver, calls these people "self-aggrandizing go-getters."

As we discussed in the chapter on conflicts of interest, everyone has an interest in enhancing his or her aggregate compensation package, or ACP. It's only human nature to want to do so—and without this aspect of human nature, companies would have a tough time figuring out how to incentivize corporate priorities. The problem is that some people view enhancing their own ACPs as the be-all and end-all of their business lives.

History is replete with examples of such relentless self-aggrandizers. My favorite has always been Napoleon Bonaparte. There's really never been anyone like him, and I confess to a lifelong fascination with his character. Blessed with one of the most powerful intellects in history, and an imagination and store of energy to match, the young Bonaparte rocketed to unsurpassed prominence. He overthrew the French government a few months after his thirtieth birthday, and crowned himself emperor five years later. Within three years all Europe, except England and Russia, were within his control. Then things began to fall apart. The story of Napoleon's career as emperor from his coronation in 1804 to his downfall at Waterloo in 1815 is increasingly the story of megalomania. The good of France, of Europe, and of his soldiers all paled in significance compared with his dreams of his own glory and power, or what he called "his star." It literally was all about him.

Because Napoleon was quite short—not more than five feet two inches tall—people sometimes describe short men with a domineering personality as having a "Napoleon complex." Not being a psychologist, I don't know whether this concept has much validity. What's critical for our purposes, however, is different. I'll call it a Napoleonic syndrome. This syndrome has nothing to do with height, and can afflict women as well as men. It has everything to do with one's own aggrandizement at the expense of the well-being of everyone else, including the organization the person is supposed to be serving. You can identify a case of the Napoleonic syndrome in a company when you see a person who displays the following behavior patterns:

- Ignores the needs and aspirations of colleagues, especially colleagues who compete, or might compete, for power, a new position, or prestige within the organization.

- Jockeys for personal advantage, including manipulating the system to get there.

- Displays indifference to, or even mocks, company codes of ethics and views legal standards as important only if you get caught.

- Doesn't hesitate to lie, cheat, or steal if it serves self-enhancement.

When they're talented—and many are very talented—workplace Napoleons can dazzle us with what they can do. If they keep their hands out of the cash register, don't exploit conflicts of interest, and (if they're men) keep their hands off women in the workplace, they can be unstoppable. But when a would-be-workplace Napoleon's abilities do not match his or her ego, self-destruction is usually not far away.

Like Napoleon's dreams of power and glory, some businesspeople view enhancing their own ACPs as the be-all and end-all of their business lives. It's no surprise that self-aggrandizing go-getters of the Napoleonic type frequently fail to pay attention to the needs, concerns, feelings, and susceptibilities of lesser mortals. They are prime candidates to be power abusers, not because they're fundamentally immoral people, but because their egos are so large that either they can't see the effects of what they do, or they find those effects unimportant when measured against the grandiosity of their own talents or achievements (real or imagined).

Napoleonic self-aggrandizers, in short, differ from the bad people discussed above because they're not malevolent. They aren't unaware of right and wrong; it's just that systematically they'll choose what enhances their own ACPs. They are consequentialists of a particularly limited and perverse kind. All consequentialists care only about the consequences of acts. That's what makes them consequentialists. But the true consequentialist cares about and weighs the aggregate positive and negative consequences of everybody. Self-aggrandizing go-getters only consider consequences to themselves. The rest of us, quite literally, don't count.

In a stimulating recent book on corporate misbehavior, *Icarus in the Boardroom*, Professor David Skeel of the University of Pennsylvania Law School helps explain why. Companies whose shares are traded on the New York Stock Exchange, or in another public market, feel the need to get "followed" by influential Wall Street analysts. Whereas a generation before, a CEO at a publicly traded company had normally risen workman-like through the ranks, new conditions called for a different personality type.[1] A "celebrity" CEO who could secure the attention and garner higher ratings from analysts was hugely valuable to the company. This is because the analysts' recommendations have enormous influence in making the stock "hot," thus bidding up its price. The new conditions also played a role in the explosion of CEO compensation since the 1980s, which greatly troubles many Americans, in and out of the business world, but which is beyond the scope of this book.

For most of us, a CEO who acts like Napoleon is too exalted to be touched. The most that one can do is learn what can be learned, build up that résumé, and stay out of the line of fire so that moving can be at a time and under circumstances that are favorable. This can be more difficult than it sounds. The imperial CEO, like the Emperor Napoleon himself, can be highly charismatic. There's always that hint of a promise—rarely, of course, ever fulfilled—that *you* will be the one taken into the imperial confidence, upon whom the emperor will rely, and that some of the riches and glory will fall to you. But this can be fatal, like making a pact with the devil.

Short of cases where CEOs go too far and find themselves in the sights of federal prosecutors, the only readily available control mechanism is the board of directors. If you know anything about the governance of companies, including large corporations whose shares are traded on public exchanges, you may have already snickered. In strict legal theory, the business of a corporation is managed by or under the direction of the board of directors.[2] In practice, members of boards of directors are frequently the hand-picked buddies of the CEO, chosen to sustain rather than seriously to oversee the way in which the CEO is running "his company." Yet, because directors have the legal obligation to manage the corporation's business, they are the targets when shareholders file civil suits to recover losses when CEOs such as Bernie Ebbers of WorldCom have looted the company for their own personal profit. In the WorldCom case, directors ended up settling with the aggrieved shareholders for $20.25 million, to be paid from their own pockets.[3]

Where the CEO isn't the problem, it's the job of any boss to spot the self-aggrandizer lower down in the hierarchy and tone him or her down. The most important point is, NEVER promote someone who behaves in this way. Don't give highly visible rewards. Don't heap honors on him—à la Kidder, Peabody and Joe Jett. It's really the same point we've discussed with the efficient, productive and dynamic sexual harasser. If you honor those who dishonor the company, or promote them, the company's reputation may suffer. You'll be the one who has to answer if or when the word is out, both inside the business and on the street, that yours is not a good company to work for.

Now, don't misunderstand me. A company needs exceptional performers, especially in key positions at or near the top. Without innovative thinking about marketing, product development, financing, and the like, a company will have trouble competing against other companies. But the list of exceptional performers isn't identical to the list of workplace Napoleons. One of the principal reason companies succeed, at least in the long run, is because of finely honed cultures of teamwork. Recognizing that the TEAM comes before the stars is the mark of the outstanding team player. Not so with

Napoleons of the workplace. While their abilities are sufficient to accord them star status—and there certainly are many whose talents do—it's their STARDOM, and not the team, that comes first. Napoleons of the workplace pollute the environments in which they work. There are a number of ways in which they do this, but I think what sums it up best is that they do not value the ideas and efforts of others, thus dehumanizing their subordinates.

Yet many power abusers aren't dominated by outsized egos, or obsessed with their own advancement. So let's turn to the third category of power abusers. Some people derive enormous satisfaction from bending others to their will. I call them the humiliators. In a way they are most sinister, because of the difficulty in identifying them and the dangerousness of their effects on the company. They're not out of control or inappropriate all the time. But they do regularly abuse and humiliate people who work for them.

THE HUMILIATORS

When people think about abuses of power in a company, it's common to focus on the characteristics of the abusers. After all, it's their conduct that's the issue and people who exercise power (like Napoleon) are interesting. But I think that to understand the ill effects on a company, it's important to focus on those who endure the abuses of power. I define this third category by looking at them through the eyes of the victim. It harks back to the fourth prong of the foursquare protocol, thinking about issues from the viewpoint of the person on the receiving end. The general term that encompasses what it feels like to suffer power abuse is "humiliation." I like the word because it focuses us on the way that abusers make their victims feel about themselves. Here's a true story, modified to disguise the participants.

Arlene worked for a construction company. The company's office was in one of those cities where Good Friday is a public holiday. The company traditionally closed on that day. This pleased Arlene, because she was serious about her Roman Catholicism, and Good Friday for her was simply not a day for business. One year as Easter approached, Arlene was working for Myrna on a particular project that was going out to bid. Myrna's reputation was that she had to have her own way.

One morning a week or so before Easter, Myrna stopped by Arlene's office and told her that she needed her to come in on Good Friday to help get certain cost information in final shape so that she could study it over the weekend. When Arlene told Myrna that the office was closed, Myrna sloughed her off. "We've worked holidays before and we'll have to work this one here. We won't get the raw data till Thursday, and if I don't have the weekend to put it together, we won't be ready for the Wednesday bid deadline."

Arlene was adamant. "I'm sorry, Myrna," she said. "It's Good Friday and I need to be in church."

"Well, church isn't all day, is it? What about 1:00? I can wait till then. If we push, we can get through it."

"You don't understand," replied Arlene. "I'm not going to work on Good Friday. It's a very holy day for me and I'm just not coming in." Myrna's face grew red. Before she could reply, Arlene continued, "Let me see if I can get some people to help you out."

"Whatever," said Myrna as she stormed out of the room.

Later that day, Arlene and Myrna participated in a team meeting on the project. As if the morning's conversation hadn't happened, Myrna said, "We'll get the data compilations done on Friday, so I can draft the report over the weekend. I have asked Arlene to come in to get the job done."

Flabbergasted, Arlene burst in. "I told you I couldn't come in on Friday because it's Good Friday. I said I'd round up some people to help you."

"And I said that's not good enough," snapped Myrna. Everybody in the room shifted uncomfortably in their seats. You could hear a pin drop.

Don, the president of the company, broke the silence. "If Arlene can't come in," he said, "we'll find someone else. Let's drop this and move on."

Fortunately, Don diffused a situation that had every chance of getting ugly. But the effects lingered with Arlene. Myrna's conduct has two different troubling aspects. The most obvious is the naked assertion of power. Myrna claims the right to tell Arlene what to do, even when the "what to do" involves requiring her to come to work on a day when the company will be closed and which is among the holiest days of the year in Arlene's religion. Yet there's something else, something more sinister. What's motivating Myrna is her desire to bend Arlene to her will, to make Arlene feel *subordinate*. How else to

explain why she doesn't want to consider Arlene's proposed alternatives for getting the work done? Whatever Myrna might *say* about
the need to get the work done, she has another agenda, an agenda
having to do with her relationship with Arlene. Myrna's agenda is
about power. We can assume that Myrna was genuinely interested in
collecting the information so the bid would be ready on time. But
there has to be more, because she spurned Arlene's offer to try to
find someone else who could pitch in. Mryna's rejection of that
offer was about her power and her desire that everyone, most especially Arlene, recognize that power. She wants Arlene to buckle, to
accept her subordination. It's like two male elk fighting for domi-
nance over the herd. This is apparent from the way Myrna sought
to embarrass Arlene and aggrandize herself in front of their colleagues. Although Don did a good job in diffusing the situation,
Myrna sought to *humiliate* her. At a minimum, Arlene had to have
been embarrassed.

Humiliation is the umbrella term for the harm that stems from
power abuses within organizations. Victims experience anger, stress,
and depression. Let's investigate this subject more closely.

THE POISON OF HUMILIATION

Humiliation diminishes its victim. In the examples I want to discuss, a person feels peculiarly and uncomfortably conscious of his or
her own relative powerlessness. To be humiliated is to feel belittled.

Humiliation stories won't make the business pages of the newspaper or get on the TV news. Inside an organization, however, people
know what's going on. Frequently, senior managers are involved in
the abuses themselves. Sometimes, and far more sinisterly, when
they aren't, they don't take tales of such conduct seriously and use
their power to do something about it. There can be a conspiracy of
official silence and, apart from whispers to trusted friends among
fellow employees, these are cases where husbands or wives bear the
brunt of the frustration. "The pay is good," employees in an
environment that permits humiliation to flourish say. "The work is
interesting. But I just can't stand it any more." Let's look at four
situations that create this kind of undercurrent of discontent. Senior
management has no business tolerating this, much less participating
in it.

HURRY UP AND WAIT OR THE MAKE-BELIEVE DEADLINE

Toni had been working hard. Her bank was in a growth mode. Her job was to put together the data that the marketing VPs would use when they called on *Fortune* 500 companies, trying to secure their business. Her bosses had kept her hopping, and she'd worked late most of the week so that she and her boyfriend could take a much-needed weekend of rest and relaxation together with no cell phones and BlackBerrys. On Friday around 3:30, she was finishing up some paperwork and planning to take off a little early to pack for the weekend. Her phone rang.

"Toni?"

"Yes. Oh hi, Mark."

"Hey," the voice on the other end said, "I hate to ask this, but have you got anything going on this weekend?"

Toni's heart sank. She could see the freight train speeding down the track toward her. But she was a cool customer and said, "I do. My boyfriend and I have rented a cabin at a lake and we're off for some quality time."

"I'm sorry to be the bearer of bad news," said Mark. "You'll have to cancel. You know that defense contractor in Texas where we've been looking for an in? Well, Henry's got one. The meeting's next week. Wednesday, I think. Henry wants a report on his desk by 8:00 Monday morning."

"But our deposit...," said Toni lamely, caring a whole lot more about the lost time than the money.

"Not a problem," said Mark. "Get me the receipt and I'll get you reimbursed. I've canceled my plans. I'll be here to help you."

Toni sucked it up and called her boyfriend. He was disappointed, very disappointed, but he was a good sport about it.

So Toni worked through the weekend. Fortunately, she and Mark finished in time for her to get home to relax with her boyfriend and watch his favorite team play Sunday night football. And she was happy with the report. Henry didn't get to the position of senior vice president without having high standards. He was spare with compliments, but she thought she just might garner some praise for the quality of this report—and some thanks for giving up her weekend on short notice to get it done.

Toni usually didn't get to the office until 8:30, but she made it through early morning traffic on Monday morning to get there at 7:30 so she could give her report one final look and be ready with a summary presentation if (as he sometimes did) Henry asked for one. Promptly at 8:00 she arrived at Henry's office, report in hand.

"I'm here to see Henry," she said cheerily to Jeanette, his assistant. "I've got the report for the Texas meeting he wanted."

Jeanette looked puzzled. "Henry's not here," she said. "He flew to Chicago last night. He should be in tomorrow morning. I'll make sure it's with his mail when he comes in."

"But, but," stammered Toni. "He said he needed it at eight today."

"Oh, that's Henry," said Jeannette, smiling. "You know him. He was probably afraid that if he said Tuesday morning you might be late. He's so meticulous, you know."

You can imagine how Toni felt. We'll talk about it after we consider three other stories.

DON'T TELL ME IT'S IMPOSSIBLE: *THE DEVIL WEARS PRADA*

Some of my friends seemed surprised when I recommended *The Devil Wears Prada* to them. "Isn't it about the fashion industry?" they seemed to say. "Surely not your thing."

"No," I replied. "It's *set* in the fashion industry. It's *about* abusive management."

As those who've read the book or seen the (not nearly as compelling) movie know, the plot turns upon the tribulations of Andrea, a young woman just out of college who goes to work for an out-of-control boss, Miranda Priestly, the editor of a top-of-the-line, trendy fashion magazine. Andrea's job is to do whatever Miranda wants for the company and to assist her personally. While the personal service aspect in itself is offensive, her insistence upon it isn't what earns Miranda a place in this chapter. She takes particular delight in asking the impossible. If Henry, in the previous story, gave a false deadline, Miranda insists that things get done in time frames nobody on the planet could manage. It's as if she were a god, and could snap her fingers and have her wishes fulfilled. For Miranda, deciding that she wants something is equivalent to saying that she wants it done *now*.

Henry manipulated Toni's personal time; Miranda acts as if time doesn't exist. If Miranda, instead of Henry, were Toni's boss, she'd probably have called her and said, "I need a complete report on the prospective client in Texas right away. I'm leaving in exactly an hour and I must take it with me." Of course, since Toni labored all weekend to get the job done, her only realistic reply would be, "No way." Miranda's stock response, not atypical of many bosses whose power has gone to their heads and who don't understand the difference between being demanding (a good thing) and being unrealistic, is "I don't want excuses. I need it now."

"GUESS WHAT I MEANT"

A close relative of the boss who makes impossible demands is the boss whose approach follows upon the words of Chicago's mid-twentieth-century mayor, Richard J. Daley—the father of the current mayor—when he was unhappy at a quotation some newspaper printed: "Don't quote what I said. Quote what I meant."

Let's call this executive Herb. If Miranda thinks that her wanting something done makes it possible that it be done right then and there, Herb's way of showing his lack of concern for his employees is different. He's the kind of boss who believes that his wishes are automatically beamed into someone else's head. He knows what he wants (or at least thinks he does) and assumes everyone who works for him automatically understands his needs. No matter how vague his instructions are, it's up to the person who works for him to figure out what he wants or what he means.

Suppose Herb asks one of his division managers to provide him with the figures on last quarter's costs. If there's no context for the request, or history behind what Herb means, the division manager asks herself, "What does he mean by 'costs'? Expenses? Costs of raw materials? Labor costs? Extraordinary one-time costs? Total costs?" If a boss is easy to get along with, the division manager can ask him. Or she can ask someone else who might be clued in to Herb's thinking. But that won't work with Herb. He's the boss and he assumes that everybody must be able to devine his meaning. "What kind of an idiot are you if you can't figure out what I want?" ("Idiot" is a favorite word of this kind of power-abuser.) If, like Miranda, Herb has a sharp tongue, or if his temper is like a barrel of gasoline waiting for a lit match, the request for clarification will produce a firestorm of its own. "What's the matter with you? Costs? You don't know what costs are? How'd we ever give you this job?" The manager is damned if she does and damned if she doesn't. Not a good place to be.

OLD YELL-ER AND THE E-MAILER

You can't talk about abusive management styles without talking about old yell-er. At an unpredictable moment, he (usually not a she) yells at a secretary or a junior colleague for having made some mistake "that any idiot would know how to do right." Sometimes this happens in front of others, sometimes it's behind a closed door, so that only part of the tirade is audible to passersby. For the victim behind the closed door, it's hard to bear.

Our modern technological world permits a particularly demeaning parallel, the widely circulated abusive e-mail. Some bosses find cc'ing distribution lists on their criticism of an individual who works for them irresistible. It's quick, it's easy, and there's none of the risk of a retort or the discomfort that can come from interpersonal confrontations. And it's a really effective way to humiliate the person to whom it's directed. Here's a story I saw happen in a law firm. A client called a young lawyer, let's call him Todd, who had done some work for him to complain that the bill the firm sent was too high. Todd and the client talked on the phone for about twenty minutes and came to a resolution about how much to reduce the amount due. Todd thought it had been a fair, frank, and open resolution of the problem. The client to whom Todd spoke was required to run the agreement by *his* boss, Kristen. *She* didn't think the offered write-off was sufficient. She then called Todd's boss, who reduced the amount still more. Todd's boss then sent him a scathing e-mail, criticizing him for not having taken the client's concerns sufficiently into account and—in a bit of executive hyperbole—claimed that Todd's mistake jeopardized the entire relationship. Naturally, there'd be no circumstances in which Todd would like to receive this e-mail. But Todd's boss turned criticism that was (at least possibly) fair into the humiliation of Todd by cc'ing a couple of distribution lists, consisting of thirty of Todd's colleagues, on the email. Todd, like the other humiliation victims we've been discussing, felt about four feet tall. Management by intimidation is a good name for this.

"C'MON, GET OVER IT"

To some people and, I'm afraid, many managers, the stories just discussed sound like the complaints of the tenderhearted. "Working in business is not like attending a garden party on a spring afternoon. It's tough, it's fast paced, and executives need to find a way to get the job done." Henry's got a large potential client in Texas. He can't afford to risk receiving the report at the last minute as he races to the airport. How many people do you know who actually meet deadlines? He can't take the risk that Toni and Mark will be late. If he said he needed the report Tuesday morning, they might have taken the weekend off, and not finished on Monday and he, Henry, and the bank would be stuck and unprepared. Isn't it trivial or even whiney of Toni not to recognize the reality in which he works? Shouldn't the message to her be, "C'mon, get over it"?

The answer is a resounding NO.

PRIVILEGING DIGNITY IN THE WORKPLACE

We're talking about dignity. We're talking about the right of a subordinate to be treated with respect. There's really no price you can place on it. We all need to be paid for our work. We all want time to engage in the personal lives we choose, spending time with family or friends, and taking part in those recreational activities we enjoy. The United States has a hard-working culture, much more so than those that prevail in many European countries. I spend more of my waking hours working than doing anything else, and the odds are you do the same. If our places of work are places where we feel disparaged, belittled, or humiliated, there's something radically wrong with the quality of our lives.

There was an easy and direct way that Henry could have conveyed the urgency of having his report ready for his Texas meeting. He could have done so in a manner that showed his respect for Toni, and for Mark, both as employees from whom he needed work and his respect for each as a human being. He could have told them the truth.

Suppose that Friday afternoon, Henry had called Toni and Mark and said, "It looks like this defense contractor in Texas we have been pursuing is ready to talk. They've asked me to fly down there for a meeting next Wednesday morning. I hate to spring this on you on a Friday afternoon, but I have got to have the report I'll need for the meeting on my desk Tuesday morning, so I can look it over before I head to the airport, in case I find I need anything else. I know this may mean it'll take some of your weekend, but I'm in a bind."

What a difference! Toni still might have lost her getaway weekend. She might have had to work late that Friday evening, come back early on Sunday, or cancel her Monday appointments. The critical point is that would have been for *her* to decide. She could figure out how long the task would take, and what would have to give. Now, she'd have to get it right. If she values her job, wants to stay on the good side of her boss, hopes to advance, and so on, she'll have to make sure to give herself enough time. She may need to build extra time into what she allots, because things have a way of taking longer to get done than people think they will. She might still have had to give up the weekend at the lake. But an environment that allows her to make that choice is better, by orders of magnitude, than one where she feels coerced—and cornered. And that's especially true where part of the coercion is a false deadline. She would have had a choice—and the responsibility to make the correct one. Most importantly, she'd have been spared the humiliation of knowing that she'd been "had" by the 8:00 Monday morning deadline and of standing outside Henry's empty office "on time" with the report in her hand when he wasn't even in the city.

Serving the customer or the client is crucial. If you don't do that consistently, you won't be in business long. That's obvious. That's why most common excuse by those who use their power to abuse their subordinates is "I'm just trying to get the job done. The customer (or the client) comes first." Miranda's requiring Andrea to do various kinds of personal tasks for her are exaggerated, but *The Devil Wears Prada* is, after all, a novel meant to get a laugh. Unfortunately, requiring personal service isn't rare. The boss's excuse is usually that he or she is so busy doing critical work to advance the company's goals that it's necessary. That's BS, by which I mean, of course, as sociologist and historian James Loewen puts it, "bad sociology." It's about power, and the rush that power freaks get by exercising it.

Many of the demands of the bosses we've been discussing are irrational, and the unstated requirement that their temper tantrums or other forms of abuse have to be endured is just the opposite of the what should occur in an exemplary business setting. Serving the customer should never become an excuse for a boss to flaunt his or her ability to exercise power.

The very irrationality of so much of it, however, is a part of the power trip itself. An employee has to put up with a boss's yelling, or the false deadlines, or the garbled instructions, or the widely circulated e-mail chastisement because the boss has the power to get away with it. Period. The arbitrariness of the demands themselves, the very fact that there really is no good business reason for the boss's conduct, is a power freak's way of emphasizing that only one thing is really at stake: his or her power. After all, what can be more of a display of the extent of one's power than that you don't have to account for your misuse of it?

DON'T TOLERATE THE INTOLERABLE

Deliberate and constant actions by bosses that humiliate those who work for them should not be tolerated. The excuse of bosses who tolerate such misconduct by others is typically the same as that of the humiliator himself: "Henry does a great job; we can't afford to get him angry because we'd be up a creek if he left."

This way of thinking can't be justified. It's an excuse, pure and simple; an unwillingness to confront a power abuser in the company or a person whose performance, otherwise, is good, perhaps even stellar. The fear that management can't confront humiliators is entirely based on speculation—and speculation that's given more weight than treating employees with respect. Will Henry really leave if senior management tells him to stop playing his control games? If he did, would his replacement certainly be worse? On a consequentialist point of view, is what a manipulator like Henry contributes necessarily more substantial than what Toni and her colleagues could contribute if their Monday dreads didn't prompt them to leave? Not necessarily. It's a mind game designed to excuse executive misconduct.

There's another reason that helps to explain why the Henrys and the Herbs and, yes, even the Mirandas get away with what they do. The law isn't involved. Now, we've moved in and out of law throughout this book. And we've made it clear that it isn't OK to do something inappropriate—or to permit those whom you manage or supervise to do something inappropriate—simply because you won't get sued. We've got to admit, however, that the absence of the hammer of a plaintiffs' lawyer or a prosecutor banging on the door takes off some of the pressure. It shouldn't, but it does.

Humiliation can, however, move into an area where the law is very sensitive. One area is sexual harassment. The other is racial discrimination.

ASCRIPTIVE CHARACTERISTICS

All of the situations we've talked about so far are characterized by bosses whose sense of their own power has allowed them (encouraged them) to trample on the dignity of those who work for them. Toni had to deal with Henry's power-tripping false deadline because she worked for him. It didn't matter whether she was Asian, African American, or white, and it wouldn't have mattered if she'd been Tony and not Toni. We'd be very naive if we doubted, however, that sometimes people are humiliated simply because of who they are.

Before we go further, let's stop to clarify some terms. What we're talking about are people's unchangeable characteristics, sometimes called their "ascriptive characteristics." In the way Americans ordinarily talk, race usually refers to skin color. A person's ethnic or national origin is equally an ascriptive characteristic. Although a person can change religion in a way he or she can't change skin color or national origin, many people feel unable to make such a change. Therefore, ill treatment because you're a Catholic is not unlike poor treatment because you're African American. (Judaism presents a dual situation. To say that someone is "Jewish" may be a statement about a person's ethnic origin, which is unchangeable, or it may be a statement about religious beliefs and practices that one can choose to abandon.) For purposes of what we're about to discuss, there's no difference between "race," "ethnic origin," or "religion." (Sex or sexual orientation are also characteristics that can't ordinarily be changed. These areas raise their own additional issues arising out of the human sex drive and how culture has mediated attitudes relating to it. That's why we dealt with them separately.)

THE SPIRIT OF THE FOURTH OF JULY

Jeff was the manager of the research and development department in a high-tech company. The company CEO was big on "team building"—lectures, workshops, outward bound trips—the whole nine yards. Jeff, too, was into it. One June he decided to invite the folks from his department over to his backyard for a Fourth of July picnic. He liked the people he worked with, and he wanted them to like him. He enlisted his wife's aid, and together they began making arrangements. They were having fun planning it, and were looking forward to the occasion. They decided to send old-fashioned invitations in the mail, rather than the now-customary e-mail attachments.

Then Jeff realized something. Or actually, his wife Cathy did. One of the people who worked in the department was Sanjay, a twenty-four-year-old engineer. Sanjay had been born in India and had come to the United States to attend one of the nation's best engineering schools. He had maintained his Indian nationality and of course, he'd also retained his Indian ethnicity. He was fluent in English, but spoke with a noticeable accent. Jeff's wife, who was writing the invitations because she had better penmanship than Jeff, paused when she came to Sanjay's name on the department list. She knew Jeff's feelings about Indians. He didn't like them. Any of them. It was a case of pure prejudice. She didn't share his feelings, but she was aware of his. She showed him the envelope she'd started to address with the name of Sanjay and his wife. Jeff shook his head. "Nope," he said. "It's my house. Private party. I can do whatever I like."

"I thought, because this was a gathering for your team, that you were going to get permission to turn in the expenses for the beer and food to the company," she asked. "Do you—"

"Then I won't do it," he interrupted. "Private party."

So that's how the picnic was planned, and that's how it took place. Except for a couple of people who went out of town to visit family, everybody in the department, together with a spouse or significant other, was present, except for Sanjay and his wife.

Sanjay learned about the party beforehand, and heard about it afterward. He had no difficulty guessing the reason for his exclusion. You can imagine how he felt. He was angry, he was upset, and he felt belittled. It was humiliating to be singled out for exclusion.

He liked his job—or had liked his job—but if this is how the company was, no way was he staying. He pulled up his résumé on his home computer just to see how it looked.

Bigotry, prejudice, racial discrimination, racial disadvantaging— call it what you like—is ugly. Is it uglier than the abuse-humiliation power-tripping scenarios we discussed earlier? I think most people would say yes. Why?

If you're in a cycle of humiliation by a boss like Henry or Herb or even Miranda, you can always say to yourself, "Maybe it will change. Maybe he or she is simply going through a bad patch. It could get better." It could. It might be unlikely, but at least it's possible. There's a second thought as well. Even though the power-tripper abuses you, and even if you're made to feel bad because of it, you may come to recognize that the problems really belong to the other person.

Many victims of racial humiliation understand that it's not really about them. That's surely true. It's about the people who experience the poison of their own bigotry, and, more exactly, the group stereotyping in which they engage. And yet, at some level, it's hard to feel that it's not about you. Your mistreatment isn't about what you did or didn't do, or could have done differently or more effectively. It's entirely unrelated to your job performance. It's about who you are. Sanjay was singled out because he's Indian. He'll always be Indian. And he'll always have to confront the fact that some of the people with whom he'll deal—hopefully a small and diminishing percentage, but still a percentage—won't give him a chance, and won't accord him the respect they accord to others. There's a feeling of powerlessness about being mistreated because of one of your non-behavioral characteristics about which you can do nothing.

Of course, Sanjay couldn't take Jeff or the company to court because he didn't get invited to the Fourth of July party. It's like the inappropriate sexual byplay that the law doesn't have the time or resources to treat as sexual harassment. But Jeff's actions weren't like Henry giving Toni a false deadline. Because race and national origin are involved, Jeff crossed the line into territory where, when substantial enough, legal strictures are severe.

ADDRESSING RACIAL HUMILIATION

Sanjay wasn't the only person to find out about the picnic he wasn't invited to attend. So did Abby, the VP to whom Jeff reported. She was livid. Abby didn't summon Jeff to her office the moment she heard about the incident. She was too good a manager not to know that you shouldn't confront an employee who's been out of line when your anger is white hot. She did her best to calm down. But her best wasn't very good. As soon as Jeff sat down in her office, her fury rained down upon him.

"What the hell is the matter with you?" Abby demanded.

Jeff stammered, pretending not to know what she was going on about. "What's 'Jeff' short for?" she demanded.

"Jeffrey," he said, looking at her quizzically.

"Obviously not Jefferson," she replied. "None of that 'all men are created equal' stuff for you."

"It was a private party," Jeff said, knowing where she was coming from and getting hot under the collar himself. "Last time I looked it was still a free country."

"Oh, a private party. I see. And who did you happen to invite?"

"Friends. Some friends. It's none of your business."

"None of my business?" asked Abby. "Do you happen to know where these 'friends'—she gestured with two fingers on each hand to indicate quotation marks—"where these 'friends' work?"

"I said, it's none of your business," replied Jeff. But, sensing he was in a little too deep to stonewall, he said, "mostly here."

"Mostly?" Abby asked sarcastically.

"All do," said Jeff, "but it was a private party. I can ask who I like. I didn't turn in any expense receipts to the company. I didn't take a penny from my entertainment budget."

Abby had expected the "private party" excuse, and she was not at all mollified. She was angry. She was right to be. Jeff's way of trying to get out of responsibility for the situation simply won't work. From both legal and ethical perspectives, Abby shouldn't buy his "company life"/"private life" excuse. This is an important distinction. It helps us to understand what we think about issues involving matters of sexual orientation and a woman's right to be free of sexual advances in the workplace, allowing a person to attend to religious observances that are important to him or her, and in drawing the line against those bosses who treat their employees as if they are effectively on call twenty-four hours a day, seven days a week. We want frequently to privilege the distinction between private sphere and company sphere. But not here.

It's clear that Jeff is using "private party" as an excuse to justify bigotry and his discriminatory exclusion of Sanjay. The fact that he could label the Fourth of July picnic "private" wasn't the real reason Sanjay wasn't invited and everybody, including Jeff, knew it. It sounds like the kind of argument lawyers sometimes try to make to get their clients out of trouble—which juries generally are smart enough not to buy.

Jeff hosted a party for his coworkers, that is, all his coworkers save the one he did not wish to invite to his home because—let's not pull our punches—of his racial prejudice. Therefore, what he did is the company's concern, and Abby would be entirely justified in making that 100 percent clear to Jeff.

Abby's most obvious way of asserting her authority to criticize Jeff *as an employee* is to use what's called an "opening the floodgates" argument. If she allows Jeff to get away with this, he may understand—and others may think—that, practically speaking, the company tolerates discrimination against racial minorities. She can't allow Jeff's action to be interpreted as a reflection of company attitudes. If not faced up front, sooner or later, the line from the unpleasant to the illegal may get crossed. In Sanjay's own case, assuming he stays at the company, he could understand any denial of a promotion or other disadvantageous work-related assignment as an instance of illegal discrimination—especially if Jeff were involved as the decision-maker. As an ethically attuned manager with her eyes on the law, Abby can't give Jeff a complete pass on his Fourth of July party on the technical grounds that it was at his house and no company funds were involved, because that approach tacitly endorses racial discrimination that no company should tolerate.

This is a good reason. But I think there is better one. During the early days of the Civil War, when he was struggling with whether he had the constitutional power to abolish slavery, and whether public opinion would permit it, President Abraham Lincoln said, "If slavery is not wrong, nothing is wrong." I believe the same can be said of bigotry—whether racial, ethnic, or religious. Now, I'm not, of course, saying that a company has any business trying to police the thoughts of all its executives and managers, much less its employees. To do so would be impractical, and would itself be wrong and an unfortunate invasion of employees' own private spheres. What I am saying is that a company should not put up with conduct that exhibits prejudice or bigotry in which the company is implicated. It was here, and Jeff's feeble effort to claim otherwise doesn't change Abby's understanding, or ours. This is true apart from the absence of a risk of legal liability, at least if the racial discrimination goes no farther. Rather the point is that racial humiliation poisons the atmosphere of a company. It makes the aspiration to ethical excellence not only unachievable. Tolerating it makes rhetoric about such a goal entirely bogus. If ever there were a fact pattern that undercuts the argument—criticized in Chapter 2, that the law, and only the law, defines what's right and wrong—this is it.

FOSTERING AN ABUSE-FREE ENVIRONMENT

Is Jeff's humiliation of Sanjay by not inviting him to the Fourth of July party any different from what Toni's boss, Miranda, and Herb have done?

Yes and no.

You know the reason for "yes." Sanjay was a victim of racial discrimination. Not illegal race discrimination, but race discrimination all the same.

Ask any person who's a member of any racial group, or any woman, if it feels different—bad in a particularly cutting way—to run into hostility *because* he's Polish or Jewish or Italian or Salvadoran or African American, or *because* she's a she. It's not the same. It's different than when someone just happens not to like your personality or your political ideas. You're disadvantaged because of something ineradicable. There's nothing you can do or change. Jeff humiliated Sanjay because of Sanjay's ethnicity.

But at a different level, the answer is no. All of the situations we've discussed in this chapter involve abuses of power—more particularly, abuses of power where the power-holder belittles the person who lacks the power.

Power is inevitably present in any organization, large or small. Somebody's got to be in charge, and some people have got to help the person in charge run the organization, whether it's a government, a business, a university, or a church. Someone must have the practical ability to get things done. But none of this implies that an organization needs to put up with power abusers. It's a question of respect.

We began Chapter 1 with a story about two managers, one of whom respected that the subpar performance of one of her salesmen was a consequence of a personal tragedy, the slow death of his wife. The other manager didn't care, which is one way of saying that he lacked respect for the bereaved employee. We can end this chapter with the same idea, an idea we have seen recur throughout the intervening pages. The business of managers committed to fostering ethical excellence must be to promote respect for everybody, most commonly inside the organization but also of the people with whom it deals externally, notably the company's customers. We haven't tried to specify exactly how Abby should manage Jeff in the last story we considered. Jeff is entitled to be treated with respect, notwithstanding the unpleasant side of his personality. The foursquare protocol provides the structure for the way that Jeff's boss, Abby, should decide how to handle the case. And the same would be true of abusers like Henry and Herb and even Miranda.

What's critical is that something must be done. An ethically excellent company must not permit sexual harassment or conflicts of interests, it must not put shoddy and dangerous products into the hands of the people upon whom it ultimately depends, its customers, and it should not permit many of the other kinds of wrongdoing this book has discussed. But it's equally important that the infrastructure of an ethically excellent company includes complete intolerance of practices that humiliate or degrade employees.

We still have a long way to go, as a society, to eliminate sexual harassment, gender discrimination, conflicts of interest, the sale of dangerous products, and all the other subjects discussed in this book. But a mark of the progress that has been made is the fact that business culture, and in many cases the law, no longer says such abuses are OK. Now is the time to rise to the challenge that workplace humiliation somehow has to be tolerated. It does not have to be tolerated and it should not be tolerated. Going forward, it is the next frontier for business ethics.

NOTES

1. David Skeel, *Icarus in the Boardroom: The Fundamental Flaws in Corporate America and Where They Came From* (New York: Oxford University Press, 2005).

2. See, for example, Section 141 of the Delaware General Corporation law. Delaware corporate law is particularly important because a majority of America's largest companies are incorporated there.

3. *The Washington Post*, March 19, 2005, p. E01.

Conclusion: Face the Facts, Tell the Truth, Run on Time

"What does it take to run a railroad?," a wise old former business school professor asked me when I first went into business. I shook my head. I couldn't guess what he had in mind. "Only three things," he said. "Face the facts, tell the truth, and run on time."

"Sounds like that works pretty well for our business, too," I replied.

"Or your life."

I hope you come away from reading this book with an acute sense that making ethical choices you feel good about requires that you understand clearly what the facts are. More exactly, you need to be aware of the subtle nuances of what you're dealing with. What is it that turned Myrna's request to Arlene to work on a day off to get a project ready from a legitimate effort to get the job done in a time-pressure situation into an abuse of power—and a lack of respect for Arlene's religious views? Was it disrespectful to Arlene's original statement that Good Friday was not a day of business for her? Or was it the public nature of her boss's criticism? Or both?

There's only one way to answer questions like these in real-life situations. Face the facts—all of them, including the unpleasant ones—and their multiple details and nuances. If you want your company to be admirable for its ethics, one of your mantras must be, "Ostriches not wanted here."

Facing the facts has another dimension, too. The law, as we've seen, provides guidance about what we should do. But it does more than that because it reflects society's collective sense of what people ought to do. Its effect is to tell us what we must do to avoid unpleasant consequences. The law, in other words, is a part of the world. Business people have to treat this as a fact.

Thus, facing the facts means treating the law as a reality, and by law I mean not just its particular dos and don'ts, but also its costs in terms of time and energy that you can expend even if ultimately you prevail before a court of law. So, don't play any mind games with yourself about "what you'll be able to say"... if you fire an employee who's a woman (or a member of a racial minority group or a person who's over forty or disabled), or if you cut corners on product safety. Treat the law not as threat, but as an invitation—or a small kick in the backside—to do what's right.

Facing the facts is about dealing with reality, even in these cases where what you have done, or what you want to do, or what the law says you shouldn't do, isn't to your liking.

TELL THE TRUTH

There's no substitute for a culture of trust and honesty. If it's true that where there's no vision, the people perish, it's equally true that where there's no integrity, the semblance of ethics perishes.

We've discussed a number of issues in which truth telling is critical. The point to emphasize here is that management needs to set high standards and impose strict accountability, especially where money is concerned. A sinister, suspicious apparent conflict of interest often disappears with early and honest disclosure. If a company wants to establish or maintain the highest ethical standards, one of the easy rules to adopt, publicize, and live by is zero tolerance for financial dishonesty. That extends to everything from delivering inferior goods to executive self-dealing.

RUN ON TIME

The final prong of the triad of how to run a railroad is to run on time. Of course, it means barring the kind of "hurry up and wait" power-gaming abuse of too many managers. But I think it means more.

Running on time, if you're a railroad, means keeping a commitment to your customers. Running on time in the world throughout this book means keeping the commitment to ethics strong and per-sistent. It means maintaining it when times are tough, when profit margins are down, or when employees are dissatisfied. It's easy to talk the talk when times are good. It's more difficult when they're not.

So running on time is my metaphor for managing a business with a sense of the highest commitment to ethical values always, not just when it's convenient. The time to start running on time about ethics is now.

Index

Schembechler, Bo, 151
Securities Act of 1933 (The 1933 Act), 111, 121
Securities and Exchange Commission (SEC), 52, 111, 121–23, 128 nn.4, 5, 139, 140, 145, 155 n.3
Sexual harassment, x, xiv, 7, 21, 23, 29, 43, 60, 64, 70, 73–85, 87–105, 132, 135, 179–80, 195, 197, 201
Sherman Antitrust Act, 110
Skeel, David, 183
Skilling, Jeffrey, 42, 108, 180
Smith, Adam, 14, 15, 16, 26, 27, 31
Snyder, Kirke, 181
Socrates, 28
Sternberg, Elaine, 57 n.1

Stewart, Martha, 44
Sutton, Robert, 178

Traub, James, 162
Traynor, Roger J., 167, 168, 176 n.12
Tyco, 163

Wal-Mart, 38
Washington, George, 19
Weill, Sandy, 150
Welch, Jack, 132, 141, 142, 146–48, 155 nn.1, 8, 13
Wolfowitz, Paul, 100–101, 104, 107
World Bank, 101–2, 107

Zero-sum games, defined, 114

About the Author

STEPHEN M. GOLDMAN is a lawyer, law professor, and businessperson. A graduate of Duke University and the University of Michigan Law School, he holds a Doctorate in Political Theory, with a concentration in Ethics, from Oxford University. He is on the faculty at the Catholic University of America School of Law, while also maintaining a law practice.